THE ART & DESIGN SERIES

For beginners, students, and working professionals in both fine and commercial arts, these books offer practical, how-to introductions to a variety of areas in contemporary art and design.

Each illustrated volume is written by a working artist, a specialist in his or her field, and each concentrates on an individual area—from advertising layout or printmaking to interior design, painting, and cartooning, among others. Each contains information artists will find useful in the studio, in the classroom, and in the marketplace.

BOOKS IN THE ART & DESIGN SERIES

The Complete Book of Cartooning, John Adkins Richardson

Drawing: The Creative Process, Seymour Simmons III and Marc S. A. Winer

How to Sell Your Artwork: A Complete Guide for Commercial and Fine Artists, Milton K. Berlye

The Language of Layout, Bud Donahue

Painting and Drawing: Discovering Your Own Visual Language, Anthony Toney

Photographic Printing, Ralph Hattersley

Printmaking: A Beginning Handbook, William C. Maxwell, photos by Howard Unger

Silkscreening, Maria Termini

Milton K. Berlye, a former special consultant
to the New York State Department of Education,
is the author of *The Encyclopedia of Working
With Glass* and *Your Career in the World of Work.*

HOW TO SELL YOUR ARTWORK

A COMPLETE GUIDE FOR COMMERCIAL AND FINE ARTISTS

Milton K. Berlye

A SPECTRUM BOOK

PRENTICE-HALL, INC., Englewood Cliffs, New Jersey 07632

51749

Library of Congress Cataloging in Publication Data

Berlye, Milton K.
   How to sell your artwork.

   (A Spectrum Book)
   First ed. (1973) published under title: Selling
your art work.
   Includes index.
   1. Art- -United States—Marketing.   2. Commercial
art—United States—Marketing.   3. Art schools—United
States—Directories.   I. Title.
N8600.B45   1978   658'.91'7   77-20496
ISBN 0-13-432617-2
ISBN 0-13-432609-1 pbk.

Prentice-Hall International, Inc., *London*
Prentice-Hall of Australia Pty. Limited, *Sydney*
Prentice-Hall of Canada, Ltd., *Toronto*
Prentice-Hall of India Private Limited, *New Delhi*
Prentice-Hall of Japan, Inc., *Tokyo*
Prentice-Hall of Southeast Asia Pte. Ltd., *Singapore*
Whitehall Books Limited, *Wellington, New Zealand*

To my wonderful lifelong models,
Ruth,
Jay,
Sharon,
Judy,
Michael,
Tara,
Dana,
and Little Ryan

Contents

HOW TO SELL
YOUR ARTWORK

Introduction

Artists can be roughly classified into two groups—those who prepare their work for sale and those who do not. This book is for the former group—those who are willing to place their talent and ability in the marketplace for what it will bring in dollars and cents.

There are close to 300,000 markets willing to pay for your work if it is of the right kind, quality, and subject—and ready for delivery when needed and wanted. And the demand is increasing each year. That is why *How to Sell Your Artwork* is published. It helps to answer the question: What part of this vast market is for me?

Selling artistic talent is much the same as selling dramatic talent, musical talent, or any of the others. In fact, it is much the same as selling girdles, garages, and garden hoses. It involves a product, sales ability, styling, timing, and the good old law of supply and demand. However, as in all fields of endeavor, there have developed certain accepted procedures and formalities that are peculiar to artwork. It

This painting, "Le cypres et l'arbre en fleurs," by Vincent Van Gogh, was sold at Parke-Bernet for $1,300,000, a world record for Van Gogh at auction (Courtesy: Sotheby Parke-Bernet Galleries, Inc.).

is these special procedures, formalities, and peculiarities inherent in the sale of artwork and talent that are discussed in detail in this book.

There is no *one* way to sell art. Each artist must do it in his or her own particular manner. It is for this reason that many different techniques and devices have been included. Each artist must interpret these techniques and devices in terms of his or her own personality, ability, needs, and desires and work out a presentation accordingly.

Experience has indicated certain truths concerning the selling of artwork and talent. Your chances for success are greatly enhanced if you will do the following:

First, frankly admit that you want to make money from your artwork if that is the case. Conviction is one of the most important qualities of a successful artist. If you want to sell your artwork, honestly admit it to yourself and to anyone who cares to listen. There is nothing more pitiful than the shallow remark, "I do my artwork for my own amusement," when such is not the case. This is not to say that there are not people whose only interest in artwork is self-realization and satisfaction. However, if you really do want to sell, then stand up and be counted. You will feel better and do better.

Second, realize that selling your work (and yourself) requires the organization of a carefully prepared campaign and cannot be left to chance. Hoping and dreaming alone won't do it. Selling is a competitive occupation requiring skill, ingenuity, ambition, and "know-how." The success you will realize will be in direct proportion to the degree to which you possess these qualities plus the amount of time you devote to planning and presentation.

Third, decide on the kind of artwork you like and want to do. It is folly to go into a field you dislike. You must prepare your work directly for the field you want to impress. This is not to say that experimentation and change should be avoided. On the contrary, these must be a constant part of your artwork. What is meant here is that you are not ready to be a selling artist until you have a quantity of one type of artwork that has been developed to a professional level.

To properly use *How to Sell Your Artwork*, read it through completely first. Following this, go back and study those sections that are concerned with the activities and topics you find most interesting. Then, as you prepare your sales campaign, keep it at hand for constant reference.

WHEN AM I READY TO BE A SELLING ARTIST?

The question of readiness cannot be answered in terms of age, time, education, inclination, or any of the set dimensions we like to use. The answer must be given in terms of your point of arrival and actually has little relationship to your means of getting there. What is meant is simply this: you are ready to be a selling artist when you have developed your artistic ability to the point at which someone will pay for your services. It is just that simple.

For some, this point of arrival is reached at a very early age; others are not ready to be selling artists until later in life. Some people "arrive" when they have completed art school or college training; others need less training or no formal training at all. Some develop varied skills in several art fields; others develop a single artistic capability. The important thing for the artist to remember is this: the answer to this question lies within yourself. Make an honest evaluation of your art capabilities. Study the field of art in which you are interested as thoroughly as you can. When you feel that your ability is sufficient for the art field of your choice, then make your move.

Just one word of caution: don't wait for perfection. There is plenty of room for a lot less than perfection. This is not a contradiction of the statement that perfection should be a constant goal. It simply means that you should not endlessly delay your decision to enter the art field until you have reached pinnacles of perfection beyond reason. To all successful artists, perfection is a guiding beacon, not a point of arrival. Many extremely successful artists readily admit in private that they do not feel they are as capable as they might be.

Trying to sell your artwork or skills before you are really ready is not nearly as objectionable as waiting too long. If you are not ready it will be made known to you in no uncertain terms by those whom you approach. You can learn a lot from being refused, provided you put this knowledge to a useful purpose. Try to find out why you were refused. Make the necessary corrections in your ability or personality if either was at fault. Then try again.

Doesn't graduating from an art college make a person an artist? Not really. All it gets you is a diploma—whatever that means. If you wish to be an art teacher in a public school then the diploma is important. In all other art fields it has little meaning or value. In the art fields outside of the school, it is the money you can earn that determines your worth. And whether you do it with a diploma or without a diploma or in spite of a diploma is of no concern. It is only results that count.

THE FINE ART FIELD

Fine art is generally defined as *a painting, drawing, sculpture, or print that is used exclusively for the pleasure of observation.* Within each art grouping may be found several different media, materials, processes, and styles. No matter what the form, if when completed it serves no other function than to be looked at, it is then in the realm of fine art.

The difference between fine art and commercial art is not clearly understood by many people. The reason for this is that the only thing distinguishing one from the other is approach. Both are art in every sense of the word. The fine artist prepares an art rendition and then attempts to sell it. The commercial artist is required to prepare artwork to certain predetermined specifications. *The fine artist sells what he has created. The commercial artist creates for what he has sold.* We will discuss commercial art in greater detail in Part Two.

If you consider fine art as your field of work, then there are some facts you should know. On the plus side you will find the work most satisfying in terms of personal emotions. There are few pleasures to equal that realized when you have completed a work of fine art.

Portrait of Juan de Paveja by Velazquez
sold at Christie's on November 22,
1970, for $2,310,000
(Courtesy: Christie's, St. James' London).

Auction (sak) room scene at Christie's during sale of the famous
Velazquez (Courtesy: Christie's, St. James' London).

There is a genuine excitement in having your work exhibited for all
to see.

On the other hand, this can be a less than satisfactory financial experience if you plan to live on what you earn from the sale of fine
artwork. Only a limited number of artists are able to do this. These
are the outstanding or those whose works are presently in vogue. The
number in this category today is far more than ever before in history.
And today, there are several fine artists who are amassing large sums
of money solely from the sales of their artwork. However, the greatest majority of fine artists carry on their art activities as a sideline
and must depend on other occupations for their livelihood.

In Part One we will discuss some of the major concerns of the fine
artist, particularly the important area of selling, which may involve
agents and dealers, galleries, art shows, museums, and special commissions.

1 Selling Fine Artwork

WHERE CAN I SELL MY FINE ARTWORK?

When you ask the question, "Where can I sell my fine artwork?" you automatically imply a second question: "*How* can I sell my fine artwork?" Where you can sell your artwork will depend, to a large extent, on the sales techniques you are capable of and willing to apply. In selling there are set procedures. This is true whether you are selling artwork, smoked hams, or garden hoses.

Display Your Work

First, you must let it be known as far and wide as possible that your work is available for sale. People cannot get excited about or even mildly interested in something they know nothing about. Display your work wherever and whenever you feel it can do you some good. Enter art shows and exhibits for which you qualify and which

(a)

Fig. 1.1 (a) A section of the twenty-fourth annual arts festival in Atlanta's Piedmont Park that has attracted as many as 500,000 people in a single year. (b) Art in the park in Middletown, New York (Courtesy: The Times Herald Record).

(b)

you estimate will be of value. Display your work in galleries at every opportunity. A great deal more is said about shows, exhibits, and galleries later in the book.

Take advantage of local opportunities to exhibit your work. In every community there are local stores, shops, banks, offices, restaurants, libraries, and other concerns and organizations that are partial to artists and readily willing to offer their facilities for exhibit purposes. Most places that permit you to use their facilities to exhibit your work will do it gratis. There are, however, some places that will insist on a regular financial arrangement that will bring them a return. Some will insist on a commission on sales. Others will buy your paintings outright and resell them on their own. More will be said concerning these financial arrangements.

If there is a local television station, seek an opportunity to show your work over its facilities. Make sure the program manager knows of your work and knows you would like to appear on one of his/her programs. That individual probably will not devote an entire program to your work unless you have a degree of prominence in the art field. He or she may, however, let you appear as a guest on an interview show, or on unusual citizen programs.

Talk About Your Work

Second, speak about art and your particular artwork at every opportunity. Become actively involved in clubs and organizations where you can meet and speak to people. Prepare a talk on art and then let it be known that you are available to speak before service clubs, local groups, and the like. In all communities such organizations are constantly searching for interesting speakers.

Speaking before groups is a learned ability. And what is true of the development of all other skills is true of this one—namely, *practice makes perfect.* If possible, enroll in a public speaking class in the local evening adult education program. Here you will get a good groundwork in the fundamentals. First accept invitations to speak before small groups and then work up to the larger ones. Remember always that you are invited primarily to entertain, and not to lecture or moralize.

There are some excellent books on public speaking in almost all libraries that you can use in preparing an effective talk.

Where a local radio station exists, it would be wise to let the program manager know you are available. Radio programs frequently need interesting people to interview. As is true of newspapers and TV

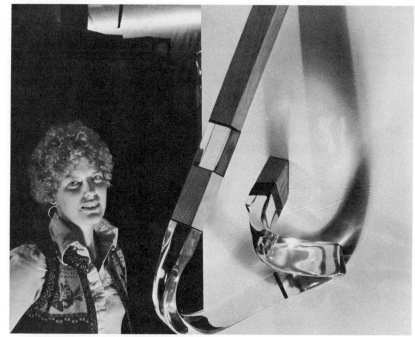

Fig. 1.2 Artist Caroline Montague with her untitled wall sculpture of carved laminated acrylic and ash in her warehouse studio in Atlanta, Georgia.

programs, you are of the most interest when you are involved in a newsworthy event. Let station managers know when you have won an art award, scholarship or fellowship, been assigned an outstanding art commission, placed high in a competitive art show, had a one-artist show, signed with an outstanding gallery to act as your agent, contributed some of your artwork for a worthy cause, completed an outstanding assignment, or spoken before an organization or meeting.

Accept the opportunity to teach art in the adult education program in your local school system if this is possible. And you will never know whether or not such an opportunity is available unless you inquire after the position. In most states you do *not* need a teaching certificate to be an adult education teacher. Any person with an acceptable background, who is approved by the local school superintendent, can usually secure a special certificate from the state education department. Teaching adults can be very satisfying and at the same time enhance your image in the community. It is also a nice thing to include when listing your qualifications for different considerations.

Third, write about your artwork whenever the opportunity presents itself. The local newspapers can be a strong asset in the development of your reputation. Keep them notified of all important events of which you are a part. We have already mentioned several events that are newsworthy. These and any additional events that set you apart from the crowd and improve your "image" should be brought to the attention of the newspaper for consideration.

Publishing news is the newspaper's job; good newspaper personnel are constantly in search of interesting, newsworthy items. So, if you are willing to "blow your own horn," it is usually not difficult to get something published about your work. Where such an item will be placed in the paper, and the amount of space it will be given, will depend entirely on the editors' judgment.

A copy of the same news article that you send to the newspapers can be sent to the news departments of both the local radio and TV stations. These latter two will give it the same treatment as the information will receive at the newspapers.

One word of caution: do not bother the news media unless you actually have a newsworthy item. If you pester them with a great deal of worthless information at frequent intervals, they may not give you the proper consideration when and if you deserve it. Remember the old story of "the boy who cried wolf."

One of the things you can do to help develop a reputation as an artist is to write articles for one of the several art magazines, or to be the featured subject of an article. Appearing in these publications carries a great deal of prestige. Full-length feature articles in such publications are usually reserved for the outstanding members in the art field—those who are well-known. However, the novice who has developed something unusual, or who has made an unusual accomplishment, can be featured in or can write smaller articles. In the appendix are listed the leading art magazines. Secure copies of these and study them for the type of articles that are accepted before you do any writing. If your article is of the type that fits in—the kind the magazine customarily uses—your chance of acceptance is greatly enhanced.

Price Your Work Well

Fourth, price your work attractively. Your asking price should make the purchaser feel he or she has received value for money spent. This is not always easy. Pricing is one of constant problems in selling fine artwork. It plagues the experienced artist as well as the novice. The only guiding rule in this regard is that you should ask whatever the traffic can bear. This is where a good agent can be of real value. Agents usually know the going prices and can milk the deal for all they can get. If you have no agent, then you must search out on your own as much pricing guidance as you can. A great deal more is said about pricing in the section devoted to this topic alone.

SELLING LOCALLY

Selling locally will mean different things to different artists, depending on the size and type of community in which (s)he lives. It will also depend on the initiative, imagination, and sales ability of the particular artist.

Small, local art galleries are being opened in increasing numbers in all kinds of communities. If one exists in your community, it may be a good place for you to try and sell your work. If you have a quantity of your paintings, it might be wise to locate a low-rent space and set up your own gallery.

There are store owners in almost every community who like to liven up their establishments by exhibiting original artwork. Furniture and interior decorator shops are especially interested. Other places that often display paintings, prints, and sculptures are bookstores, drugstores, clothing shops, banks, restaurants, and insurance offices. Almost any location that caters to people is a good place to exhibit artwork.

Some shopkeepers will let you exhibit your work in their places at no expense to you. Others will demand a percentage of the sales price should you sell the painting they are exhibiting. There is no set percentage given. You should be willing to offer from 20 to 33⅓ percent, depending on the exhibiting conditions available, the type of clientele that frequents the establishment, and the responsibilities the proprietor is willing to assume.

The outdoor exhibit is another location where artwork can be sold. The lawns in front of libraries and museums are given over for such use at regular intervals in many communities. In some places, the artists are permitted to set up their easels right out on the sidewalks of the main streets.

It is important that you let the local architects and interior decorators know, at frequent intervals, that you are available for art commissions. These two groups are recommending more and more artwork in their proposals. It is the artist they recommend that most frequently gets the commission.

Much locally sold artwork is done from the artist's studio through personal contacts. Here is where a wide local reputation and large circle of friends and acquaintances will pay off.

SELLING NATIONALLY AND INTERNATIONALLY

The selling of artwork in the national and international markets is accomplished through the large galleries. These galleries are located in the major art centers such as New York City, Paris, London, Boston, San Francisco, Chicago, and other large cities. Later in the book we will discuss these major galleries and how to contact and negotiate with them.

Fig. 1.3 Atlanta artist Hans Godo Fräbel is shown next to his "Profile," selected by the Corning Museum of Glass in Corning, New York, for inclusion in its contemporary collection. Fräbel's work is found in museums and private collections all over the world, and even on the desk of President Jimmy Carter in the Oval Office.

"How much shall I charge for my artwork?" This is the question most frequently asked of the author when he makes the acquaintance of an artist. This is asked of art critics and others who are supposed to be "in the know." There is no set answer to this question simply because there is no precise value that can be placed on any piece of artwork. There are so many intangibles to be considered in the pricing of fine artwork that it is impossible to prepare a pricing system. What are these intangibles?

The Quality of Your Artwork.   One of the intangibles involved in selling your fine artwork has to do with your skill, ability, talent, or whatever word you choose to describe how well you prepare your art rendition.

It is fairly easy for most people to distinguish between poor and very good artwork. But it is not so easy to differentiate between good and very good. This requires the development of an ability to distinguish between subtle differences that most people do not even understand. These differences may concern technique in handling the equipment, the selection of color, the presentation of the subject, or any of a hundred other variables. And even when these can be distinguished, they are usually subjective personal reactions. As evidence, read the different critics' reactions to an artist's work. There is frequently so great a variation in their reactions that you wonder if they are speaking about the same artist.

Public Esteem.   What does the general public think about art at the time you are trying to sell? This directly affects the price you can charge for your artwork. For the past few years art prices have been riding the crest of a buyer's market. Thousands of people—in all walks of life—are now buying fine art to grace their homes or for speculation, hoping prices will rise so they can resell for a profit. But there is no assurance that this will continue. Many people reading this book will remember a time when an artist would give a completed work in return for a square meal. Generally, the price of artwork is directly related to the prevailing economic atmosphere. In good times art prices go up; in bad times art prices are one of the first to be depressed.

Reputation.   This is another intangible to consider in pricing artwork that is hard to estimate. The reputation of the artist has a marked effect on the price of an art piece. This may sound objectionable to those who feel that artistic skill alone should be the sole consideration. The fact is that an artist's reputation has a very important bearing. The author has among his acquaintances two persons who purchased paintings from the same artist. Both paintings were the same size and same general composition. The first one paid $35 for the painting. The other paid $1,000 for his painting three years later. A close study of the paintings will reveal that there was no appreciable change in the artist's ability in that time. The change in price was due solely to the artist's increased reputation. Reputation can also work the other way. A painting was recently purchased for $5— it sold for $750 not too many years ago.

Location. An art item offered for sale in New York City will bring one price, in Chicago it will be another, and in a suburban or rural area it will be still another. In big cities where people are accustomed to purchasing art they will usually pay higher prices. In more rural areas, where art is looked upon as a luxury, the prices will generally be lower. Prices will vary from city to city and community to community.

There are several other conditions that affect the price of art in unpredictable ways but they need not be of concern at the present. The question you want answered is, "How shall I determine the price for my artwork?" Your best bet is to try and get a gallery to handle your work. Dealers there know pretty well what the traffic can bear and will usually get the most for your work. How to go about trying to interest a dealer, and the business arrangement you should make with that person, are factors that are covered in another part of this book.

WHAT IF THE DEALERS AREN'T INTERESTED?

The next question is, "What if I cannot interest a dealer in my work? Then what?" In that case you must determine the price on your own. This is not as hopeless as it might sound. There are certain indicators you can look to for help, such as the following:

1. Attend exhibits and galleries as frequently as possible. Search out artists you consider to be in a category with yourself. Note the prices they are charging and charge the same.
2. Place a few pieces of your work on the market at different price ranges. Analyze the response to determine the highest price you can charge and still sell your paintings.
3. When a person is interested in your artwork, find out as much as you can about his or her financial situation. Also try to find

out if (s)he has previously purchased artwork and what (s)he paid. This information can be a valuable guide in determining price.

Determining Your Asking Price. There is no easy, fast, or sure way to price artwork so it will sell. You will suffer the frustration that comes to all artists when selling their work. After a sale is made you will have the feeling that you could have asked a little more for your art piece. By the same token, when you do not make the sale you have the feeling that the sale might have been finalized had you asked a little less than you did. Do not let such frustrations discourage you. Look upon each sale or possible sale as an experience in learning. And do not get panicky and drop your prices as a result of

Fig. 1.4 Ouida Canaday with two of the oversized figure studies (done in oils) for which she is famous.

one rejection—or get overly elated and raise your prices as a result of one sale. *Fluctuate your prices up or down in response to a trend resulting from a* series *of sales or rejections.*

Reviewing Your Pricing Schedule. Frequently review your pricing schedule to get the most out of your sales. Your prices should rise or fall depending on (a) the degree of skill you have developed, (b) your reputation, (c) the type of clientele you have interested in your work, (d) your own financial needs, and (e) the impressions you are trying to create. Any one or more of these five conditions may change. If you do not review the situation frequently, these changes can escape your observation, with the result that you will be charging unrealistic prices.

DETERMINING THE MINIMUM PRICE TO CHARGE

The information given above helps you to determine the maximum to charge for your fine artwork. The remaining question is, "What is the minimum I should charge?" When you are first entering the field as a selling artist you must be concerned with minimums, for that is about all you most likely will be paid. *The base minimum you should accept is an amount equal to your actual cost for producing the item.* This amount is usually more than the artist imagines. For a realistic figure you should estimate your costs much as a commercial artist would and include the following:

1. *Out-of-pocket costs:* This should include all cash payments you made in connection with the particular art item, such as cost of materials and supplies, model fees, special props and devices, etc.

2. *Overhead costs:* This should include *monthly continuing expenses,* such as equipment replacement, rent, phone bills, heat, light, etc. The only practical way to use this figure is to break it down to an hourly overhead rate and add it to the overall cost on that basis. To figure the hourly overhead rate, (a) estimate the number of days you work in a month; (b) multiply this by the number of hours you actually work at your art each day; (c) divide this figure into the total monthly continuing expenses.

3. *Time charge:* This is determined by placing an hourly rate worth on your work and multiplying it by the number of hours you actually worked on the particular art rendition being priced. Here again, the big variable is what you are worth an hour. Frankly, your answer is that you are worth what someone is willing to pay—no more, no less.

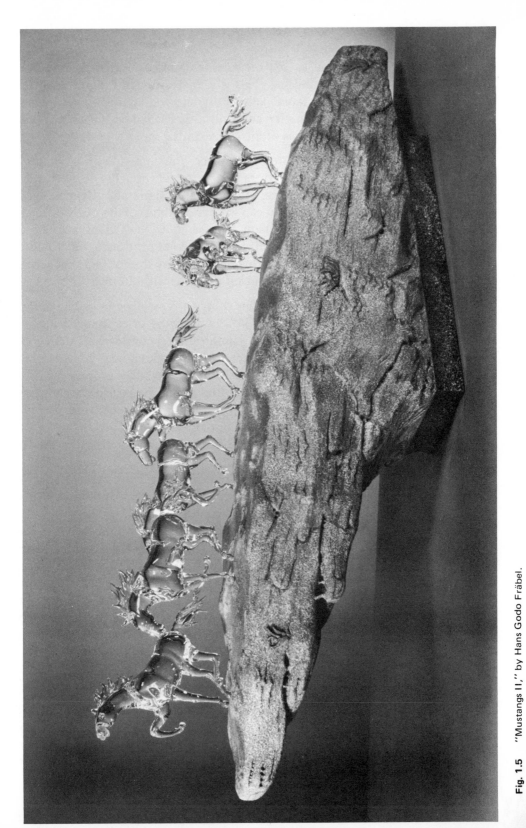

Fig. 1.5 "Mustangs II," by Hans Godo Fräbel.

When you come to sell the artwork you have created, you enter the field of merchandising. This is a different world requiring different thinking and different actions. To succeed in merchandising may require as much creativity and skill as is needed to create works of art, but they are abilities of different kinds.

The Hypothetical Customer.   When you come to selling your artwork you must eliminate from your mind all thoughts of its creation —for this has no relevance. All you must think about is the hypothetical customer; how you can get her or him to like your work; and how you can get this person to give you a sufficient amount of money for its possession. This may sound cold and base, but whether you like it or not, it is merchandising. If you do not feel you can do what is required, then get yourself an agent without delay.

Wide Price Range.   Another thing to remember in selling is that your work should be offered in a rather wide price range. Those art pieces you and your agent (if you have one) consider less than good should be priced comparatively low (depending on your market, etc.). Those you consider good should be a little more expensive. Those few you agree are outstanding should be priced substantially above the others. Ranging your prices in this way accomplishes a few things. First, it gives those with limited means an opportunity to purchase your less expensive work. Second, it encourages the sale of your modestly priced art pieces, for they appear to be good buys when compared with your high-priced work. Third, you encourage the people of means to buy your higher-priced work because it is out of the range of those with less wealth.

The great majority of your artwork will and should be in the low and medium price range. This is the "bread and butter" range where you will sell the greatest number of paintings. You will sell only a few in the high-priced range, but do not let it bother you. If you stay in the fine art field you most likely will improve and build a reputation. Later on, when your reputation permits you to charge more for your work, these more expensive, outstanding paintings will bring a handsome return.

One final word: *The only price that is right for artwork is the one that will permit and encourage people to buy.* Let's face it, the only artwork that is worth anything is that which is bought and placed where people can observe and enjoy it. If you place unrealistic prices on your work and as a result wind up with a studio full of unbought pieces, what have you accomplished?

21

To be afraid to part with a piece of your work because you fear it will be worth more at a later date is to be shortsighted and without faith in yourself. It is the people who are buying your artwork *now*— who are showing it and praising it to their friends—that are building your reputation. And you should have the faith that when you have the advanced reputation you will be able to create better and more work in keeping with your fame.

2 Agents and Dealers

There comes a time in every artist's life when she or he feels the need of an agent's services. The fact is, the professional artist does need one. The questions are: When is the proper time to get an agent? Do I need an agent? What type of agent is best for me? Where do I find an agent? How do I pay an agent? What agreements do I make with an agent? These are a few of the more important questions that must be answered. Let us take them one at a time.

WHEN AM I READY FOR AN AGENT?

The first question is improperly phrased. It should not read, "When is the proper time to get an agent?" but, "When is an agent ready to accept me?" The fact is, until such time as you become an artist of outstanding reputation you will have little to do with the selection of an agent. The best you can do is hope a reputable agent will accept you as a client. There is no point in looking for an agent until you have developed a dominant style and medium and can produce work of a professional quality with regularity, and when you have at least fifty or more pieces of artwork to display. To hope that an agent will take you on before such a time is unrealistic.

You may think it unreasonable for an agent to place these requirements on you before (s)he will handle your work. But is it? Put yourself in the agent's position. Would you devote the time, energy, and money necessary to publicize an artist if you had only a few pieces to sell? Agents are businesspeople. Unless they can see a reasonable financial return for their efforts, they are not interested. If there are a large number of art pieces to sell, plus some assurance that more of professional quality will be forthcoming, the agent has reasonable assurance that money can be made.

DO I NEED AN AGENT?

An answer to the second question, "Do you need an agent?", will depend on three considerations: time, latitude, and income. If you have a great deal of free time on your hands, if you are only interested in selling your work in the immediate vicinity, and if you are satisfied with a very limited income from your artwork, then you do not need an agent. The information given in this book plus a little ingenuity will supply you with the know-how.

There are advantages to being your own agent. For one thing, you will work more conscientiously to sell your own work. Second, you can save the 33⅓ percent commission usually paid an agent. Third, you may enjoy the challenge and experience of selling art. There are many part-time artists who act as their own agents and do a satisfactory, though limited, job.

On the other hand, if you want to work full time at your artwork or if you are working at a job and doing your artwork in your free time, then you will not have the necessary time to act as your own agent. You will also need an agent if you want to expand your reputation beyond your immediate vicinity—and if you do not care to get involved in sales and related experiences. Under these conditions an agent is absolutely necessary.

There are other things an agent can do for the busy artist. In dealing with customers he or she can mention complimentary things about your background, outstanding accomplishments, and honors you have won. An agent can display complimentary reviews and use similar devices to influence potential customers. These are things you could not do yourself without appearing to be conceited. The competent agent could also keep your financial records in order, collect money that is due, arrange social meetings that will help to further your reputation, and arrange to have your work appear where it will do you the most good.

WHAT TYPE OF AGENT DO I NEED?

Should you decide that you have sufficiently progressed, and your situation is such that the services of an agent are necessary, then your next logical question is, "What type of agent is best for me?" In this context, type refers to *level or sphere of operation.* Before you start your search for an agent, you must first make some basic decisions about what you wish to accomplish:

1. Do you want to sell your work in the large art centers such as New York, Philadelphia, Chicago, Los Angeles, etc.? Or, if you live in a modest-size city or community, would you be satisfied to sell in your local vicinity? By local vicinity is meant not only your immediate community but also a reasonable surrounding area that includes at least 40,000 people or more. It is doubtful that a population of less than this could offer sufficient, consistent demand for an artist's work.

2. Do you wish to ask high prices for your work and be satisfied with a few sales? Or do you prefer to price your work modestly (between $10 to $100) and try to appeal to the larger middle-class market?

The above questions are for you to consider; but the answers may not necessarily be available to you. For example, you may decide that you would like to sell your work in New York City. To accomplish this you would have to be "handled" by a New York gallery. And this is only possible for artists who are prominent, popular, and outstanding. If you have evidence that you fit into this category (awards, prizes, large sales, published articles, etc.) then this is for you. Details on how these galleries operate are given later.

If you are a competent artist, but not yet outstanding or well-known, then you should plan to sell in your local vicinity. This is not to imply that you have been relegated to an inferior position. On the contrary, you may be much further ahead. Having your artwork offered by a gallery in one of the art centers does not carry with it any sales guarantee. Generally, the stilted presentations of galleries sell few of any one artist's work. A vigorous local presentation can

Fig. 2.1 Gaugin painting, "Nature morte a l'estampe Japonaise," 28$\frac{1}{2}$ by 36$\frac{7}{8}$ inches, which was sold at the important Impressionist and Modern paintings and sculpture sale on March 17, 1976 for $1,400,000 (Courtesy: Sotheby Parke-Bernet, Inc.).

frequently accomplish more sales for you. More will be said about this later.

The question on price, mentioned above, is entirely up to you to answer. Before you make your decision, however, there are a few things you should consider. There are two popular impressions (or misconceptions) among artists. One is that the higher you price your work the more prestige you have. The other implies that the higher prices will attract the wealthier people to your work. Both of these impressions should be closely examined.

It is true that in our society there is a relationship between price and prestige. However, it is the price that is actually paid, not what appears on the price tag, that makes the difference. You can charge anything you like but if no one will buy, how much prestige is involved? High prices on artwork that doesn't sell may do something for your ego but can raise havoc with your pocketbook.

The impression that only the wealthy purchase artwork is questionable. Although this was true in the past, the fact is that our present-day economy bears no relationship to that of the past. In those days you either sold to the wealthy or to no one, for there were only the rich or the poor. Today, in the United States, neither of these groups is significant when compared with the vast middle class that controls the economy. It is this group that earns approximately $190 billion each year and spends it for drapes, rugs, appliances, TVs, and dozens of other necessities and luxuries for the homes. And it is this constantly growing group of approximately 30 million families that constitutes the art buyers of the present and the future. These people can be found in all communities.

WHERE DO I FIND AN AGENT?

There are basically three possible decisions you can make concerning the art market you wish to approach, and your decision will determine the kind of agent you will need and where to look for that person: (a) You can sell your artwork locally to the luxury-minded middle-class market. (b) You can try to sell to the local wealthy market. (c) You can try to sell through the art galleries in the large art centers. A different approach is needed to secure an agent to cover each of these situations.

THE LOCAL DEALER AS YOUR AGENT

If you decide you want to sell your work locally, your search for an agent should start with an investigation of the local art galleries—if one or more exists. At the outset, you should inquire if they are interested in new artists in general and you in particular. The proprietor (dealer) will most likely question you in detail about your *reputation as an artist* and less about your work. This is because local galleries are interested in securing artists who they feel will enhance their own prestige. Even the most insignificant gallery can get all the unproven artists they wish. This is not to say that local galleries do not take the work of any unknowns. They do, but are very careful to pick only the most promising. So it would be wise to get this point of acceptance cleared up before you spend any more time on your investigation.

If the dealer who owns the local art gallery is interested in seeing your work, accept the appointment. You should prepare for this interview the same as you would for a large gallery in New York City. The preparations are described in detail in the section devoted to galleries. Whether you are accepted or not, it is good experience to be interviewed by a dealer. If you are refused, you have lost nothing. If you are accepted, do not be in a hurry to sign an agreement.

Before you accept the local dealer as your agent you should check carefully. Is this dealer experienced in handling your type of artwork? What type of people does this gallery cater to? What is its average price range? Is it a busy place? Does the dealer have a genuine interest in art or just in money? What is the dealer's reputation in the community?

Fig. 2.2   Auctioning the "Portrait de l'artiste avec sa palette" by Paul Gaugin at Parke-Bernet Galleries May 5, 1971. The painting sold for $420,000 (Courtesy: Sotheby Parke-Bernet Galleries, Inc.).

Most local galleries are seldom located in the main business areas. They are usually in an attractively set-up, quiet place. The dealers are usually pleasant, interesting, dignified people. The whole atmosphere is usually keyed to a slow, limited type of operation, primarily organized to attract the luxury-minded middle class and the relatively wealthy. If you could be satisfied with only an occasional sale of your work at a fairly good price, then this is the place for you. This is the most you can expect from so limited an operation.

The artist who is looking for consistent sales of his modestly priced artwork will find that the remote, local art gallery will not meet his or her needs. (S)he must find a place where her/his work can be regularly observed by large numbers of people. It is a fundamental law of business that the more people who see your product the more there will be who will buy. Thousands of studies by industries of all kinds statistically prove this point. And it is just as true with art as it is with TVs, tomatos, and tea sets.

Where can you find such a location if the art gallery is not satisfactory? There are a few good possibilities depending on where you happen to be located. In the past, the only place that a large pedestrian traffic could be found was downtown where everyone went to shop. Today there are shopping malls in the suburbs of all large cities and the outskirts of all smaller communities. This expansion has increased the sales opportunities for the artist as it has for everyone else.

In every busy shopping area you will find a series of stores that cater to a clientele that is likely to be interested in art. Such places as bookstores, fine furniture shops, the better department stores (discount stores will not do), gift shops that carry a better line of home items and jewelry, music shops, and the card shops that handle the more expensive lines of cards and related items are good places.

Investigate the shops that interest you by spending time in them. Note the numbers and types of customers—are they nicely dressed? Do they take the time to browse? Approximately what percentage make a purchase? The shop itself should be neatly organized, clean, sufficiently illuminated, furnished in good taste, and generally inviting. The clerks should be mature, pleasant, dignified, friendly people who appear genuinely concerned with each customer. Take note of the parking lot outside. Do the customers drive cars of recent vintage? Are the cars well-cared-for and clean? The makes of the cars are of little importance. Some of the people who drive the most expensive cars use all their spare money for such purchases and have little left for art or anything else.

Fig. 2.3 Wood sculptures of Marc Schriebman showcases, at the Todd Gallery at the Woodbridge Center, Woodbridge, New Jersey.

When you find the shops that are appropriate for the sale of your artwork, approach the proprietor or manager—whoever is responsible for merchandising—and present your proposition. (Details on what your proposal should include are included in a later section.) When a store shows an interest, inquire as to the amount of space it will devote to your work; where the space will be located; who will be responsible for properly setting up and maintaining your exhibit; and how much promotion the store is willing to give your work.

Most artists consider themselves fortunate if they find one appropriate shop to take in their artwork. However, should you be lucky enough to find a few possibilities and must select one, then choose

29

Fig. 2.4   Todd Gallery at the famous Concord Hotel,
at Kiamesha Lake, New York.

the one that caters to the greatest number of the type of customers who will be interested in your work; the shop that will give you the greatest amount of space for display and the best location, whose salespeople have a sympathetic understanding of art and are willing to push its sale.

THE INDIVIDUAL AGENT

If you cannot find an appropriate art gallery or shop that will handle your work, where can you then turn for an agent? In this case, you will have to find an individual of the proper temperament, background, and experience. Great care will have to be exercised in the selection of this person. Lacking a business establishment in which to sell your artwork, this individual will have to make up for it with different sales promotion methods. This takes time, energy, determination, and know-how.

Having the necessary time, and a desire to earn money, are two of the major qualifications for an agent. He or she must also be friendly, able to approach and converse with people of all types, must be pleasant, cultured, intensely interested in art in general, and particularly fond of your artwork. Your agent must have a wide circle of friends from all walks of life—engineers, doctors, lawyers, teachers, banking personnel, merchants, etc.—and must be able to speak convincingly.

Your agent will have to be able to convince people that your artwork would add a great deal to the beauty and joy of their homes or places of business. Bank presidents, lawyers, doctors, school principals, businesspeople, etc. will have to be persuaded that your work will improve the decor of their offices, homes, and/or establishments. Architects, interior designers, and interior decorators must be impressed with the value of including your artwork in their recommendations. Merchants must be convinced that occasionally displaying samples of your work will bring "class" and prestige to their places of business. The newspapers, radio, and television media must know of all your accomplishments; this too will be up to your agent.

It will not be easy to find the proper person with all the necessary qualifications. You may make mistakes in your first few selections, but don't give up. There are good agents available. If you cannot find one among your friends and acquaintances, check the staff of the local college or secondary school. A notice on the faculty bulletin boards of these institutions may bring results. Officers of local clubs are good prospects. Retired school teachers who are still vigorous often serve as excellent agents. If all else fails, a small ad on the art news page in the local paper may bring surprising results. If you do resort to an ad, have the interested parties write or call. In that way, you can eliminate a lot of unnecessary lengthy interruptions.

When you have found the proper agent you will have little trouble recognizing that person. He or she will be a genuine asset, helping and supplementing your career where needed. Your agent will advise you and make suggestions concerning the advancement of your career *but must not tell you what artistic creations you are to make.* The artwork you create must be your responsibility and yours alone. It is the agent's job to develop the most favorable sales situation for that which you produce.

FINANCIAL ARRANGEMENTS

The most commonly used sales procedure between an artist and his sales representative (who may be called a dealer or agent) is quite simple: the artist turns over the completed artwork to his/her representative, who gives the artist a receipt. When the artwork is sold, the sales representative turns over to the artist the agreed-upon price less commission. The artist is also given a copy of the bill of sale.

THE COMMISSION

The amount to pay a sales representative is customarily 33⅓ percent on all sales. There is no point in trying to offer less. An agent or dealer will remain with you as long as (s)he is making a fair amount of money for her or his efforts. Experience has shown one-third to be a fair and equitable commission. An exception may be in the case of sculpture, where there is a foundry cost, and in murals, where there are excessive material costs, installation, etc. These deductions should be considered before commissions are determined. On those occasions for which the sales representative grants special commissions to encourage a sale, the monies should come from his or her percentage and not from the two-thirds due the artist.

A point of contention that arises more often than it should in the artist-agent relationship concerns the amount of commission, if any, the artist should pay to the agent on his or her own sales. To avoid any unpleasantness, this point should be covered in the artist-agent contract. Agents should be given the full commission on *all* sales made in the territory assigned if they agree to the following: (a) to give the artist at least a minimum amount of promotion; (b) to guarantee a certain minimum amount of sales; and (c) to perform certain services without charge to the artist.

The commission paid on charitable sales will depend on the amount received. If the full price is received then the full commission should be paid. If the price is substantially below the regular price, then no commission should be forthcoming. Prizes are not subject to commissions, except purchase prizes which are sums of money awarded to an artist by a sponsoring organization in an art show in exchange for the winning artwork. On the latter the agent should receive one-third of the regular selling price.

The transactions between you the artist and your agent (dealer) should be covered *in writing.* Only in this way can you avoid the misunderstandings that can arise in the course of events. The written contract should be prepared no matter how close a friend your agent might be. Friendship has a way of deteriorating as misunderstandings creep in.

You as the artist, or you in combination with the agent (dealer) can have a lawyer draw up a contract for your particular need. If you feel capable enough, you can draw up your own contract. Sometimes the artist and agent will exchange letters in which they spell out their agreement. And this will be sufficient. The important thing is that there be a *written* understanding that can be referred to when there is a question involved.

The artist-dealer contract should cover all the important issues that might interfere with a desirable relationship. It is wise to consider issues before they become problems charged with emotion. A well-conceived contract lets everyone involved know where (s)he stands—what (s)he can and cannot expect to take place. Following are some of the main issues that should be covered:

1. The *percentage of commission* paid on sales. This should also include the commission paid the dealer for murals, portraits, and other special assignments the dealer secures for the artist.

2. The *basis for figuring commissions* on purchase prices.

3. The question of whether the dealer should get *commissions on the sales made by the artist* should be settled. Dealers are usually given commissions on such sales if they first give the artist a minimum guarantee of sales.

4. The question of *royalties, commercial assignments, and sale of reproduction rights* should be covered. It is customary for the dealer to receive a commission on only those that he or she arranges.

5. When sculptures and murals are involved the artist should indicate the *installation, supplies, etc.,* that are deducted before the commissions are figured.

6. When the dealer has a gallery available, the contract should indicate the *amount of exposure* the artist's work will be given— how frequently there will be a one-person show; how many of the artist's pieces will be in the group show, and how many in the permanent exhibitions. It should also indicate the number of pieces of the artist's work the dealer will keep on hand in storage.

7. *Expenses* should be considered, including (a) the percentage of expenses for the one-person show that will be paid by the dealer; (b) the extent of the expenses of packing and shipping work to clients and exhibitions that the dealer will bear; (c) the amount of insurance the dealer will carry on the artwork in his possession.

8. *Financial arrangements* should be carefully spelled out. Who shall set the prices on the artwork? This is usually a written agreement between artist and dealer. The dealer should realize that money for works sold is received in trust and the net proceeds (after agreed-upon deductions) shall be immediately deposited in a special trust bank account for the artist. A specific time (usually twice a month) should be indicated when the dealer should give the artist the money due her or him. Some dealers give the artist a set amount each month, then have an accounting periodically to even out money due. Written receipts should accompany all artwork that passes back and forth between artist and dealer. There must be a final and complete financial accounting at the end of each year.

9. There should be a positive statement on the *sphere and latitude of the dealer's coverage*. If the dealer does not have exclusive rights over the artist's work, the contract should indicate the conditions and degree to which the artist can have others represent him or her.

10. The *period of time covered by the contract* should be indicated. It should also include a statement on conditions under which it may be canceled.

The above are the basic arrangements that should be considered in the artist-dealer relationship. Some artists may have special interests or problems that call for additions to or subtractions from the contract. Some of the customary fees, commissions, and regulations vary in different parts of the country. These are but a few of the reasons why contracts have to be varied to fit each artist-dealer/agent relationship.

A rather inexpensive artist-dealer contract form that can be altered to meet most artists' needs can be purchased from the Artists Equity Association, Inc. This is an organization of fine artists that has branches in the large cities across the country. The central office is at 2813 Albemarle St. NW, Washington, D.C. 20008. This group also sell other forms that the fine artist can use to his or her advantage.

Artwork Sold to the Dealer. The artist-agent financial arrangement described to this point is the most popular but by no means the only one used. A second is the artist-dealer arrangements in which the artist sells his work outright to the dealer who, in turn, resells it to the public. This arrangement may have some variations: (a) the dealer may contract to purchase, and the artist may agree to sell all the art work (s)he produces; (b) the dealer may contract to purchase a certain portion of the artist's work; (c) (s)he may purchase all the artist's work in a certain medium; (d) in return for promotional publicity the dealer may be given the right of first refusal; (e) or, the dealer may agree to buy an occasional piece of work from the artist.

Any of the above arrangements that are committed to a written contract bind both the artist and dealer. In a contract that says the artist *must* sell and the dealer *must* purchase there can be no variation. If a contract permits either the artist or the dealer a chance for refusal then the rejected artwork may be sold to a third party.

In an agreement in which the artist makes an outright sale of artwork to a dealer, (s)he retains no rights regarding to whom or for what amount the work may be sold unless the contract so specifies. Once the artist has made a binding contract with a dealer (s)he may not withhold or restrict the sale of any work that is within the authority of the dealer. On the other hand, if the contract specifies

Fig. 2.5   View of the Ann Jacob Gallery located in the famous Peachtree Center in Atlanta, Georgia.

that the dealer must sell at a certain price (s)he may not vary it for any reason.

Informal Contract. What is the situation if the artist leaves artwork with a dealer with whom there is no formal contract? In this case, the artist has entered into an informal contract with the dealer. By leaving the artwork the artist has said, "I am willing to accept the contractual arrangements you normally grant." The dealer, in accepting the artwork, has replied, "I agree to grant you all the benefits that I customarily grant to others in your situation." This informal relationship automatically continues until it is formally terminated. By formal termination is meant that either of the parties notifies the other in writing that the relationship is ended and such notification is made public so no one will be misled.

The objections to the informal contract arrangement are quite obvious. For one thing, it is not always easy to determine that which is a dealer's "normal" procedure. Legal battles between artists and dealers concerning an informal contract are extremely uncommon. But when they do occur they are usually very expensive and time-consuming. The artist should try to avoid the informal contract situation by sending the dealer a letter outlining the financial arrangements as they are understood to exist. If the dealer replies that the arrangements as outlined in the letter are correct, then a formal contract exists. The combination of the two letters represent a contract. If the dealer does not answer, the artist has lost nothing, for the informal status continues.

In all artist-agent or artist-dealer contracts that grant the agent/dealer complete or substantial control over the sales of an artist's work, it is implied that the agent will make a "reasonable" effort to publicize and sell the artist's work. Test cases in the courts have indicated that the artist is not bound by a contract until such reasonable effort is made.

The artist should not be apprehensive about terminating a contract with an agent or dealer who fails to sell his or her work. In most cases, agents/dealers are happy to oblige. By releasing you, they make room for another whose work might sell.

Final Recommendations

(1) Whenever you hand over a piece of your artwork to a dealer/agent, make sure you get a *signed receipt*. This is not necessary, of course, if you have made an outright sale. (2) Insist on a *duplicate copy of the bill of sale* whenever a piece of your artwork is sold.

Following are suggested forms that might be used for these purposes. The artist who has a very limited need for these forms may type copies on his or her regular letterhead. Those who have a ditto-type duplicator available can, for only a few cents, prepare a carbon and run off a couple hundred.

SUGGESTED RECEIPT FORM

Artist's Name

Address   Phone Number

The following art pieces have been released to the custody of ....

(Name)

Title	Size	Medium	Selling Price	% Commission

1. ....
2. ....
3. ....
4. ....
5. ....

(Use back of sheet if necessary)

The above is to be used for the following purpose:

(Sale, exhibit, reproduction, etc.)

The above art pieces must be fully insured against loss or damage for the benefit of the artist, until such time as they are returned to the possession of the artist. Such insurance to be in an amount equal to the selling price less commission. All above works are to be returned to the artist on demand. The artist reserves all reproduction rights.

(Signature of dealer or agent)

(Date)

None of the above listed artworks may be sent out on approval unless this statement is signed below.

---------------------------------   --

(Date)   (Artist's Name)

SUGGESTED BILL-OF-SALE FORM
(To be filled out in duplicate)

Artist or Dealer's Name
Address of Above   Phone Number

Date of Purchase ....   Price ....

Sold to ....
                              (Name)

Address ....
Terms of payment ....
Description of artwork: ....

....

All reproduction rights for the artwork described above are reserved for the artist.

(Signed) ....
                    (Purchaser)   (Artist or Representative)

3 Selling To and Through The Galleries

THE ONE-PERSON SHOW

Just as it is the dream of every actor to see his/her name up in lights above a Broadway theater, so it is the dream of every artist to have a one-person show at a large city art gallery, particularly in New York City. The artist's chance of realizing this dream is far greater than the actor's. The fact is that almost any artist can have a one-person show in New York City or in most of the leading art centers.

The one-person show is available to two groups of artists: those with outstanding talent and those with sufficient capital. The benefits such a showing brings to the artists in each group varies greatly.

The dealer who runs a gallery, whether it is located in New York City, Chicago, San Francisco, or Podunk Corners, is interested in artwork that can be sold. If a dealer believes your work can be sold, you are in. If not, you are out. It is just that cut and dried. The questions are "How do I get my work before the dealers?" and "If my work is accepted, what kind of sales deal do I make?"

FINDING THE RIGHT GALLERIES

The galleries in the leading art centers can be located by looking in the national art magazines (see list in Appendix, pp. 249-253) that can be found in almost all libraries. Here, too, can be found art yearbooks that include extensive listings of galleries. There are always the yellow pages of the telephone directories. You can borrow the New York City telephone directory or that of any city in which you are interested from your local telephone company or the library.

When people in the fine art field speak of the major art centers they are referring to New York City, Paris, London, Boston (and vicinity), Chicago, Los Angeles (and vicinity), San Francisco (and vicinity), and Washington. It should not be assumed that these places are anywhere near equal in art opportunities. New York City alone has about twice as many art galleries as there are in the rest of the United States.

Fig. 3.1   Entrance to the M. Knoedler Galleries on 70th Street in New York City.

In each of the locations listed above, approximately 75 to 85 percent of the galleries exhibit the work of contemporary artists. This will give you a rough idea of the number of gallery opportunities that are available. It also explains why so many budding artists head for New York City. Although it is true that New York City has the greatest number of gallery opportunities, it is also true that it has the greatest competition. Before embarking for New York, the developing artist would do well to first investigate an art center near her or his home. Success in a gallery outside New York can be every bit as rewarding.

Galleries specialize in certain types of artwork. Some will handle only paintings, or sculptures, or prints, while others will include a few different kinds of artwork. There are galleries that offer only the masters, while others specialize in contemporary American artists or foreign artists. Still others offer a particular style of artwork. Some galleries search out and encourage new art talent; others have only a passive interest in new art, while still others will have nothing to do with new and/or contemporary artists. Contact only those that handle your type of work and accept new artists. It is a waste of time to bother with the others.

GETTING YOUR WORK SEEN

When you have carefully located the right galleries for your work, you are ready to write or phone for appointments. If you phone, try to do it at a time when the dealer is not busy. Late morning in midweek is probably best. If you write, keep your letter brief and to the point. Dealers are not interested in your life history, only information that will help them understand your artwork and standing in the art field. If you have some good photographs of your work, include about ten or twelve in the letter. If you have a personal reference that will be meaningful to the dealers, don't forget to mention it. It can help to open doors that might otherwise stay closed.

When you are granted an interview by a gallery representative, select your showing carefully. Don't take along everything you ever painted. Choose one dominant style to put across and select your best representations of this style. The number you should take along will be determined by the size of your work. Generally, from six to twelve will do. This is a sufficient number for the experienced dealer or curator to evaluate. If that individual is impressed, (s)he will come to your studio or make another definite arrangement to see the rest of what you have to offer.

Fig. 3.2 Installation, Vieira da Silva exhibition,
M. Knoedler & Co., New York.

If your work is too large to take along on the interview, photographs will have to do. However, make sure the photos are of excellent quality. Colored slides make an excellent presentation.

Place your work before the gallery representative, then step back and be quiet. Don't try to explain your work. These people know what they are looking for and no amount of talk will change their mind.

What do dealers look for when they view the work of new applicants? This question was put to a number of dealers and curators from galleries that specialize in finding new art talent. Every last one responded that they could not give a detailed answer. Their reaction to new art was an immediate "reflex" and not at all dependent on prolonged reflection.

After looking over your work, the dealer or curator may offer you

one of the following alternatives.

1. Refusal. You may be told politely that your work is unacceptable.

2. The "For-Hire" Show. You may be told that the gallery will not accept you as a permanent artist member but will give you a one-person show. *This type of offer must be examined with extreme caution.* Such an offer can have many ramifications and unless the artist is careful, she or he can end up paying a great deal of money for very little in return.

The one-person show is discussed in detail in Chapter 4. At this time, however, you should become familiar with the so called *for-hire show* that some galleries try to sell to the unwary.

There are galleries in New York City (and in other leading art centers) that are typical art galleries in all respects except one—they are for hire. Here, money is the dominant consideration. These galleries will hang a single picture, a dozen, or fill the entire gallery, depending on how much money you are willing to pay. If you can foot the bill you can also have a fancy catalogue, elaborate advertising, cocktail party, and any of the other trimmings. (Incidentally, cocktail parties are not customarily included at exhibits any more.

Fig. 3.3   Reinhardt "Black Paintings,"
Marlborough Gallery, New York.

Only a very few outstanding galleries retain this practice.) A full-dress one-person show with all the trimmings can cost from $700 to $1500 for a two- to three-week show. The difference in cost will be determined by location of the gallery and the number of "trimmings" you want.

In appearance, the "for-hire" gallery can be as impressive looking as any of the others. The trouble is that the people of stature in the art field—the ones you wish to impress—are not likely to frequent the place. They have so often seen these galleries filled with poor work that they have given up on them. If you can afford it, the "for-hire" gallery can do your ego some good, give you a fancy gallery name to include in your record, and give all your friends and relatives a chance to see your work, but it will do little to further your career.

If and when you are offered a one-person show by a gallery, make sure you are given a *written contract.* Study the contract very carefully to make sure it covers all details. Make sure you understand your responsibilities, the things for which you must pay, and all the costs. This should be done no matter which gallery makes the offer.

The art gallery proprietor who makes you an offer of a one-person show because he or she has a sincere belief that your work will sell, will be willing to share a portion of the costs. The amount of the investment that person will assume will be in direct proportion to the faith (s)he has in your work. This individual may take full responsibility for preparing and presenting the show and only require you to pay a minimum guarantee against future commissions. When the dealer has a maximum of faith, (s)he will be willing to accept your paintings, at a predetermined price, in lieu of all or part of the cash payment.

An offer of a one-person show that does not include an offer on the part of the gallery to share the financial risk on an equitable basis is of very questionable value. If a gallery is not willing to make an investment in your show you can be quite sure that it will bring you little, if any, returns in money or prestige.

3. Consignment Offer. You may be offered the opportunity to submit some of your work for the gallery to sell on a consignment basis. This is not the same as being given a permanent gallery contract. All the dealer agrees to do is make an effort to sell your artwork. If this effort is successful, you will get the sales price less the dealer's commission. No money will change hands until a sale is made. The dealer may require that you provide some guarantees concerning sales territory, commissions, minimum prices, etc. These agreements are usually included in letters exchanged between artist and dealer.

Fig. 3.4 Art auction at Todd Gallery in Beverly Hills, California.

The most desirable feature of this particular arrangement is that it gives you an "inside track" with the gallery. If your work sells in an amount at least equal to its expectations, you will undoubtedly be given a full, permanent contract.

4. Contract Offer. Finally, you may be offered a contract to become a permanent member of the gallery's stable of artists. This is a *very* rare occurrence. When it does happen you can be sure that the gallery representative believes you have unusual abilities to produce artwork that is highly likely to sell.

The artist-dealer contract you will be offered will entitle you to a continuing exhibit of samples of your work in the gallery; a one-person show at certain specified periods of time (usually every third year); a set financial arrangement, etc. No matter which gallery offers you the contract, you should have your lawyer examine it carefully before you sign it.

Having your work exhibited in a New York gallery, or in a gallery in one of the other major art centers, has two positive advantages. First, it enhances your prestige. Second, it offers you an additional market for your work. What the artist must realize is the magnitude of these advantages. The erroneous impression harbored by most artists is that a New York showing is the opening to the "big life," "big money," "big fame," etc. This is *not* so more often than it is.

In the final analysis, the acceptance of your work by any leading gallery is an indication of a point of arrival. It indicates that you now are capable of producing fine artwork of professional quality. It guarantees nothing more. Just what it will mean in terms of your income will depend on several things—your personal popularity, the prevailing financial atmosphere, the effort exerted in "pushing" your work, the prevailing modes and moods in artwork, and the pricing of your work. If you wish to live off the income of your fine artwork, then you cannot relax once you have been accepted by an important gallery. Your important work has just begun.

Fig. 3.5   Upper gallery of the Roberts Gallery in Toronto, Canada showing an assorted collection.

4 Selling Through Art Shows

The value of the art show as a means for selling artwork is strongly questioned by many prominent people in the art trade. The fact remains, however, that this type of exhibit, with all its shortcomings, is still the artist's biggest showcase. Directly or indirectly, it is responsible for the sales of more different types and grade levels of artwork than any other means. The wise artist tries to understand the shortcomings of the exhibit system and then goes on to make the most of the good it has to offer.

There are three general types of exhibits: the open juries exhibits, museum invitational exhibits, and one-person shows. Artists should strive to enter all kinds. They should, however, go into all art shows with eyes wide open, knowing the advantages and disadvantages of this method of exhibiting one's artwork.

Juried exhibits are usually sponsored by some art gallery, organization, museum, or art group. The entries may be limited by skill, location, type of medium, group affiliations, training, or any of a half-dozen other regulations. There is usually an entrance fee ranging from 50 cents per picture for small local exhibits to $10 or more for large national or international shows. Some small local exhibits will hang any picture for which the fee is paid while the more advanced have a jury carefully choose each entry.

Some sponsoring organizations require that you deliver your work in person to the exhibit center. Others insist that the artwork be properly packed and shipped. In many cases both means of transportation are accepted. In all cases, however, you will have to assume the expenses involved in packing, shipping, handling, and insurance. To ship a single painting to a national exhibit can cost you $20 or more if you carefully record every expense from the entrance fee to the return of the painting. Cumbersome sculpture, requiring special packing and handling, can go far above this amount. A recent trend is for sponsoring organizations to pay for the return of artwork selected for inclusion in their exhibit. This was brought about when many artists objected to their ever-increasing expenses.

There is always a group of "experts" assigned to choose the outstanding among the entries. The number on the jury may vary from one to a dozen or more depending on the method of judging employed. Usually the jury consists of three or four members. A few different methods of judging have been used but none seem to please everyone or even a small fraction of those who enter the exhibit.

The art pieces judged best in the exhibit are given awards. In small local exhibits the award may be a ribbon, medal, certificate, or a combination of these. The regional and national exhibits may offer a scholarship (to students) but usually they give a cash award or a purchase prize. A purchase prize is a sum of money given to the artist by the sponsoring organization in exchange for the winning artwork.

Announcements of forthcoming exhibits can be found in a few of the leading art magazines such as *Art News, American Artist, Art Magazine.* These will list the location of the exhibit, who to contact for entry information, the date the exhibit will take place and the deadline for entries, entry fee, who the exhibit is open to, nature and medium of the work to be shown, number of entries permitted, and

whether there will be a jury and prizes. Sometimes, the prizes will be indicated as well as the names of those who will be on the jury. These announcements usually start to appear several months before the exhibits are scheduled to go on. (See the Appendix, pp. 249-253, for a more complete list of art periodicals.)

Advantages of Juried Exhibits

So much for the mechanics involved in the juried exhibit. What are its advantages and disadvantages to the artist? There are a few of each.

The exhibit acts as an excellent measuring stick for the artist at all stages of development. Novice artists may enter local exhibits where they can compare their artwork to that of others. As artists advance in ability they can submit their work to exhibits with more stringent entrance requirements. A definite indication of advancement is the type, nature, and number of exhibits for which an artist's work is accepted. It must be emphasized that numbers alone are not indicative of advancement. The type and stature of the exhibit at which your work is accepted is a truer measurement of your ability.

Another advantage exhibits offer is maximum exposure. Every exhibit, no matter how limited, offers an opportunity to let your work be viewed by interested persons who might extend your reputation. Dealers, curators, and collectors attend exhibits regularly. There is always a chance that they will select your work. There is also the chance that your work might be judged the best of the show. This can do your reputation and morale a great deal of good. Then too, there is the chance to sell. At every exhibit there are many people who come not only to look but also to buy.

Disadvantages of Juried Exhibits

The objections most frequently voiced about exhibits are that they are expensive, overrated, and biased. Artists who keep careful expense accounts can show that the paying of entrance fees, plus the packing, insuring, and shipping of entries to exhibits, can be an expensive proposition.

Those who say that exhibits are overrated charge that comparatively few pictures are sold in relation to the number exhibited. Even the prestige factor, they contend, is frequently not all that the sponsors of the exhibits would like you to believe.

The charge of bias is the most prevalent and widespread. It is contended that bias exists on two levels: the juries who originally select the artwork to be exhibited are frequently partial to certain style, kind, or type and this will be reflected throughout the exhibit. Then the judges who select the final winners are frequently victims of the same condition.

SELLING AT ART SHOWS

The actual selling of artwork at juried exhibits is carried on in several different ways. At some exhibits the artist or his/her dealer is permitted to be present on the floor of the exhibit when the artwork is on display, and may try to sell to those who show interest. At other exhibits all selling is done only through an individual or committee empowered to do this. Many exhibits require that persons interested in purchasing contact the exhibit committee, which then refers them to the artist concerned.

Selling is an integral part of all exhibits. The selling procedure permitted is made known to the artist when (s)he applies for entrance. Some exhibits permit price tags to be placed on the art pieces that are for sale. Most do not. In almost all cases the sponsoring organization for the exhibit takes a percentage of all sales made. This may vary from 10 to 25 percent, depending on the prestige of the exhibit.

Are juried exhibits worthwhile? There is no simple answer to this question. This is for sure: they play an important part in the development of all artists. They do offer opportunities that cannot be realized in any other way.

MUSEUM INVITATIONAL EXHIBITS

Only artists invited by museum staff may participate in invitational exhibits. The museum may insist on selecting the exact pieces to be shown. Sometimes the staff draws up very confining specifications for the artwork that will be accepted; the final judgment is then left to the artist. There are never any final judgments made as to superiority of one participating artist over another.

Before an invitational exhibit the museum staff decides on the general theme for the exhibit, then invites artists whose work is in keeping with the planned theme to participate. In selecting artists, the members of the museum staff rely on their memories and notes they have compiled on artwork they have seen at galleries, juried exhibits, one-person shows, other museums, or in the leading art magazines.

Is it possible for the unpublicized artist to be invited to participate in a museum's invitational exhibit? The answer is yes. If you feel that your work would qualify, then it is up to you to convince the responsible parties. Some museums will arrange an individual interview if you contact them. Others will have special days set aside for new artists. In all cases it is best that you first write and send about a half-dozen photographs of your work. If the museum administrators are impressed with your work they will extend you an invitation.

The sales at museum exhibits are arranged by or through the museum. Sometimes the museum staff will try to sell your works. When they do, they receive a predetermined commission for their effort. Other times they will refer interested customers directly to the artist.

ONE-PERSON SHOWS

The one-person exhibit is a show where only one artist's work is on display. It is the ultimate desire of all artists to have such an exhibit, especially if the show is sponsored by a leading gallery or museum in New York City, San Francisco, Paris, or another of the other famous art centers.

The mechanics of the one-person show are very much standardized. A dealer who maintains a gallery devotes the entire place, or a major portion of it, to your work. Your work is carefully framed, mounted, and presented. From this point on the procedure may vary a little, depending on where the show is being offered.

In local galleries—those in small communities outside a major city—price tags are placed right on each piece displayed. If the local newspaper has an art section it will usually announce your shows in this section. An ad is sometimes placed in the local paper. Notices are sent to interested groups and individuals in the community.

In New York City and other leading art centers, the art pieces are numbered (never priced) after they are placed on display. These numbers, plus the name of each piece, are listed in a catalogue prepared just for the show. Ads are placed in the prominent art magazines and local newspapers. News releases are sent to newspapers. Announcements and catalogues are mailed to persons the dealers feels might be interested. Special comments and sometimes photos are sent to art critics, museum directors, and persons of similar stature. On rare occasions there is a cocktail party on opening night.

Fig. 4.1   A. J. Casson one-man show on the main floor of the
Roberts Gallery in Toronto, Canada.

On the local level a one-person show may be presented at any
opportune time and run for any length of time. Such presentations
are sometimes planned to coincide with special seasons or events. In
New York City the art season runs from early fall through late
spring. A show usually goes from three to four weeks. Dealers
schedule their shows from six months to a year in advance.

Who pays the bill? This varies from artist to artist and dealer to
dealer. The unknown artist may be required to cover all expenses.
The popular artist presently in vogue may be required to pay none.
Most agreements between artist and dealer fall somewhere between
these extremes. In some agreements the dealer will advance money
to the artist against future sales or accepted artwork in lieu of
money.

When is the artist ready for a one-person show? As we mentioned earlier, you are ready when you have a large number of art pieces, most of which are in one particular style, and this style is developed to a degree of maturity. Note that this description includes three important elements: number, style, and maturity.

Number of art pieces is important because a one-person show is a fairly expensive business venture, and unless there is a large number of items to sell, a profit cannot be realized. *Style* is important because it sets the artist apart from and above other artists. *Maturity* is vital because it means that the artist can repeat his or her particular style with authority and regularity.

Fig. 4.2   A variety of works by major name artists are featured at the Todd Gallery in the Fashion Center in Paramus, New Jersey.

There is nothing to be gained from rushing into a one-person show before you are ready. The best person to let you know when your time has arrived is an experienced dealer. Contact such a person at regular intervals—every year or two, depending on how fast you are at producing and how much work you do. If the dealer thinks your work can be sold, (s)he will let you know soon enough.

How frequently should you have a one-person show? Here again, it is an individual matter depending entirely upon the ability of the artist. One who works with speed and accuracy may have a show every year. Slower performing artists may wait two, three, four, or even five years between shows. Every two or three years is the average.

The one-person show in a reputable gallery in New York City stands a good chance of being observed by the outstanding people in the art field. This in itself is very desirable and important. It does not, however, carry with it any guarantee of success or advancement. Most shows are forgotten the day after they are closed.

The museum one-person show differs in several respects from those sponsored by galleries. First, it is never "for sale." The museum extends an invitation to the artist it feels is worthy. Second, it is reserved only for important artists who have made or are making an unusual impression on the art world. Third, there is no cost to the artist of any appreciable amount. Fourth, all sale possibilities that arise at the show are referred to the artist, who completes the sale at a location away from the show.

No art exhibit of any kind offers as much prestige to the artist as does the museum one-person show. Such an opportunity is usually available only to experienced and seasoned artists.

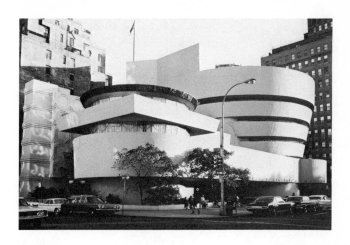

5 Selling To and Through The Museums

Museums are interested in offering for exhibit only artwork rendered by important artists. If a museum purchases your work you can be sure it feels that you are making an important impact on art, or will be in the very near future. It is this implied distinction that makes the sale to a museum so desirable. If the museum that purchased your work is a large, important one, you can be certain that dealers and collectors will soon follow suit.

The amount of money you will receive from a museum for your work will not be great. Museums are well aware of the prestige they offer and expect you to accept this as partial payment.

When are you ready to sell to museums? Only after your artwork has been given complimentary recognition in a few important exhibitions and shows. How do you make the sale? Usually the staff will contact you when the museum is ready to buy. It is sometimes possible to hasten this interest by tactfully keeping the museum staff aware of your advancement.

Fig. 5.1 Exterior view of the Solomon R. Guggenheim
Museum on Fifth Avenue in New York City (Courtesy:
The Solomon R. Guggenheim Museum).

Museums cater to certain types, schools, or periods in art, and to
particular types of artists. It is quite useless to try and sell to a
museum artwork that is not in keeping with their presentations.

Rental Services

Many museums operate rental services. This is done to bring contemporary art before the public, and also to gauge the development
of the up-and-coming artist. Museums invite artists who they feel will
appeal to their patrons to submit their work for such services.
Patrons will rent a number of pieces of artwork for an exhibit. The
fee they pay will vary with the value of work included in the exhibit.
They are permitted to exhibit the art pieces in a single, predetermined location for a set period of time.

All museum rental services have a set artist's contract. Such a
contract usually stipulates that the artist will set the sales price on
his or her art contributions. It also specifies the length of time
56   the rental service will be permitted to retain the artwork, determines

amount of commission and/or service charges that will be paid in the event the work is sold, and requires the artist to assume the responsibility for transporting the artwork in good condition to the rental service's terminal. The rental service usually assumes the responsibility for insuring the artwork against deterioration, destruction, and disappearance. The artist should not assume that because the contract submitted by the museum's rental service is printed it cannot be altered. On the contrary, it can and should be changed so that it is satisfactory to both parties concerned.

A rather complete listing of museums can be found in the *World Almanac, Information Please Almanac*, and similar publications. Write directly to the museum to secure information on its policies concerning exhibits, purchases, and lending services. Addressing the letter to "Director of Public Relations" will get it to the proper person.

Fig. 5.2   Internal view of the Guggenheim Museum showing the famous ramp arrangement of the viewing sections (Courtesy: The Solomon R. Guggenheim Museum).

6 Art Commissions

Special commissions are those *art renditions that are made in response to a predetermined assignment.* They might include architectural murals, mobiles and sculptures, monuments for civic parks and buildings, portraits for individuals and organizations, and paintings for special needs and occasions.

Such commissions are available only to the competent artist. Competence alone, however, is not enough. Sales ability on your part, or that of your agent, is every bit as important.

If you are interested in selling murals or sculptures to enhance buildings, then extend your reputation among architects and interior decorators as far and wide as you can. If you are interested in preparing monuments, then let this be known to the civic groups responsible for the selection of such monuments.

Some architectural and monument commissions are assigned on the basis of open competition. In most cases, however, it is the architect, interior decorator, or responsible committee that hires **58** the artist for the special commission.

Get to know personally as many architects, interior decorators, and responsible committee members as possible. Make sure they know you are available for art commissions of the type they can recommend. For the great majority, whom you cannot meet personally, prepare a direct-mail campaign.

Art Commissions

The Direct-Mail Approach

A direct-mail campaign should include a first and at least three carefully prepared follow-up letters and inserts to each potential client. (Sending only one letter is a waste of time. Surveys have shown that it is not until the third that you realize any results from

Fig. 6.1 Artist Manville B. Wakefield working on the 36-ft-long historical mural for the Marine Midland Bank in Liberty, New York.

direct mailings.) The letters should be concerned only with the *important facts and information about your ability and background* that particularly qualifies you for the kind of art commission you seek. All other incidental information should be left out. It is wise to include in each letter an insert showing pictures of your work, reprints of articles about you that have appeared in print, pictures of you receiving awards, etc. If you have successfully completed *any* previous assignment similar to the kind you seek, play it up in a big way. Remember, nothing succeeds like success.

Fig. 6.2 (a, b, c) Sculptor C. O. Perry makes an adjustment during reassembly of "Early Mace," a major sculptural work in Peachtree Center, Atlanta. Perry, a native Montanan, created the stainless steel sculpture in his Rome, Italy studios. He visited Atlanta to supervise reassembly and installation of the 11-ft-tall work. The sculpture was commissioned by architect John Portman, Atlanta.

(a)

(b)

Just one more suggestion: architects and interior decorators who have used artwork successfully in one rendition tend to use it again. Make a special effort to search out those who are partial to artwork.

If portrait art is what you want to sell, circulate among those who can afford your work. This is the cocktail party, country club, prominent service club set. Your toughest job is securing the first commission. Once you have a good piece of art to display, and a satisfied customer to vouch for you, the following portrait commissions follow quite easily.

Every commission you accept should be covered by a written agreement. This is especially true if a substantial amount of money is involved, and the artwork prepared cannot be sold on the open market in the event that it isn't acceptable to the person or group for which it was originally prepared.

62

THE COMMERCIAL ART FIELD

As we mentioned early in the book, the commercial artist works for the specific purpose of selling what she or he has created. But the expression "commercial art" has never had a single definition. For the present, we will say it is *any art rendition or design function applied to the display, publishing, advertising, visual education, and manufacturing fields.* It is a business in every sense of the word.

Commercial artists can be broadly divided into four major groups: illustrators, designers, letterers, and layout people. The illustrators prepare the graphic representation of an object, incident, scene, person, place, or idea. Designers develop the styling of such items as packages, appliances, textiles, displays, books, and wallpapers. The letterers determine and draw the type, style, and size of lettering that is to accompany a commercial art rendition. Layout people determine the arrangement and form for various units of illustrative material on the printed page.

All four of the above categories are divided and subdivided many times into many different techniques, types, kinds, and forms of specialization. The tremendous demands of modern industry require this variety. To be a successful commercial artist you must discover your best capability and develop it to the point of perfection. You may be an ''airbrush'' person or a ''tempera'' person or an expert in some other medium. You may be a specialist in cloth styles, landscapes, animals, athletes, or what have you. Or you may slice your specialization in another direction—but specialize you must if you are going to be a part of big-time commercial art.

Peter Max, whose special brand of artwork
started a new trend in commercial art.

7 Getting A Job in the Commercial Art Field

The selling of artwork in the commercial art field is accomplished on two general levels. First, there are those who seek a salaried job. This is true for most beginners in the trade, and for those experienced artists who seek a change in position. Second, there are the freelance artists who seek clients to purchase their work on a contract basis.

Much advice given to the job seeker can be of value to the freelance artist. On the other hand, there are sales procedures and techniques used by the freelancer that are of little value to the job hunter. For this reason, we will discuss job hunting in this chapter.

LANDING THE ART JOB

Securing a job of value in the commercial art field must be looked upon as a campaign. Like any campaign, it will only reach a successful conclusion if carefully planned and intelligently executed. A well organized plan for securing a job in the commercial art field must include the following ingredients:

1. A carefully organized portfolio.
2. A clear, concise personal data sheet (résumé).
3. A well-organized plan for contacting prospective employers.
4. A carefully planned interview strategy.
5. A well-timed follow-up.
6. An up-to-date record on all activities.

The Artist's Portfolio

The artist's portfolio (which is frequently referred to as a "book") is his or her sample case and as such should include only the very best work. Also it should be presented in the most attractive, most flattering manner possible. It certainly should not include everything the artist has ever done, for there is much that is done by beginners and experienced artists alike that is better forgotten. Quality is a far more important consideration than quantity regarding the selections for your portfolio. Any of your art renditions that require even the slightest apology should not be included.

The successful commercial salesperson carefully prepares this sample case before (s)he calls on a prospective customer. The artist would do well to follow this same policy. Before going to an interview, learn as much as you can about the prospective employer, especially about the kind of artwork he or she prefers. Then place in your portfolio those examples of your work which will appeal to the prospective employer. Showing a great number of samples that are not pertinent or appropriate is a waste of time; most prospective employers are too busy for that.

Everything about the portfolio should receive your careful attention—for every part of it is a reflection on you. If you present a sloppy, disorganized portfolio, the prospective employer will assume that this is characteristic of you—that any work you will do will be sloppy and disorganized. For this reason, it is important that you give consideration to the binder and mounting sheets that make up the binder as well as the art presentations themselves.

The type of binder that will be best for your needs will depend on the type of material you are going to display and the amount of money you care to spend. If you specialize in jewelry or similar work that requires only small sketches or photos, then a neat 8½" × 11" looseleaf folder will do. If you are an illustrator you

Fig. 7.1 "The World of Peter Max" exhibit at the DeYoung Museum in San Francisco (Courtesy: Peter Max).

probably will need a large binder to hold $16'' \times 20''$ samples or even larger.

Each sample in your portfolio should be well matted, crisp, and perfectly clean both front and back. The illustration should be mounted above center on the sheet and should not be crowded. Leave large borders when possible; but related work may be mounted in groups.

Place the samples in the portfolio with your best work in front. Arrange them so that only one sample is exposed at a time as a person thumbs through it. Samples too large for the portfolio should be photographed to a reduced size. The photographs should be entered in the portfolio with the same care given originals. Line originals can be photostated instead of photographed.

A portfolio that is gaining in popularity is one consisting of **67** *excellent quality* color slides of the artist's work, mounted in an appropriate case accompanied by a small, good quality projector. This type of portfolio is compact and easy to transport, and at the same time can include a maximum number of samples.

When the time comes to show your portfolio in the course of an interview, place it open before the prospective employer then settle back and relax—or at least appear relaxed. Don't offer any alibis, excuses, or explanations.

The Résumé

The *résumé* is an important job-hunting tool and should be given considerable attention. It is often the deciding factor in determining whether the job seeker gets that coveted interview with an employer.

What is a résumé? It is one or two sheets of typed information which "sums up" everything about a person that his/her employer would care to know. It should be a clear, concise summary of all the pertinent information concerning your person, experience, education, and outstanding accomplishments. It should contain brief but sufficient information to tell a prospective employer (1) what you can do, (2) what you have done, (3) what you know, (4) who you are, and (5) what kind of job you would like.

The actual work on your résumé starts with a preliminary analysis of facts. The best way to do this is to prepare an "asset list" under these headings: work, history, education, personal characteristics, and resources.

1. *Work History:* List all your employment—full-time, part-time, vacation jobs, and freelance experience. Don't leave any gaps in time.

2. *Education:* Under this heading, you should list not only your formal education, but you should also include any evening, home study, correspondence, or special courses that might possibly apply to the work you plan to do. Don't forget to mention any diplomas, scholarships, certificates, or awards you may have received. If you attend college, there is no point in listing any previous education.

3. *Personal Characteristics:* Evaluate your personal characteristics for their selling points and job significance. Be as objective as you can.

4. *Resources:* List all the possible resources—that is, leads, sources of information, contacts, and aids—you may want to use in planning your campaign, such as personal friends and acquaintances, business associates, school friends and instructors, professional organizations, firms that may have the kind of job you want, employment agencies (public, private and school), and trade directories.

Note: A word should be added at this point concerning the things that should be left out of the résumé. Don't mention money. At the time you are interviewed you will most likely discuss money but don't include it as a part of your résumé. Salary may be a point you are willing to negotiate. Placing a figure in your résumé may "close the door" before you are given a chance for discussion.

Organizing Your Résumé. Now that you have assembled all of this raw material you must process it—grade, select, and reject—so that you can produce an effective finished product, your basic résumé.

There is no one best organizing principle for a résumé. Nevertheless, all good ones will highlight the important points around a specific job problem. In most cases your goal (the job, that is) will help you determine the most suitable method—whether to build around your professional training, the types of firms you were employed by, your specific skills, or the fields of work for which you believe you are best suited.

In general, however, your résumé can be organized in one of two ways:

1. *By job*, in inverse chronological order—start with the most recent job and, going back in time, give employer, type of firm, and work performed.

2. *By function*—start with the most relevant function you can perform (from the prospective employer's point of view) and continue with others in the order of their pertinence. Describe each function or skill with specific illustrations from your experience.

SAMPLE RÉSUMÉ FOR NEW GRADUATE

Date Submitted. . . . .

Sharon Kay   Art Studio Assistant or
321 Bay Street   Advertising Art
Chicago, Ill. 46201   Department Assistant

Area Code (212) 551-7072

OCCUPATIONAL GOAL:
   Major interest is a job in an art department where I can further develop
   my art skills and will have opportunity for further specialization later.

EDUCATION: 1974-78
   Compton College, Chicago, Ill. B.A. in Commercial Art. Courses included advertising design, basic design and color, crafts, fashion design,
   graphics, history of art, interior design, painting and drawing, sculpture,
   and ceramics.
   Extracurricular activities: Member of Design Club that prepared
   illustrations for school publications (president 1977-78). Taught art
   to handicapped children in local community center. Designed brochure
   for college art shows for two years.
   Awards: Prize for best art brochure, 1976. Secretary Students' Council
   1976-77. Graduated top quarter of class.

WORK EXPERIENCE:
   J. Taub Studio, Chicago, Ill., summer 1977, general assistant. Helped
   prepare spot illustrations, magazine ads, lettering, pamphlets.
   Grant Company, Chicago, Ill. (manufacturers of greeting cards), summer 1976. Prepared paste-ups for offset. Designed gift wrappings,
   cards, stationery.

PERSONAL DATA:
   Age: 21
   Marital Status: Single
   Health: Excellent
   Hobby: Fine art. Awarded three first places in area art shows.

SAMPLE RÉSUMÉ FOR EXPERIENCED ARTIST

Date Submitted. . . . .

Jay Berlye
36 York Avenue
Monticello, New York 12701   Illustrator

Area Code (915) 794-5435

GENERAL BACKGROUND:

Six years of experience as an illustrator for outdoor magazines. Specialized in watercolor and black and white hunting and fishing scenes. Set up and directed the art activities of an advertising agency which prepared posters, record album covers, pamphlets, and manufacturer's catalogues. Elmira College, B.A. in Art. Veteran—age 35—willing to travel.

EXPERIENCE:

1965-Present   *Outdoor Magazine, Inc.* Middletown, N. Y., illustrator. Member of illustration team that prepares pictorial presentations for stories in the magazine. Determine number, type, and size of illustrations, and supervise their preparation. Prepare watercolor and black and white illustrations for each edition. Consult with the printers for the proper reproduction of the illustrations.

1957-65   *White & Pierce Advertising Agency, Inc.*, Chicago, Ill., art director. Started as general art man for small agency. Grew to a four-person art department with myself as director. Supervised all artwork produced by the agency. Met with clients and administration to determine presentation desired. Roughed out illustrations. Supervised final preparations. Consulted with marketing and graphic design departments.

EDUCATION:

Elmira College, Park Place, Elmira, N.Y. 1949-53, B.A. in Art. Major: design and illustration. President of art club. Art Association scholarship, senior year.
Hartman School, Chicago, Ill., 1953-54. Evening course specializing in commercial art.

PERSONAL DATA:

Age 35. Married. Three children. Would like to locate in New York City or Chicago areas. Willing to travel.

Covering Letter. *A covering application letter* should accompany every résumé that is mailed to a potential employer. It is the combination of both the covering letter plus the résumé that makes up the application. It should be noted at the outset that although the résumé may be reproduced in quantity by some method, *the covering letter is always a typed original.*

The main purpose of the covering letter is to convince the prospective employer to read your résumé. It must be convincing enough to indicate that you have certain specialized qualifications that can be of value—that you can improve the potential employer's organization or make them more money. Keep the letter brief so it will not compete with your résumé. Use simple, direct language and correct grammar. Avoid hackneyed expressions; and, of course, type neatly.

The letter should consist of three or four paragraphs. It should open with a direct statement indicating that your training or experience may be profitable to the prospective employer. This should be followed by a paragraph amplifying this opening statement or stressing additional qualifications. A reference to the résumé should be included. Finally, there should be a direct request for an interview.

In every library can be found books concerned with letter writing. The inexperienced letter writer should refer to such a book for guidance in preparing the letter of application.

Just a few more pointers on your covering letter:

1. Address your letter to a specific person by name when possible.
2. With local firms take the initiative in suggesting that they telephone you for an interview.
3. Let the letter reflect your individuality, but avoid appearing aggressive, overbearing, familiar, cute, or humorous.
4. If you are a newly graduated student sell what abilities you have. Stress education in your résumé and covering letter. In this regard, indicate the courses you have completed that are related to the work for which you are applying, the grades you received that were good, the extracurricular activities in which you participated that particularly qualify you, the related work you did while at school and during vacations, offices you held or any indication of the high esteem in which you were held, and any honors or scholarships you received.

Contacting Prospective Employers

The job seeker's plan for *contacting prospective employers* must be well-thought-out and carefully organized. Start by making a list of promising organizations, shops, and studios. Such a list can be compiled from the classified telephone directory (out-of-town copies may be borrowed from your local phone company or library), membership lists from professional organizations, professional magazines, and lists of concerns and organizations found at large libraries (such as *Standard Directory of Advertisers, Literary Marketplace, The Stores and Shops Retail Directory, Madison Avenue Handbook,* etc.). One of your best sources is suggestions made by friends and acquaintances. Don't be afraid that your list might be too long. The more people who know you are looking for a job, the better.

Never just "drop in" on a prospective employer. Always arrange for an interview beforehand. Separate your list into those you will phone and those you will write a letter. Arrange these lists from the most desirable, and, if convenient, make your contacts in this order.

Whenever possible, try to contact a prospective employer through a mutual friend or acquaintance. Lacking this opportunity, you will have to go it "cold turkey" through a phone call or letter.

The Interview

The employment interview is the most important event in the job-seeking campaign. Everything you have prepared before—portfolio, résumé, covering letter, organizational plan—was keyed toward securing this important person-to-person meeting. The 20 or 30 minutes you spend with the interviewer may determine the entire future course of your life. For this reason you should secure every assistance possible in preparing for this event.

Here are some of the things you can do to get yourself ready:

1. Find the exact place and time of the interview.
2. Get the full name of the company straight, along with its address.
3. Be certain you have your interviewer's full name, and find out how to pronounce it if it looks difficult.
4. Do some research on the company interviewing you.
5. Prepare some questions before you go in for the interview. (There are a number of publications that can help you research a company. Most of them can be found in any good-sized college or public library.)
6. Plan to arrive at the designated place at least 15 minutes early, if you can.
7. The essentials of neatness and cleanliness scarcely need to be mentioned.

Fig. 7.2 "Tiles," by Olga de Amaral, is an all-wool 83- by 14-ft artwork, and is located at the Peachtree Center Plaza Hotel, Atlanta. It was commissioned by John Portman.

Each of the above suggestions is meant to be helpful, but it would be a mistake to become unduly worried over too many details. A genuinely attractive personality and a good record will overcome most small errors. Be friendly, honest, and sincere and you will always make a good impression.

You cannot rehearse your role in an upcoming interview, because you don't know what cues will be given to you. Your best guide is to rely on your own native courtesy and good sense. There are, however, some basic rules and situations common to most interviews that may help you if you know about them ahead of time:

1. Nervousness: It's normal for many people to be nervous, particularly in an interview. And there are many jobs open for which a little nervousness isn't looked upon negatively. It does help, however, to dry a damp brow or a clammy hand just before meeting your interviewer.

2. Greet the interviewer by name as you enter his or her office if you are sure of the pronunciation.

3. If the interviewer shakes hands with you, use a firm grip—a "limp fish" handshake will make a bad impression. However, don't try to prove how strong your grip is by grabbing his/her hand and mashing it.

4. Don't chew gum, and don't smoke unless the interviewer invites you to do so.

5. Offer the interviewer a copy of your résumé at the opening of the interview. It will serve as a point of departure which the interviewer will appreciate and will make a number of questions unnecessary.

6. Be ready for at least one surprise question right from the start—a few interviewers favor one of the following gambits:

   a. What can I do for you?
   b. Why don't you tell me about yourself?
   c. Why are you interested in this company?

If you think those are easy questions to answer without some previous thought, just try it. You don't have time to flounder around. This is where preparation will count.

7. Keep following this lead. Don't answer by just saying "yes" and "no." On the other hand, don't talk too much.

8. Look your interviewer directly in the eye—and keep doing it from time to time during your conversation.

9. Sit up in your chair and look alert and interested at all times.

10. Make sure that your good points get across to the interviewer. (S)he won't know them unless you tell him/her. But, try to appear factual and mention your best qualities in relation to something concrete.

11. Even if the interviewer does much of the talking, remember that you can lead him or her by asking questions which call in turn for a question you want to answer. Example: You are strong in extracurricular organizations. The interviewer hasn't mentioned that point and you want to go into a little detail you couldn't cover fully in your résumé. You simply watch for an opening, and ask, "Are you interested in my extracurricular activities?" The answer is not likely to be "no."

12. Be ready to give an answer to the question "What do you plan to be doing ten years from now?" It's a favorite. A popular alternative question is "How much money do you expect to be earning in ten years?" The purpose is to determine your ambition, ability to plan ahead, and the soundness of your thinking. Do you want, vaguely, to get ahead? Or are you going somewhere in particular?

13. Never make a slighting reference about a former employer or a professor. If something went wrong, suggest that at least some of the blame must have been your own.

14. Conduct yourself as if you are determined to get the job you are discussing. You have other irons in the fire, of course, and the interviewer is aware of that. But (s)he wants to think that you want this job. If you play coy, nobody may take you.

15. Try to avoid giving the impression that you have come in to look over the possibilities, and that you are not yet sure what you want.

16. Show the interviewer that you are interested, that you appreciate the opportunity you are being given to present your case, and that you realize the demands on his/her time.

17. Ask some definite questions about the company. Don't ask so many that the interviewer thinks you are afraid of work or are hesitating at the thought of joining the company. But do show your interest.

18. If you are asked if you've ever been fired—and you have been—frankness again is the answer. Tell the interviewer you've learned from your mistakes. Also, there is the possibility you got into a wrong job through a misunderstanding.

19. If you get the impression that the interview is not going well and that you have already been rejected, don't let your discouragement show.

20. Don't take notes in an interview if you can help it. If you are given application forms, be certain that they are filled out completely and neatly.

21. What if you so impress the interviewer, or the company is in such need of recruits, that you are offered a job on the spot? If you are absolutely sure it is the one you want, accept with a definite yes. If you have the slightest doubt—if you do not want to accept without further thought (or further interviews), play for time. You must not embarrass the person who has made you the offer. Be courteous and tactful in asking for time to think it over. Try to set a definite date when you can provide an answer. This will reassure the interviewer that you are giving the offer serious consideration. Above all, don't create the impression that you are playing one company off against the other to drive up the bidding.

22. Avoid accepting more than one offer. If you do you will reflect badly upon yourself.

23. You may be asked why you left your last two or three jobs. Return to school, better pay, more responsibility, are acceptable reasons.

24. What about salary? Many people believe that an applicant has to ask as much as the traffic will bear, or more, in the hope of gaining a bargaining position, and that companies always offer as little as they can. However, interviews have a certain number of jobs to be filled in definite salary brackets. The interviewer may not choose, unfortunately, to tell you what (s)he has to offer. He or she may ask you how much you want. The usual answer in that case is to indicate that you're more interested in a job in which you can prove yourself than you are in a specific salary. This politely passes the question back to the interviewer. If (s)he is interested, (s)he will generally suggest a figure. In most cases reputable corporations will offer the standard salary for the type of job in question. It is in your interest, of course, to have found out what the rate is. You know, also, the level beneath which your needs and responsibilities will not permit you to go.

25. Don't be too discouraged if no definite offer is made or no specific salary is discussed. The interviewer will probably wish to communicate with his/her office first or interview more applicants before making any offers.

26. Most interviews last between 20 and 30 minutes. Be alert to signs from the interviewer that the session is almost at an end. (If (s)he looks at his/her watch, you can be sure of it.) If you still want the job, sum up your interest briefly, say you are interested, and stop.

27. Be certain to thank the interviewer for his/her time, and consideration of you. Resist the temptation to flatter him or her. Smile and show as much confidence in leaving as you did in arriving.

28. If you don't "connect" immediately, remember that interviewers, companies, and jobs differ greatly. You will learn much from your first interview and you will almost certainly do better in succeeding ones. The important thing is to keep trying.

Follow-Up

Follow up each interview with a note in which you thank the potential employer for his/her time and consideration. Do this within a day or two of the interview. Try not to make this letter trite and ordinary. Make an effort to remember something that took place in the interview that could be used for special comment.

Subsequent follow-up letters should be planned. The number and frequency of the follow-up letters should be determined by the possibilities for the position. This can only be determined by the facts available to you, the results of the interview, and the subsequent information brought to your attention. Remember the old adage, "Rome wasn't built in a day." Some positions involve a lot of working and coaxing before they come through. Be ready and willing to carry on the courtship.

Record-Keeping

Keep up-to-date records on everything that took place during the interview. Record the following information: concern involved, interviewed by whom, date, impressions, potential, record of follow-up. Each interview should be recorded on a separate 3″ × 5″ card for easy reference.

GETTING A JOB THROUGH AN AGENCY

Employment agencies can be of service to you if you are in search of regular weekly employment. The extent of their service and the amount you will have to pay will depend on the position you seek.

Placement services are maintained by many art schools. If you are a newly graduated art student this is the best sort of placement agency for you.

If a school placement service is not available, you may apply to either a private or state employment agency for placement. Such agencies exist in all large cities. The problem is not in locating the agencies (for they are listed in the yellow pages of the local telephone directory). The problem is in finding one that will serve your needs well.

Fig. 7.3 "The Eclipse," by Charles Perry, is 30 ft in diameter and weighs about six tons. It is located in the lobby of the San Francisco Regency (Courtesy: John Portman).

The sole purpose for the employment agency is to bring together an employer who has a vacancy in his concern with a potential employee who can qualify for the vacancy. For this service the private agency charges a fee that might be paid by either the employee or employer. The size of the fee is determined by the salary paid for the particular job. State employment agencies charge no fees.

Private employment agencies vary greatly in the quality of service rendered. Low-paying jobs result in a corresponding low fee and therefore tend to receive less consideration. Beginners in the field who apply for such jobs will usually be subjected to this lack of consideration and find it very disturbing. Applicants who qualify for more responsible, higher-paying jobs, are usually treated with more deference.

State employment agencies have changed substantially in character and service in many parts of the country in recent years. Originally they were primarily concerned with placing people in the more menial occupations. This is the impression that still remains in the minds of many people. The fact is, state employment agencies now place substantial numbers of white-collar workers. It would certainly be worthwhile to check the nearest state employment agency when you are in the market for a job. Service is always free and such an agency tends to give equal consideration to all applicants.

Applicants for vacancies in the top positions in the art field are usually secured by *placement consultants*. Placement consultants employ investigative personnel to thoroughly check all possible applicants. Employers almost always pay the placement consultant. This is an expensive service and therefore used for top personnel.

Before applying to an agency, check it out as carefully and completely as you can. Talk with your friends and acquaintances. Find out if they have had successful results with a particular agency, and if so, apply to the same one. Do not have anything to do with an agency that requires a registration fee. Pay only after you have been placed in a job.

When you apply to an agency, act as if you were going to have an interview with a prospective employer. Do everything you can to impress the agency. Sometimes, when you particularly impress an agency interviewer (s)he will go out of his/her way to recommend you.

Always inquire about whether you or the employer will pay the fee. If it is you, find out what the fee will be. If you find an agency that serves you well, be fair with it all along the line. You don't know when you will need an agency again.

8 Specialization in Commercial Artwork

The answer to the question of specialization is more one of geography than choice. You will specialize or not depending on where you live and the type of market you want to serve.

At the outset, it must be pointed out that the most successful commercial artists are specialists. There are, however, many who make a very satisfactory living as general practitioners of the arts.

The general practitioners are usually only found in small towns. The person who is accepted as the town artist may be called upon to paint signs, design costumes and sets for plays, paint murals, do an occasional portrait, touch up old paintings, teach an adult class, and any other thing that can conceivably be classified as artistic. If small-town living is your preference, it will be to your advantage to develop as many art capabilities as possible.

The broad field of commercial art is so complex and demanding that generally, an artist must specialize if he or she is to realize any success. The commercial artist as a general practitioner is practically nonexistent in the large city. The novice is advised to learn to do one thing well. When this area is developed to the point where it can be done well and fast, then employment can be sought in this field. When you have established yourself as a competent professional in one field, you then can try other artistic endeavors.

Choosing your particular field of art specialization can be a momentous thing. It should be preceded by careful study and

Fig. 8.1 Elmer C. Plumb, specialist in advertising art to the shoe industry, and some of his popular line and color wash samples (Courtesy: Elmer C. Plumb Studio).

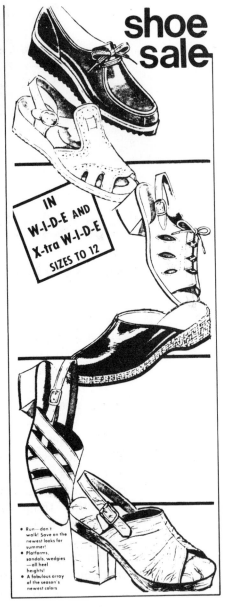

investigation. First, you should become familiar with the customary fields of specialization in commercial art. Second, you should decide which fields appeal to you in terms of working conditions, financial returns, promotional possibilities, and so forth. Third, you must decide in which field your particular type of art talent will realize its greatest fulfillment. Making your final decision will not be easy. It is recommended that you seek as much assistance as possible.

Following are listed the generally accepted fields of commercial art. In large communities and art concerns, most of these fields are broken down still further. There are several books that explain these occupations in detail, such as Head's *Careers and Opportunities in Commercial Art*, Keppler's *Your Future in Photography*, Dalrymple's *Careers and Opportunities in the Theatre*, and Hopke's two-volume *Encyclopedia of Careers and Vocational Guidance*, to mention only a few. Such books should be referred to for closer study.

ILLUSTRATOR

The illustrator prepares paintings and drawings to adorn, emphasize, and explain a publication, story, or advertisement. Almost everyone in this field is a specialist of some type. You may specialize in illustrations for certain kinds of stories, such as love stories, adventure stories, science, fiction, etc. Or you may specialize in certain subjects, such as cars, planes, boats, dogs, cats, etc. In the fashion field you may do only women's fashions or men's or children's. Or you may specialize in a certain technique like watercolor, or pen and ink, etc. You may illustrate a certain sport like baseball, football, boxing, etc. There appears to be no limit to the degree of specialization possible in the illustrator's field.

POSTER ARTIST

Poster artists prepare pictures or sketches that are used primarily for advertising purposes. They are meant to sell products, events, and places. Typical are the travel posters in travel agencies, movie posters outside theaters, product advertisements in train stations, and so forth. In large poster studios, advertising agencies, and poster departments of department stores, a single poster may be a combined effort of two, three, or even four people—one may do the layout, another the lettering, another the details, etc. In the small studio—consisting of the poster artist and one assistant—the poster artist must be capable of handling design, layout, and color.

LETTERING ARTIST

Lettering artists place the lettering on posters, advertisements, packages, labels, letterheads, etc. They give to lettering the infinite variation, the flexibility, the subtle rhythm that cannot be accomplished by standard-type designs. The specialization in this field is concerned with size and use rather than shape and type. There are the lettering artists who specialize in preparing the careful lettering that appears on advertisements, labels, letterheads, etc. This is slow, exacting work accomplished with special instruments used in the trade.

There are those who specialize in show-cards—hand-lettered display cards usually used in window displays and for special announcements. These artists often produce their work freehand, using the brush in a particular rapid manner. There are lettering artists who specialize in lettering on windows and still others who work on very large displays such as outdoor signs.

GRAPHIC DESIGNER

The graphic designer compiles the printed page in its final form. He or she is the one who determines the kind of illustrations, photos, type, lettering, and drawings that will be used. This person may specify the paper or material on which the printing is to be done and determine how it is to be folded or bound together, and make any other decisions necessary to the proper completion of the job. The graphic designer's "layout" may be prepared for an advertisement, newspaper, record jacket, television commercial, billboard display, film strip, book, catalog, etc.

Graphic designers tend to become specialists in the field in which they are most frequently employed. Some specialize in advertisement layout, others work in books, television, newspapers, typeface, exhibits and displays, packaging, etc.

On some occasions, graphic designers choose to freelance. In such cases they do almost any layout their clients request. Very few graphic designers have sufficient demand for any one type of work enabling them to specialize.

84

FABRIC DESIGNER

The fabric designer is the artist who prepares artwork that is particularly suited to enrich the design of a surface. The designs may be used on fiber or plastic fabrics of all types, as well as such diverse categories as wall coverings, linoleums, floor tiles, shower curtains, table cloths, rugs, lamp shades, towels, wrapping papers, wallboard, bedroom linens, etc.

Most fabric designers work for a single manufacturer and specialize in the field represented by the manufacturer. For example, some individuals only create designs for fabrics used in women's dresses or fabrics for men's suits or upholstery materials or wall coverings, and so forth. A large number of fabric designers work for art studios, while a few freelance. These artists will specialize or do several types of surface artwork, depending on the type of clientele served.

Fig. 8.2 "Sisal Weaving," by Françoise Grossen, is a 14- by 36-ft work executed in reds and golds and located in the San Francisco Regency (Courtesy: John Portman).

Fig. 8.3 "La pell d'un poble," by Jose Grau Garriga, is a weaving in wool that is $6\frac{1}{2}$ ft high by 5 ft wide. It is located in the San Francisco Regency (Courtesy: John Portman).

INDUSTRIAL DESIGNER

The industrial designer designs or redesigns products so that they are more attractive, more efficient, safer, and more comfortable. In the normal course of their work, these artists design everything from planes, transporting equipment, appliances, furniture, lighting and plumbing fixtures, to toys, tools, machines, etc. Today, almost every product that must have the acceptance of the general public has passed through the hands of the industrial designer.

Almost all industrial designers work on a freelance basis. They are either paid per assignment or given a yearly retainer. The industrial design field is becoming more specialized all the time. While it is still true that most of the leaders in the field will take on any product, there are prominent designers who specialize in certain types of products or materials.

Fig. 8.4 Graphics by Bruce Dell of John Portman & Associates, located on the wall of a stairwell in Embarcadero Center's Hyatt Regency, San Francisco (Courtesy: John Portman).

CARTOONIST

The cartoonist is an artist who specializes in line drawings. There are several different forms of specialization in this field. There is a gag cartoonist whose rendition may consist of one panel or a series of panels leading to a dénouement. The strip cartoonist prepares the familiar "funnies" that appear in thousands of newspapers. There is the editorial cartoonist, whose offerings supplement the editor's views of the news. The political cartoonist helps to define the characteristics and issues that distinguish one candidate or political group from another. Such an artist emphasizes a person's physical characteristics by exaggerating them in the drawing. The sports cartoonist reflects the dynamic activities of the sports world. Then there are special-interest cartoons such as the famous Ripley's "Believe It or Not." The cartoonist who prepares animated cartoons draws thousands of individual "frames" that are eventually put together in a consecutive sequence.

PACKAGE DESIGNER

Package designers prepare structural and decorative designs for all types of packaging. This work is done by studios that specialize in this field, or individual artists who do it on a freelance basis. Some artists who have developed a reputation in the packaging field work on a contract retainer basis which places their services at the disposal of a manufacturer. On rare occasions, designers may work on a royalty commission basis.

The package designing field has grown tremendously, and currently a great deal of specialization is taking place. There are artists who specialize in quality boxes for such things as perfume and jewelry, while others design more practical packaging, for, say, groceries or pharmaceuticals.

STAGE AND TELEVISION ARTIST

The theater and television fields require the service of many different types of commercial artists: specialists in scenic design, scenic painting, fashion and costume designers, make-up artists, cartoon animators, letters and titlers, and mural artists, among others. Every phase of artwork concerned with the professional stage and television productions is carefully specialized. This is so for two reasons: because of the exacting quality of the specialized type of work required and because of the tight unionization of the trade.

PHOTOGRAPHIC ARTIST

When the photographer has mastered the technical requirements for taking good pictures to the point where these are accomplished almost by reflex, she or he is then ready to be considered an artist. The photographer who can create pictures that are meaningful, exciting, lifelike, that virtually "speak" in positive, forthright statements to whole groups of people, is in every sense an artist. There is no limit to the need for the services of such a person. Photographers are needed to augment the written words in magazines and books with interpretive pictures, to supply imaginative sequences for TV, to create rich, sensitive scenes for motion pictures, to offer chic presentations of the latest fashions, to communicate news of history in the making, to create eye-catching advertisements, and on and on. Photographers are needed wherever anyone has a story to tell, a message to convey, a product to sell, or an incident, situation, or person to remember.

Photographers tend to specialize in one particular field and this usually determines whether they work on a salary or a freelance basis. Those who work for publications, large studios, businesses, and agencies usually draw weekly salaries comparable to the pay of other artists. More accomplished photographers move up to executive positions or go out on their own on a freelance basis.

ARTIST EXECUTIVE

The more skilled and experienced commercial artist may choose to accept one of the many executive positions available in the field. The kind of position such a person might be offered would depend on background, experiences, skills, relationships that have been developed, personality, and desire to advance. As in all other fields of endeavor, the artist may aspire to several executive positions at all different levels of responsibility and compensation. Some of the more popular higher-level art jobs are advertising agency art director, magazine art director, head of the art department for a publisher or

89

for a large store or chain stores or mail-order concern, art studio owner or director, and art service owner or director.

The artist who moves into an executive position spends little if any time at the drawing board. His other responsibility is to develop new ideas, or coordinate the development of ideas by others. (S)he then plans the execution of the ideas and passes them on for others to prepare. After the finished artwork has been completed this individual has the responsibility of deciding on the acceptability of the work. In very large art departments or studios these responsibilities may be subdivided among a few executives.

9 Selling Commercial Artwork

FREELANCING

Freelancing means that an artist maintains his/her own studio and performs work in response to assignments or in anticipation of future sales. The alternative of this is working at a 9-to-5 job with the customary pay check at the end of the week. Which alternative an artist should choose will depend on many things: artistic abilities, financial obligations, business connections, field of work, sales abilities, production speed, plus a dozen other related considerations.

Freelancing is the ultimate desire of almost every commercial artist. This is so because freelancing offers the vision of wealth, independence, and easy living. It is true that it does offer all these, but only rarely. Most freelance artists just make a living, work long hours, and are always thinking about maintaining their clients.

Two positive things can be said for freelancing. First, it does offer the greatest opportunity for making money in the art field.

Fig. 9.1   Moik Schiele, "Untitled tapestry," 100 by 80 inches, hanging in the Fort Worth National Bank, Texas (Courtesy: The Fort Worth National Bank).

Second, it allows for control of one's own working conditions. Both of these are subject to the fact that the artist has sufficient business of the proper type. Mediocre freelancers generally earn between $8,000 to $15,000 a year. The more competent, successful free-lancer may earn from $15,000 to $30,000. There is a small group of outstanding artists who earn from $50,000 to $100,000 or more a year. These figures fluctuate greatly in response to changing business conditions.

The salaried commercial art jobs—where artists actually produce artwork on a weekly basis—do not usually pay very well. Most of these positions are held by beginners and are excellent training ground for them. As the artist works at these jobs (s)he tends to eventually specialize in the field of his or her greatest ability. As the artist becomes skilled in this specialization, his/her general usefulness to any one employer tends to diminish. The reason is that few employers have constant use for a particular type of artwork. Also, only a few can pay a competent specialist enough to convince him or her to forsake the more lucrative freelance market.

Beginning commercial artists working on a salary basis can expect from $125 to $250 a week. The difference paid depends on ability, schooling, field of work, and previous experiences. After a few years, staffers with proven ability are paid approximately $250 to $350 a week. Many concerns offer annual bonuses or have profit-sharing plans that can equal as much as an extra month's salary.

Experienced artists who work their way up to an executive position can look forward to a salary of $20,000 to $50,000 or more a year. These are such positions as art directors, department heads in large organizations, studio directors, and senior designers. Such levels require executive ability, knowledge of the art field, and critical judgment in addition to personal artistic skill.

The commercial artist usually starts as a salaried apprentice and can end up as a high-income executive or freelance artist. Most stop somewhere between these extremes.

Operating a freelance art studio is a difficult business, and unless it is recognized, organized, and run as such, there is little chance of success. It is vital for the freelance artist to secure clients for his/her work, meet commitments with speed and accuracy, receive satisfactory payment for labors, and secure repeat assignments. This takes experience, ambition, capital, and "know-how." An artist lacking these four qualities should not attempt freelance work.

GETTING FREELANCE WORK

The ingredients for a well-organized plan to get a job listed in Chapter 7, "Getting a Job in the Commercial Art Field," also apply for the freelance artist seeking clients. He or she must have (1) a carefully organized portfolio, (2) a clear, concise résumé, (3) a plan for contacting prospective clients, (4) a carefully planned interview strategy, (5) a consistent, well-timed follow-up, and (6) up-to-date records. Chapter 7 is "must" reading for the freelance artist, for it discusses important tools for the freelancer's use. Here we present suggestions above and beyond those in Chapter 7 that can be used to advantage.

A fundamental principle of selling is that *it is easier to sell to someone you know than to someone you don't know.* The more you know and understand about a potential client, the more direct can be your appeal to his/her particular wants, needs, prejudices, plans, style, and other conditions. No effort should be spared to obtain all the information you can.

There are several publications that can help you in your research of a company. Most of them can be found in any large library. Among the most helpful are: *Standard Directory of Advertisers, The Stores & Shops Retail Directory, The Madison Avenue Handbook, Thomas' Register of American Manufacturers, Moody's Manuals, Fitch Corporation Manuals, MacRea's Bluebook, Standard & Poor's Corporation Records, Poor's Register of Editor & Publisher International Year Book, Directors and Executives, Dun & Bradstreet Reference Books, Kelley's Directory of Manufacturers and Merchants* and *Literary Market Place.* If possible, secure a copy of the company's annual report. And don't forget to question your friends and acquaintances in the trade.

Once you have accumulated all possible information, then analyze it for its implications. Try to determine the type of work the company is partial to, its specialty if it has any, the type of customers it caters to, the volume of business it does, the prices the company customarily pays, whether it has any particular needs at present, and who makes the hiring decisions. Once you have an understanding of your potential client, then slant everything you do—your portfolio, résumé, letters, interview strategy, follow-up—so it applies as directly as possible.

The Portfolio

The portfolio of the freelance artist should be identical to that of the job-seeking artist in all respects except one—that of *content.* Everything previously mentioned about attractiveness, binders, fillers, and mounting methods applies to the freelancer and should be read carefully. The freelancer's portfolio should be exceptionally attractive in every respect—clean, neat, well-organized, carefully prepared, and meticulously presented.

The content of the freelancer's portfolio should be guided by two considerations. First, what type of artwork is the freelance artist capable of producing on a professional level? Second, what type of work will the clients be interested in buying? Every sample considered for inclusion in the portfolio should be subject to these two considerations. To include in the portfolio an art sample of fine quality that you happened to produce, but could not repeat with professional regularity, is foolish. And to subject a client to dozens of samples that are of no interest to that person can only be detrimental to your cause.

Fig. 9.2 This 40-ft stainless steel sculpture stands in front of the Gas Light Tower in Atlanta, Georgia. It was created by Dutch-born brothers Hans and Gerrit Van deBovenkamp. The sculpture consists of 400 individual sections and stands in an oval reflection pool (Courtesy: John Portman).

Show a client what (s)he customarily buys. Don't try to change him/her—after you get to know the client better there is time enough for that. Show the client five or six outstanding samples of the kind of work that interest him/her and you will get the best response. In other words, your portfolio is not to be a morgue of all your old accomplishments. It must be an up-to-date sparkling presentation of the latest thing. This means that your portfolio should be reorganized frequently—before every single interview, if possible.

You should not have only originals in your portfolio. This gives the impression that you have not sold any of your work. It would be ideal if you could, on two facing pages of your portfolio, show the original work on one side and an ad page proof or other evidence that it was reproduced on the other. In any case, include some photographs of tone work, and photostats if in line. This suggests that some of your work is not available. In some cases, where the originals have become shabby, a photograph or photostat may make a better presentation.

Should samples of schoolwork be included in the freelancer's portfolio? Such work may be included if it indicates abilities in keeping with subsequent work and if it indicates a phase of the artist's ability important to the kind of work being sought. Samples of commercial work should dominate your portfolio. The school samples should only serve to complement and add emphasis to the other.

Some professional artists are getting away from the customary folder-type portfolio. These artists are having color transparencies made of all their work. The transparencies are carried about in a special case that also includes a viewer. The originals are delivered to the client on request. This method eliminates the need for the artist to drag around large, cumbersome originals.

The Résumé

The résumé of the freelance artist differs slightly from that of the job-seeking artist earlier discussed in detail. Again, a rereading of Chapter 7 is valuable. Both types of artist use the résumé for the same purpose—to sell their abilities. All that differs is the approach. The job seeker may accentuate his/her experience or education or blend both in a common presentation. The freelance artist does not have this choice. (S)he must enumerate his/her commercial accomplishment, listing the outstanding work done and for whom. Incidental data is kept to a minimum. Social experience is seldom mentioned. You may, however, include outstanding and unusual school experiences that have a direct bearing on the kind of work being sought.

The layout of the freelancer's résumé may be similar to the samples previously included, but not necessarily so. It should include name, address, and phone number near the top of the page. It should be concisely written and carefully organized. The layout need not be as formal as that recommended for the job-seeking artist. Originality and variation is in order for this résumé. If you can compile some clever, artistic presentation that will set your résumé off from the others, do so. But make sure it is not "corny" or overdone. If you are in doubt, use the formal layouts shown on pp. 70-71.

The freelancer's résumé, like that of the job seeker, may be reproduced in quantity for distribution. It may be reproduced by mimeograph, offset, or any of the standard printing methods. Do not use ditto. The characteristic purple color of ditto lacks the professional touch. A word of warning: do not spend a great deal of money to produce a very fancy résumé. A person who does this tends to hesitate about changing and updating the résumé. It is important that the résumé be updated at frequent intervals.

The Xerox and similar instant reproducing methods are being used by many artists who frequently change their résumés. These artists do a paste-up job and then run it through the machine. By carefully cutting out and pasting in, these artists prepare a tailor-made résumé for almost every important interview.

The Covering Sales Letter

A covering sales letter should accompany every résumé that is sent out by the freelance artist to a potential client. To be more correct, the résumé should accompany the letter, for it is the *letter* to the potential client that is of prime importance. This must be, in every sense, a sales letter; its purpose is to sell your work, your skill, your ability, your personality, your potential, your capabilities. Once you realize and accept this, the letter will be easier to prepare.

Information concerning the covering application letter is covered in Chapter 7. This should be read carefully, for much that is said applies to the freelancer's sales letter. Like the application letter, this one should be brief and written in simple, direct language and correct grammar; it should not contain any hackneyed expressions, and should be a neatly typed original.

In preparing the sales letter you must first have a very clear understanding of what you want the letter to accomplish. The vague idea that you want the potential client to buy your work is not enough. You should determine the kind of work in which you want to generate interest, when you would prefer to do the work, the price range in which you want to operate, and the working arrangements you would prefer. Once you have made these determinations you can form a clear-cut idea of what you want your letter to accomplish.

Having determined the fundamental purpose for your letter, the next question is, "How can I make the letter accomplish this purpose?" Or to state it another way, "What techniques can I use in the letter to convince the potential client to do what I want him/her to do?" Much has been written concerning the psychology of the sales letter. The subject has been covered in books and magazines of all kinds. However, if you were to summarize all these writings you would find that they agree on one thing—the letter must be oriented toward its *recipient*—the "you" attitude.

Nothing related to the sales letter is more important than this "you" point of view. To accomplish this technique, the letter writer must adopt the reader's viewpoint. For example, instead of writing about "how much I should like to have you contract for my work," the emphasis should be: "when you contract for my work, you will benefit in several ways." Some of the ways the potential client might benefit is by securing superior artwork, saving money, making a greater profit, gaining improved efficiency, and getting better customer service. The important thing is that the potential client get the impression that it will be to his/her advantage to use your services.

The structure of sales letters has taken a well-defined form. A study of such a letter prepared by professionals in the field will show a great structure similarity, even though the content may differ. The freelance artist preparing a covering sales letter would do well to follow the following suggestions. Briefly stated, the structure should follow this sequence:

1. *Attract attention*—Open with a statement or device that gets the reader's attention within the first twenty words.
2. *Create interest*—Indicate a need for your particular services.
3. *Indicate superiority*—Convince the potential client that you are the best available in your category.
4. *Encourage action*—Recommend action that the reader can perform without difficulty.

The letter may be so structured as to devote a single paragraph to each of the above, or, as is frequently the case, 2 and 3 are included

Fig. 9.3 "Renaissance of the City," by international artist Robert Helsmoortel. This is a five-piece, walk-through work of art standing 33 ft high and having a base of more than 20 ft. The sculpture weighs between 20 and 21 tons. This world's largest fiberglass sculpture is located in the plaza in front of Peachtree Center in Atlanta, Georgia (Courtesy: John Portman).

in a single paragraph. More paragraphs than four are usually not necessary; the résumé takes care of the additional details.

The question now is, *How do you attract attention in the letter?* What techniques and devices are available to the novice in this undertaking? One of the most successful methods is to open with a *slanted question*, a question that is of interest to the reader and to which (s)he would like an answer. The following might be used when writing to an art director:

Where does your studio stand financially?
How can you be sure you're buying the right illustrations until you know what so-and-so is buying?
You know about the "Wilson" technique, don't you?

Such a beginning arouses the potential client's interest in reading further in order to discover the answer. It directs his/her thinking and focuses his/her attention.

Another effective technique for seizing attention is to open the letter with a *significant fact*. The emphasis here should be on significance, for if the fact is not meaningful to the reader it will not develop interest. For example:

DESIGN makes the all important difference!
It's the lettering that sells three out of five times!
The Blank Company featured John Doe illustrations in five of its featured ads this year.

The *directive* statement is another method for beginning the covering sales letter. In this technique you tell the reader to do something that (s)he will readily accept and not find offensive.

Don't bother reading further if you have all the expert appliance designers you need!
To assure quality, choose experience!

The above are but a few of the methods that can be used for attracting attention in the covering letter. For the original and clever person there are dozens of additional things that might be done. A few popular techniques are:

1. Enclosing some unusual or clever insert with the letter.
2. Using a startling color for the letter paper.

3. Shaping the letter in an unusual manner.

4. Typing the letter with unusual colored inks and type design.

To *create interest* on the part of the potential client so (s)he will be willing to look further into your particular capabilities you must appeal to two basic wants—to make more money and to improve business reputation. If you can show the person that you can contribute to both or either one, the potential client is sure to be interested. To do this, you must present the most appealing qualifications in your résumé—qualifications that indicate you can do superior work, have developed techniques and abilities that enable you to work for less, and can offer faster and more dependable service.

To *indicate superiority* on your part for the assignment you seek, you may use a few different approaches in your covering sales letter.

First, you may present supporting facts from reputable companies concerning the sales of your work, indicate publications in which evidence of your work can be seen, mention specific data about work production and costs; and submit evidence by accepted experts. Second, you could submit names of outstanding individuals who are willing to serve as references and vouch for your qualifications. Third, you can offer to produce sample assignments for little or no compensation if they are not acceptable. Whichever of the three types of approaches used, you must be sure that your evidence supports your original claims.

Encouraging action is the final responsibility of your letter. In the case of the freelance artist the action desired is an opportunity to show the portfolio to the potential client. This should be a direct statement requesting the interview. In addition, you should suggest a procedure that will make it easy for the reader to comply with your request. Some suggested procedures would be to include a stamped, self-addressed card on which the reader could fill in the time, to provide a special phone number to call collect, etc.

A few additional things you should bear in mind as you prepare your covering sales letter are proper English, the quality of stationery used, and the proper form the letter should take. Although there are some people who do not consider these items as important as content, it is a fact that if any of these are glaringly incorrect they can ruin your chances.

If you feel you need additional help in preparing an effective letter there are comprehensive books on the subject to be found in every library.

Finally, there are a few additional points you should bear in mind concerning your covering sales letter:

1. Address your letter to a specific person by name when writing to a concern.

2. Consider a series of sales letters. A message tactfully and consistently repeated will bring better results than a single writing. As a general rule, there should be no fewer than three in the series, and they should be sent no further than three weeks apart. The ultimate number and timing will depend on the message you are trying to convey.

Contacting Prospective Clients

The freelancer's plan for contacting prospective clients must be prepared with extreme care. The freelance artist seldom has much free time and therefore must devote all efforts in the most productive channels. The freelancer is not interested in quantity, for (s)he can seldom take care of more than four or five clients at a time. More important is "quality"—those who will pay the top dollar for the work. Therefore the freelancer must prepare the contact list—first in terms of those who can use his/her type of artwork, and second according to those who reputedly pay the higher fees.

The artist who is actively involved in the commercial art fields will have a general idea of which are the most desirable accounts. The novice will not have this advantage. For general guiding rules it can be assumed that (1) concerns that give wider distribution to artwork will generally pay higher fees. For example: concerns that place artwork in leading national magazines will usually pay more for it than those that place their work in publications of limited circulation. (2) Larger, more prestigious firms usually pay higher fees. There are many commercial artists who will take issue with this last statement; however, it can be taken as a very general rule.

Your list, if you are a freelancer, can be compiled from names your friends and acquaintances give you, from membership lists of professional organizations, names appearing in professional magazines, and lists of officers of concerns and organizations found in publications available at large libraries.

Organize your list from the most to the least desirable. Then separate the names into two lists of those you will call and those to whom you will write. Whenever possible try to get a mutual friend or acquaintance to arrange an interview for you.

Details on writing to a prospective client have been covered previously. Phoning to ask for an appointment (interview) requires a technique all its own. An effective phone approach requires preparation. You must know what you are going to say and how you are going to say it. You cannot know beforehand how a telephone conversation is going to proceed word for word. However, if you have planned and rehearsed what you want to say, you can most likely slant things in your direction.

Fig. 9.4 "Untitled tapestry," by Leroy Wilce, a California artist. The tapestries hanging in the Atlanta Hilton were custom-designed for the hotel by Mr. Wilce, as well as produced by him. He works entirely alone, with no assistants. Over 200 colors were used in the tapestries, which took over forty days to complete (Courtesy: Atlanta Hilton Hotel).

The interview is extremely important for the freelance artist. It is here that the "sale" is made. Everything that was done before has been a prelude to this, and everything that is done after is the follow-up. Here, in this thirty-odd minutes, you must convince the art director or account executive that you are the best one for the job. And this will take all the skill you can muster, for you must not only sell your ability but yourself as well.

In an earlier section we listed things to be done in connection with the interview. Although these suggestions are for a person applying for employment, they apply also to the freelance artist looking for new accounts. If you study the suggestions, you will note that they are concerned with actions and responses that make you appear most receptive, reliable, competent, and desirable. All things being equal, people prefer doing business with individuals having these qualities.

For the freelance artist, the interview centers around the portfolio. This sets the tone and tempo of that which transpires. There is nothing you can do or say that will overcome the impression set by a poor portfolio. And there is little you have to do to augment a good one.

Even though you give the potential client a copy of your résumé, on which you have listed your experiences, be prepared to talk about your work in depth. The interviewer will frequently want to know how you did your work as well as for whom. This person wants to be sure that your portfolio includes examples of work that you can repeat with professional regularity.

Don't expect the interviewer to reveal any particular attitude toward your samples. If (s)he feels they are poor the interview will be brought to a speedy, and even abrupt, ending. If the interviewer thinks well of your work, (s)he most likely will not say so or even reveal it in facial expression. If you question him/her for a reaction your question may be ignored, or at best the interviewer may indicate that your work is only satisfactory. You can understand this behavior when you realize that this person may shortly be bargaining to get you to work as cheaply as possible and does not want you to have the advantage of personal reactions.

The interview may come to three possible conclusions. First, if your work hasn't made a good impression, you may be dismissed without any commitment having been made. Second, if the interviewer does like your work, (s)he will save your résumé or ask for your calling card and indicate that (s)he will get in touch with you when there is a need for your services. Or, third, (s)he will discuss with you the possibility of an assignment.

If you experience the first conclusion do not feel overly discouraged. One potential client may find your work completely unsatisfactory, while another may think it is great. If, however, four or five in succession indicate that your work is poor, then you should certainly reexamine your presentation and seek some competent professional advice. If your interview ends with the second conclusion—that you will be contacted—then you will have to carefully plan a follow-up campaign. This is discussed in the following pages. Should you be offered an assignment—as indicated in the third conclusion—then you have positive indication that you have made the grade.

The danger inherent in being offered an assignment on the spot is that you might be overly flattered and agree to conditions that are less than satisfactory. If you are offered an assignment don't be softened up by the "you're a great person" routine that some clients will subject you to.

The Follow-Up

The follow-up conducted by the freelance artist is an important part of the campaign for new accounts. The form it should take will depend, to a large extent, on the impression made by the artist at the time of the interview.

If, as a result of the interview, you are given an assignment, there is little to do as a follow-up except to complete the work in the time and for the price agreed upon.

Should you feel, as a result of your interview, that you made a good impression but did not get an assignment, then it is your responsibility to keep up the interest with a well-timed follow-up. There is no set time when and how frequently you should contact a potential client. *It should be done whenever you have something significant for the client to see*—such as work of yours that has been used in an important publication or display, new work you have completed that you feel would be especially appealing, development of a new technique or process, or an important assignment you have had. In any case, do not delay the first contact any longer than two or three months after the interview. If you haven't received an assignment within eight months, try to arrange another interview to show your new work.

When you have the impression that you made a poor showing at your interview, you should not necessarily feel that the door has been slammed. Your impression may be wrong. Some art buyers have a tendency to make all artists feel inferior. And since almost all artists feel that they can do better, they readily accept this impression. When you have this feeling, it merely means that you have a bigger job cut out for you—but not necessarily an impossible one. Your follow-up will have to be exceptionally clever and pointed. You have to impress the potential client that there is more to your ability than first meets the eye. To acomplish this requires a carefully timed, continuous campaign. This calls for time and effort and the artist should first be convinced that the account is worth it. Often it is wiser to look elsewhere.

Some commercial artists prepare a standard set of follow-up mailings and send them out during a set period of time. No effort is made to personalize these pieces—they are merely attractive and even clever. The sole purpose for this type of mailing is to keep the artist's name and type of work before the potential client. They are sent out following all interviews for as long as a year or two. The advantage of this procedure is that it makes a minimum of demand on the artist's time, inasmuch as the mailings can be handled by some other person. The disadvantage is that it fails to have the personal touch and individualized appeal.

Up-To-Date Records

Up-to-date records are a necessary part of all businesses. This is no less true for the freelance artist. Too many commercial artists look upon record keeping as time-consuming and wasteful. The opposite is true. A good set of records prevents wasteful and expensive repetition and loss of business. The records can be quite simple. The important thing is that they be kept up-to-date.

The records for keeping track of your interviews and results can be kept on 5 × 8 file cards. A separate card should be prepared for each contact and should list the following: company name, company address, type of products (the kind of work that is produced), interview date and time, interviewer's name and title, résumé information (keep a copy of every different résumé you prepare; number each and place the number of the one left in this space), portfolio features (by giving a number to each piece of work you produce, you can list the numbers here and know just what you showed), money discussed, follow-up dates and types (record here any follow-up material you sent the concern). Once you do business with a concern it should be recorded in your regular financial bookkeeping system.

Additional sales techniques and devices the commercial artist may employ include advertising in publications, articles prepared for periodicals, work donated to charitable organizations, etc. At the beginning of this section it was mentioned that freelancing is a business in its truest form. In short, the more people and businesses that know about you, the more chance you have of getting assignments. It is for this reason that you must grasp every possible opportunity to bring your name before those who buy artwork.

PRICING YOUR ARTWORK

Pricing your artwork is perhaps the most frustrating thing you will have to do when you enter the commercial art field. The ultimate price of your work will be determined by supply and demand. Your question is, "What tangible basis do I have for figuring whether I am getting a fair return for my work?"

Out-of-Pocket Costs.   First, you must figure your *out-of-pocket cost*. This must include everything that directly costs you money, such as materials and supplies, costume rentals, photographs, model fees, special props and devices.

Overhead Costs.   Second, you must add the *cost for overhead.* This includes the continuing expenses involved in the business generally, such as rent, phone bills, advertising costs, business entertaining costs, wages, equipment replacement, etc. The only practical way to use this figure is to break it down to an hourly overhead rate and add it to the overall cost on that basis.

To estimate the hourly overhead rate, proceed as follows: accurately estimate the number of days you work in a month and multiply this by the number of hours you actually work at your art each day. (Do not include time spent on related chores, such as bookkeeping, correspondence, and contacting clients.) Divide this figure into the total monthly cost for all items listed in the previous paragraphs and you have a fairly accurate hourly overhead rate.

Charge for Your Time.   Third, you must charge for your time, which is another way of charging for your skill. No artist produces the same quantity with the same skill in each equal time period. Yet the only logical basis for figuring the time rate is by the hour. You must keep an accurate record on just how many hours were required to produce the job, then multiply this by an hourly rate that you have set on your work. For example, if a job required nine hours to complete and you charged at the rate of $10 per hour, the time rate for that job would be $90.

To summarize, the total cost for the job should include the following three charges:

1. Out-of-pocket costs
2. Overhead costs (overhead hourly rate times the number of hours required to do the job)
3. Time charge (hourly time rate multiplied by the number of hours required to do the job)

It should be noted that items 1 and 2 above cannot be altered for any one job. They represent actual monies invested in that particular job and must be returned in the charges. The third consideration, on the other hand, is a variable item and the one that causes the frustration.

Fig. 9.5   Graphics by Bruce Dell of John Portman & Associates. Located on the lower mall of the Peachtree Center outdoor cafe, Atlanta (Courtesy: John Portman).

What is a fair hourly rate for your skill? This can vary from artist to artist, from job to job, from season to season, from medium to medium, and in response to dozens of other considerations. Little help can be given you in this regard. You must determine for yourself what is a fair amount. If clients refuse to give you work because you charge too much, you will have to cut down on this amount. If your estimates are accepted too readily, you probably are charging too little. This is something you must play by ear; you must constantly keep in tune with the times.

A word of caution: don't get panicky and start dropping your rate each time a client complains about your price. Many art purchasers complain about price as a general practice no matter what prices they are quoted. Alter your rate in response to a general trend and not to an isolated incident. If you get yourself loaded down with low-paying work, you will not have time to search for the better type.

Having carefully explained a method for pricing your work, it must now be added that you, the artist, may not be the one who sets the price. It is a frequent practice that the buyer set the purchase price. Usually this is undesirable, but not always. There are times when the buyer is more capable of estimating the true value of a piece of artwork and will do right by the artist. Most times, however, the buyer will try to beat down the price so the work can be obtained as cheaply as possible.

Pressure to Lower Your Price

Experienced art buyers have many techniques that they use to justify lower prices on artwork. The inexperienced artists are especially susceptible to these maneuvers. There is no one way to combat the buyer's pressures. What you can do will depend on your financial condition, and in turn, how independent you can be. The least you should do is to figure out beforehand the minimum you can afford to accept, then bargain for a price as high above this as you can get. Should the offered price be below what you have decided is the acceptable minimum, then you should refuse the assignment.

The arguments used by art buyers to pay smaller fees are quite standardized, and although the wording is not always the same, the point they make is always the same. Following are some of the more popular arguments and devices that are used.

The Big Promise. You may be assured that if you will do a good job on this particular assignment, other assignments will follow at much fatter fees. The buyer may or may not have intentions of giving you additional work. In any case (s)he will seldom pay more. This argument never justifies your accepting less than a fair price. A variation on this is the "do-me-a-favor" approach. Here the buyer feigns that (s)he has run out of money and has only a little left for artwork. If you will go along with this, the buyer implies he or she will make it up to you at a later date. If you fall for this story, the buyer will have another one for you the next time.

The Poor Work Story. The buyer explains that (s)he thinks your work is not very good but (s)he will give you a smaller fee for it and work it in somewhere. If the artwork can be sold elsewhere, you should not accept this unfair offer. If it can be used by this client alone, then you should bargain for as much as you can get but should not work for this buyer again without a written contract.

The Big Rush. The buyer convinces you that (s)he must have the work in a hurry. When you deliver the artwork on schedule, the buyer points out the fact that it took so little time, it should cost less. You should not be taken in by this rush act for it is seldom true. When you do accept the rush assignment, be sure to get a price agreement *before* you do the work.

Limited Exposure. The buyer claims that the artwork is going to have a limited exposure and therefore pay should be less. You should not be expected to give a quality rendition for a little money. It should be the other way around: the buyer should expect less exacting work for this use and the fee (s)he is willing to pay.

Limited Money. The buyer claims that (s)he has a limited budget and can pay only a set amount. Another variation is one in which the buyer claims that his/her concern has "set" fees for different types of work. The answer in this case is that the buyer will hold to a set price if (s)he can buy for that price, *if this doesn't work, (s)he will pay more.* Some buyers have worked out elaborate performances to convince you of this "set-price" policy. You should not be fooled —the buyer will pay more if and when (s)he has to.

Fig. 9.6 (Opposite) This architectural design by Bruce Dell consists of colored discs and is located in the shopping gallery of Peachtree Center, Atlanta (Courtesy: John Portman).

The Threat. This approach takes a few forms. The buyer may threaten that you will not be given any more assignments if you insist on your price, or that (s)he knows of other artists who will work for less, or that (s)he will spoil your reputation with other buyers. You should stand firm against this type of attack, and should eliminate this person from your clients at the earliest opportunity.

The success of the commercial artist is not measured by how busy he or she is or how many accounts he/she services. It is whether the artist is doing a reasonable day's work and receiving for it a fair or handsome return. You, the artist, have a limited number of hours for productive work. If you fill these hours with poorly paying jobs you will not have time for the better opportunities. The wise procedure is for you to estimate—to the very best of your ability—the fairest value of your work and not accept less. In the beginning you may lose jobs you would have liked to accept, but in the long run you will build a more stable and satisfying profession.

THE MARKET FOR COMMERCIAL ARTWORK

The market for artwork can be roughly classified into two groups: local and national. First, let's take a look at the art potential that might exist right in your own back yard.

LOCAL MARKETS

If you are competent, ambitious, and enterprising, you can probably build a demand for your artwork right in your own locality. Local art opportunities usually center around the artist's studio. This is most often a converted barn, cellar, or attic where the artist displays his/her work. Having such a studio encourages friends and people in the vicinity to come and observe your work and, in turn, make purchases. If you can locate your studio so it is easily accessible for tourist and vacation trade, so much the better. You can also use your studio as a center where you can teach art on an individual or class basis.

There are many local art opportunities outside your studio: portraits are a perennial favorite—parents like to have them made of their children; children like portraits of their parents; communities sometimes want pictures of their past and present prominent citizens. Clubs, schools, hospitals, libraries, and businesses may request portraits of their founders, officers, etc. Add to this the people who like paintings of their favorite pets, and the number can be substantial.

Businesspeople who are proud of their plants, hotels, stores, or offices sometimes have artistic renditions made to exhibit, to use as trademarks, and to advertise.

Murals are used extensively in the lobbies of hotels and public buildings, and in banks, bars, and restaurants. The walls in homes of wealthy people are often individualistically decorated by artists.

There are scores of opportunities all around you—opportunities to turn your artistic ability into a steadily increasing income. If you are enterprising and willing to "dig," you will find them. And once you have established a reputation, you will find that many profitable commissions will come your way.

THE NATIONAL MARKETS

On the national level, the markets available to the commercial artist are many and varied. There are more than 300,000 firms in our country that buy artwork on a regular basis. The individual pieces of artwork they buy can be counted in the millions. And the amount of money they pay out to artists in all parts of America is phenomenal.

Following are listed broad groupings of concerns that purchase artwork regularly. The numbers listed in front of each grouping are only approximate, inasmuch as they vary from year to year. In each grouping are listed some possible sources where information about these concerns may be located. A word of clarification concerning the suggested sources is in order.

The sources mentioned below are books and periodicals that can be found in most large libraries. Although many of the listings are comprehensive they are by no means complete. Most of the publications, like *Thomas Register* and *Dun & Bradstreet Directories*, include only those concerns that have paid to be included. Those that do not pay are left out. Among the latter are hundreds, and possibly thousands, of excellent sales sources. How you might go about contacting these concerns has been discussed.

5,500 Advertising Agencies. This is perhaps the most lucrative sales outlet for commercial artists of all kinds. It is also one of the most competitive. Almost all such concerns have an art director and many include an art department. They use layouts, illustrations, posters, package designs, displays, lettering of all types, and almost every form of artwork. They are constantly on the lookout for the new, the different, and the unusual. In all large libraries can be found listings of advertising agencies in *Standard Directory of Advertising Agencies*, which is published annually followed by periodic supplements. *Standard* includes an alphabetical list of advertising agencies including branches, personnel, and accounts. It also includes a geographical index listing names, addresses, and telephone numbers of agencies by state and city. This publication covers the entire United States plus some foreign agencies. Some smaller publications that include agency listings are *Editor & Publisher International Year Book* and *Madison Avenue Handbook*.

16,400 National Advertisers. These are large concerns that depend primarily on advertising for their business. They usually maintain their own advertising departments, headed by an art director. That person is the one to contact for art sales. The artwork such concerns buy is for catalogs, circulars, direct mailings, and displays. In one year alone, this group of firms spends approximately $465,000,000 for artwork. National advertisers can be found listed in *Standard Directory of Advertisers*. In this publication the concerns are listed alphabetically and also by classification.

3,700 Newspapers. This category includes the daily and weekly newspapers. There are also the feature syndicates that furnish the newspapers with much of their material. They use cartoonists, letterers, illustrations, "mechanical people," maps, and drawings. Listings of these concerns can be found in a few different publications. There is the *Ayer Directory of Newspapers and Periodicals*, which gives a geographic and a classified listing as well as specialized information. There is the publication titled *Newspaper Rates and Data Service, Inc.* This includes up-to-date information about the entire newspaper trade. It issues a separate publication for weekly newspapers. The *Editor & Publisher International Year Book*, published annually, lists the responsible personnel in the different newspapers as well as other pertinent information. A listing is also included in *Standard Directory of Advertisers*.

2,200 Magazine Publishers. This figure includes not only the magazines customarily seen on the newsstands but also the trade journals represented in almost every field of endeavor. When you realize that each magazine usually publishes twelve or fifty-two issues per year, you start to realize the vast demand for artwork. This is the prestige market of commercial art. Magazines purchase cover designs, illustrations, layout, and cartoons. The magazines can be classified into three broad groups: as "slicks," "pulps," and "commercials." "Slicks" are the high-grade, high-priced magazines that get their name from the smooth papers on which they are printed. "Pulps" are low-grade magazines usually printed on rough, inexpensive pulp papers. "Commercials" refers to the magazines published for individual concerns, industries, or trades. Slicks pay the most for artwork, while pulps pay the least. Commercials vary greatly from excellent to very poor. Listings of magazines can be found in the *Standard Directory of Advertisers, Literary Market Place* (annual), and *Writer's Market*. The latter two books supply information of interest to writers, but they do have addresses the artist can use. Inquiries sent to the art director in care of the magazine will usually get to the proper party.

1,150 Book Publishers. The amount of artwork used by book publishers varies with the type of books published. An adult book will usually require a cover and jacket, while a children's book may have more artwork in it than writing. Book publishers use artwork for jacket designs, covers, frontispieces, illustrations, end papers, and advertising. Listings of these concerns are in the *Standard Directory of Advertisers, Literary Market Place* and the *Writer's Market*.

79,500 Department Stores and Specialty Shops. The artist who can work with speed will find this a lucrative field. These stores offer a considerable market for fashion art and other types of merchandising illustration, as well as artwork for newspaper and direct-mail advertising. Some of the leading stores are mentioned in *Sheldon's Retail Trade* and *Stores of the World Directory*. Neither book is very complete and both list only the very large concerns.

43,000 Printing and Related Trade Shops. This group includes all the reproducing trades, such as printing lithographers, photo engravers, silk-screen houses, and poster shops. Such concerns use commercial artwork of all kinds. The modern demands in this field call for more and more artwork. Even the smallest concerns are realizing the value of attractively prepared printed material and are demanding it. The demands for artwork of all types by these concerns will be constantly increasing for many years to come. A list of some of the largest concerns can be found in *Standard Directory of Advertisers*.

400 Greeting Card Publishers. This entire business owes its existence to the beautiful, clever, and cute designs created by artists. Here illustrations, cartoons, lettering, advertising, and layouts are used, and such businesses are always on the lookout for the new and unusual in their particular kind of artwork. Names and addresses for many of these concerns are in *Standard Directory of Advertisers* and *The Writer's Market*.

1,180 TV and Motion Picture Studios. These concerns use a considerable amount of artwork for the sets, titles, commercials, and advertising both on posters and in newspapers. The increased quality of, and demand for, color television and motion pictures has substantially increased the demand for artwork. Television networks and stations are listed in *Literary Market Place.*

450 Music Publishers. In this field artwork is used for covers of sheet music, recording covers, and advertising. The names and addresses of the music companies can be found in a monthly publication called *Schwann Monthly Guide to Mono and Stereo Records.* It can be obtained from almost any record shop owner. This publication will also give an indication of the number of new materials the companies are placing on the market. As a general guide the artist should realize that the more music a company produces, the more need it has for artwork. Record companies are also listed in the *Literary Market Place* annual.

220,000 Manufacturing Concerns. Large and small businesses alike have need for artwork. Such things as company journals, catalogues, circulars, price lists, direct-mail advertising, sales flyers, and annual reports are usually prepared directly by the companies themselves. There are a few comprehensive publications that list manufacturers of all types. The more popular ones are *Thomas Registry*, which consists of a few very large books of products classification, one of alphabetical listing, and an index of advertisers. The *Dun & Bradstreet Million Dollar Directory* lists companies that have done a business of at least one million dollars during the year. The *Dun & Bradstreet Middle Market Directory* is an attempt to list some of the smaller companies. Another directory is *Kelley's Directory of Manufacturers and Merchants.*

850 Textile and Wallpaper Companies. The artwork used by these companies is very specialized in nature. The market is open only to those artists who understand the technical requirements peculiar to the trade. A close study of the popular design presently in vogue in the trade will indicate to the artist whether his or her particular capabilities are adaptable to this work. Those who feel they can make a successful contribution in this field may find addresses for these companies listed in *Thomas Registry*, mentioned above.

Fig. 9.7 (Opposite) These striking chandeliers were designed by John Portman & Associates. They are 9- by 9-ft square and are located in the Peachtree Center Plaza Hotel Ballroom, Atlanta (Courtesy: John Portman).

10 Agents and Studios

The commercial artist who wishes to devote *all* his/her time to producing artwork must make arrangements with a second party to be responsible for the sale of his/her work. It is at this time that the artist becomes involved with a representative. This may be an agent, agency, or studio, depending on the type of arrangements (s)he wishes to make.

Before going any further with the discussion of representatives, there are a few things that should be made clear. There are not very many representatives for commercial artists. These people are only interested in handling the very best. They are seldom, if ever, interested in the beginner. The beginner would be wise to get a salaried job in the art department of an agency, studio, or large company. Here (s)he can learn the latest techniques, develop a specialty, and possibly build a reputation. When this has been accomplished, the commercial artist will have less difficulty in becoming affiliated with an agent.

THE ARTIST-AGENT RELATIONSHIP

In the ideal artist-representative relationship, you, the commercial artist, prepare the artwork in response to an assignment secured and transmitted to you by the agent. The completed artwork is taken to the client by the agent. Within a predetermined period the agent is paid for the work. (S)he passes the money received on to you after deducting the commission. In this ideal form the relationship is truly simple and complete. The trouble arises from the fact that the relationship is frequently far less than ideal.

It is often difficult to find an agent who has sufficient art background and understanding of techniques to be able to properly service commercial art accounts. The transmission of limited or incorrect information by the agent may force the artist to devote an unreasonable amount of time to corrections and alterations for which (s)he is not properly compensated. Artists who cannot find an agent

Fig. 10.1 Graphics by Bruce Dell of John Portman & Associates. Located on the outside wall of the Peachtree Center South Tower, an office building in Atlanta (Courtesy: John Portman).

capable of doing a satisfactory job of servicing take this responsibility upon themselves—and alter the agent's commission accordingly. More will be said about agents' fees.

Other difficulties can be found in the way some agents operate. There are agents who will develop a close relationship with a few art directors. These directors will tell the agent what they need in the line of artwork. The agent will proceed to find an artist who can take care of these needs. If and when the time comes that the artist cannot meet the needs of these accounts, the agent will drop him/her and take on a different artist.

Another thing agents will do is take on a large number of artists and then proceed to show work from all of them to any accounts interested in seeing them. This is the "buck-shot" method of getting assignments. The artist is short-changed in this arrangement because the agent has little time or interest in promoting any one of those she or he represents.

Agents, in their desire to sign up artists of outstanding reputation, frequently represent artists who do very similar types of work. These agents will then proceed to submit two or more competing artists for the same assignment.

The attitude of the agent may also prove difficult to the artists. There are some agents who are convinced that they know all there is to know about commercial art. These individuals will not only try to tell the artist what artwork to do but also when and how to do it. This attitude is, in most cases, a defense mechanism. Such agents, when they fail to sell an artist's work, will usually blame the artist's failure to understand their instructions, and not their own lack of ability to sell. The artist should not become completely dependent on an agent in this way.

In the artist-agent relationship the artist should have complete responsibility for the artwork produced. The agent should sell the artist's work and be able to service the accounts to the artist's satisfaction. The agent who satisfactorily takes care of this twofold responsibility is customarily paid a commission of 25 percent. Agents who perform less of a service are paid less. Those who do more are paid more. Agents who only sell and leave all the servicing to the artist are usually paid between 10 and 15 percent. On the other hand, an agent who has a close working relationship with a high-paying client, and can assure the artist a substantial amount of this work, can receive a commission as high as 50 percent.

The artist should realize that the agent's commission is a negotiable consideration. The money an artist pays in commissions is directly out of his or her pocket. Every effort should be made to

Fig. 10.2   "Chiru II" is the work of Miller Yee Fong
and William Gomez. The sculpture was specially designed
for the huge lobby area of the Atlanta Hilton. It is fashioned
from 4- to 8-inch aluminum tubes of varying lengths
(Courtesy: Atlanta Hilton Hotel).

keep this payment within reason. The artist should make sure that the contract with the agent includes a clause that permits the periodic review of commission payments.

THE CONTRACT

The agreement between artist and agent should be in the form of a written contract. It is too complex a situation to be left to any verbal statement. The artist who does not have a carefully prepared written contractual agreement with his/her agent can find him/herself unwittingly involved in embarrassing and expensive situations. More will be said of this later. Your artist-agent contract should be prepared by a competent lawyer and should cover the following areas:

1. There should be a statement to the effect that all samples of your work furnished to the agent remain your property and must be returned on demand in good condition.
2. The sphere in which the agent should represent you should be determined. Agents like to have exclusive rights to the sale of your works. This is very confining to you and therefore should not be granted until you are sure that the agent can guarantee you sufficient work to merit this confidence.
3. The contract should spell out who is responsible for servicing the accounts. If this is the agent's responsibility, you the artist should reserve the right of approval.
4. The agent's percentage should be clearly indicated.
5. There should be a clear understanding as to who will collect the money from the clients and how money transactions between you and your agent shall take place.
6. You should be careful to indicate to what extent you are responsible for commitments made by your agent.
7. The contract should contain a statement to the effect that the agent should not submit to the same client work in competition with your own.
8. Procedures for securing samples of work accepted for publication should be indicated.
9. The period covered by the contract should be stipulated. This statement could also include condition for renewal.
10. Conditions under which the contract can be terminated or voided should be spelled out. This statement should indicate a period of time in which the agent should be required to secure a certain number of assignments. Each party to the

contract should be permitted to terminate the contract, after a certain period of time, by sending to the other a written statement of intentions.

The contract should be compiled so that it can be used for single jobs and for long-term agreements.

The Implied Contract

The artist must always be careful that (s)he does not unintentionally slip into an agent-artist agreement. As we will mention in Chapter 12, there are verbal and implied contracts, as well as written ones, which are accepted in courts of law. All that is needed for a contract is that an offer be made by one party, and the offer be accepted by another. In the written and verbal contract, everything is indicated in so many words. In an implied contract, no words of any kind need transpire and yet it might be just as binding. The following is an example:

Should an individual, agency, or studio display your work and as a result secure an assignment, and should you accept this assignment, you have in fact accepted this party as your agent. *It makes no difference whether you gave your permission in the first place to have your work displayed by this individual or agency.* Your acceptance is the act that completes the contract.

Such a contract includes a few implications. First, the artist by his or her actions agrees to pay the customary commission that the agent usually receives. Second, the artist must accept any agreement the "agent" makes with the third party. Third, the artist is responsible for the instructions concerning the artwork that are given the "agent" even though the instructions may not have been passed on to the artist. Fourth, an implied contract can be assumed to be in force until such time as it is dissolved by a written statement. Such a statement must also be sent to any third parties who knew of the contract.

It goes without saying that the implied contract is a two-way street—it binds the agent as well as the artist. The individual, agency, or studio that gets involved in such an agreement must also assume all the responsibilities.

If you, as the artist, sell your work outright to an individual, agency, or studio then you assume no further responsibility for the work unless you have a written contract that states otherwise. The one who purchased the artwork assumes the role of a jobber and the artist has no customary obligations to the jobber.

Fig. 10.3 "Two Columns and a Wedge" (also known as "David
and Goliath" and "The Whistle"), by Willi Gutmann. The tallest
form is $36\frac{1}{2}$ ft high; the second is $8\frac{1}{2}$ ft high; the third is $5\frac{1}{2}$ ft high.
The sculpture is made from stainless steel, and is located in
Embarcadero Center, San Francisco. It was commissioned by
John Portman.

THE ARTIST-STUDIO RELATIONSHIP

In the art service studio, art comes the nearest to industrial line
production as is possible. A few very large studios have on their
staff a number of artists with many different kinds of abilities.
Most studios, however, retain only a very few people on their permanent staff and get the great majority of their assignments filled
by freelance artists with whom they maintain special relations.

The relationship between artist and studio may take a few different forms. The most common relationship is on a desk-space basis.
Under such an arrangement the studio permits the artist to use its
facilities in return for which that person pays rent or performs
specific services for the studio. It should be pointed out, however,
that although this is the arrangement most frequently used, it is not
necessarily the most advantageous for the artist.

Studio as Agent

A second alternative for the artist is to grant the studio regular
agent's privileges under a specific written agreement. (See suggested
agreement on pp. 122-123 concerned with agents.) It is important
that such agreements be in writing and the artist not forfeit his/her
privileges by default. In addition to the regular agent's commission
the studio usually adds a "service" charge. This may up the commission as high as 40, 50, or 60 percent. The amount of commission
granted the studio should depend on the kind of facilities provided
and the type of assignments given the artist.

Time-Basis Arrangement

A third alternative is for the artist to sell his/her services to the
studio on a time basis. Such an agreement should be accompanied
by a written contract.

Selling Work Outright

A fourth alternative is for the artist to sell his/her work outright
to the studio.

There is always a fifth alternative, wherein the artist might com-
bine two or more of the above possibilities into a relationship with
a studio.

If you, as a freelance artist, are considering a working arrangement
with a studio, it is important that you give the matter extremely
careful consideration. Every percentage of commission you grant to
others leaves less for yourself.

Fig. 10.4 "Flora Raris," by Richard Lippold, is 120 ft high and is located in the lobby of the Hyatt Regency in Atlanta. It is made from anodized aluminum. The work was commissioned by the Hyatt Corporation.

||| PROTECTING ARTWORK

There are in existence, in numerous museums around the world, art renditions that are hundreds of years old. That these art pieces still exist gives the general impression that artwork and artists are endowed with a special quality that renders them impervious to the ravages of circumstances and time. Nothing could be further from the truth.

The artwork itself is subject to destruction from many sources and conditions. Just to mention a few, there is the accidental breakage or tearing, gradual deterioration, wear, damage from moths and vermin, vandalism, damage sustained due to the repair and retouching process, and last but by no means least, harm that results from improper packaging and handling in shipment and storage. A destroyed art rendition can represent the loss of countless hours of demanding work and loss of sizable amounts of money.

The artist is even more vulnerable than the artwork itself. The problems that can confront artists when they set about to protect **127** their creative efforts can be many and varied and can come from

This is a free-formed concrete fountain located in the 4.2-acre Embarcadero Plaza in San Francisco. It stands in the center of a five-sided irregularly shaped pool. It was created by Armand Vaillancourt of Canada from precast aggregate concrete boxes, 11 by 5 ft square (Courtesy: John Portman).

many directions and sources. For instance, as long as the artist is working on an art creation in the privacy of his or her studio, nothing much can happen in the way of social repercussions. But the moment the artwork is completed and placed before the public, the artist is subject to all the legal, moral, and intellectual obligations society places on all its citizens.

Should the art rendition produced for viewing offend and injure the reputation or cause financial loss to an individual, organization, or group, then the artist could be subjected to about a dozen different legal charges. If the artist becomes involved in a legal confrontation and is found guilty, this could lead to financial losses of varying degrees or even imprisonment, depending on the severity of the injury to the other party.

Another injury that is, on occasion, suffered by the artist concerns the area of finances. All too often, the artist who is meticulous about creating a worthwhile piece of art will be haphazard about the financial transaction involved in its sale and consequently can end up receiving far less than the original worth of the object. Artists, as a group, are notoriously poor in financial dealings. Many do not know what constitutes a simple contract or the commitments involved. As a result, many artists not only give up their creations for a lot less than they are worth but also give away any moral rights they may have over the ultimate fate of their work.

Finally, the seemingly most obvious way of protecting artwork is often neglected—that is, the actual physical care involved in handling and transporting pieces that may have been painstakingly created and carefully sold. We will deal with all these aspects of protection—of the artist and the artwork—in the following chapters.

11 Insurance Coverage

The completed piece of artwork represents to the artist a substantial investment in time, energy, materials, and supplies. The end product is the artist's investment.

Artwork may be protected under a few different types of insurance policies. The artist who only occasionally creates a piece of artwork of limited value need not invest in a special policy. If this artist includes his or her creation as a part of home furnishings, it can be covered under a homeowner's insurance policy, provided there is not a specific statement in the policy eliminating artwork. If your policy excludes artwork, bring it to your agent's attention. It is possible such a statement can be removed from your policy.

ORDINARY HOMEOWNER'S POLICY

To have artwork covered under an ordinary fire or homeowner's policy, the creation must be considered an integral part of the household furnishings. Artwork temporarily stored in the home is not covered. Such work could be insured if a "rider" (special endorsement) is added to the policy specifically indicating that it is covered. Such a rider is usually inexpensive.

The amount that will be paid for artwork under the ordinary homeowner's policy will vary greatly depending on the precautions the insured artist has taken. If a painting is destroyed, the insurance company will ordinarily only pay an amount equal to the cost of the materials and supplies used in making the art piece. If the insured feels the artwork is worth more, (s)he should have it appraised by an accepted authority (a dealer or recognized artist) and have the appraised value submitted to the insurance company. If the company accepts the amount and records it in the policy, then it will pay this amount if the artwork is destroyed. If the appraised amounts are very large, the insurance company may require an additional premium to cover the artwork in question.

THE FINE ARTS POLICY

The serious artist who devotes a great deal of time to his/her work and creates work of substantial value should secure an insurance policy written solely to protect that work. Such "fine arts" policies are written by many companies. Almost any general agent can write such a policy for you.

The fine arts policies usually cover all risks of loss or damage to the insured property except loss occasioned by wear and tear, gradual deterioration, moths, vermin, inherent vice, or damage sustained due to and resulting from any repairing or retouching process.

The following risks are not usually subject to the rates, rules, and coverage of ordinary fine arts policies:

1. Dealers, commercial risks, museums, art galleries, or art institutions ordinarily open to the public.
2. Property owned by and insured for account of federal, state, county, or municipal authorities.
3. Temporary exhibits of property not owned by the insured when covered for a total period of not exceeding 90 days unless further extension for such 90-day period is specifically authorized.
4. Property on exhibition at fairgrounds or on the premises of any national or international exposition unless such premises are specifically described in the policy.

If the artist desires to have any of the above risks covered in his/her policy, (s)he must have them referred to the company for a special coverage and rates. It should be noted that universities, colleges, schools, and hotels are classified as private collection risks and usually covered by the fine arts policy.

New works of the insured artist are automatically covered under the fine arts policy. Such work is covered to an amount equal to the actual cash value provided this amount is not in excess of 25 percent of the total amount of the policy. The new work must be reported to the insurer within ninety days from the date it was started and additional premiums paid if they are due.

Fig. 11.1 Olivier Strebelle's "L'Epanouie" in bronze, located at the entrance to the Sidewalk Cafe in the Peachtree Center Plaza Hotel, Atlanta (Courtesy: John Portman).

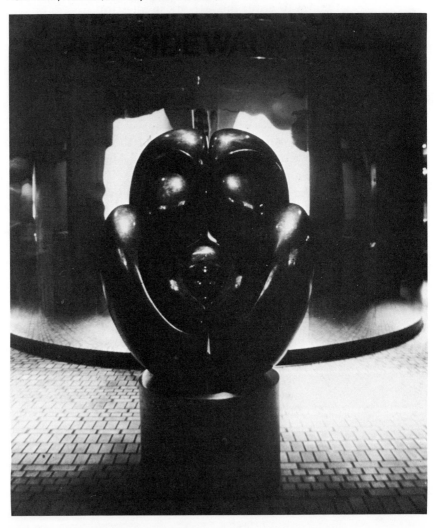

Insurance is an important item to be considered whenever a piece of artwork is entrusted to a person other than the owner. Artists frequently submit their work to exhibits, galleries, and agents. Or they may permit a potential customer to have an art piece for a trial period. The question is, who should cover the art piece with insurance while it is out of the artist's possession? There is no standard answer to this question.

Artists who regularly ship their work to galleries or agents usually cover such work in their fine arts policy. They make sure it is covered while in transit as well as when it is in the hand of the bailee (a person who is to handle or sell the work of another).

Museums, galleries, and agents frequently carry blanket insurance policies covering the artwork in their possession. The artist, however, should not make the assumption that his/her work is covered. There should be a contractual agreement indicating the type of insurance coverage that is being provided and who is paying the premium. The artist with sufficient prestige, whose work is in demand, usually insists that the bailees assume insurance costs. Artists lacking a following are usually stuck with this expense.

An important thing for artists to remember is that the value of their work may fluctuate. Any substantial rise or fall in value should be reflected in the insurance policy.

Artists should also realize that they can most likely negotiate a fine arts policy that is tailor-made to meet their own personal needs.

Proper insurance coverage is a must for both the practicing fine arts and commercial artist.

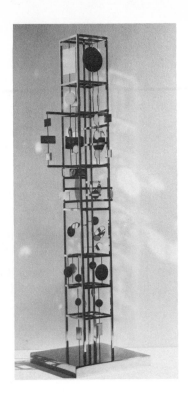

12 Financial Arrangements

As we have already seen, you, as the artist, may choose to sell your work through one or more different sales techniques. You may sell directly to a person who is going to display your art rendition in his or her home or place of business; you may arrange to sell through a gallery or dealer under one of several possible financial arrangements; or you may contract with an agent to handle your sales. There is the possibility that you will sell a completed piece of work or you may possibly prepare work to certain specifications. Many of these sales arrangements can be broken down into several additional variations. Each arrangement requires careful consideration regarding financial transaction procedures if they are to be legally correct and you are to get the money due you. If we seem to be repeating information in this section, be patient—this is important material for any artist to know. Additionally, there will be many who will read selected portions of the book for their own particular purposes.

There is one rule that is fundamental to all situations involving
immediate or eventual financial transactions—*get it in writing when-*

ever possible! A written agreement that is carefully and properly executed is always superior to a verbal implied one.

Careful and proper execution of a contract, as we touched upon earlier, implies that when there is more involved than the preparation of a simple receipt or order form, the document should be prepared, or at least reviewed, by a lawyer.

Fig. 12.1   "Tiles," by Olga de Amaral, is a 52- by 12-ft all-wool work located at the Fort Worth National Bank Tower, Fort Worth, Texas. It was commissioned by John Portman.

A written contract is not the only form that is acceptable. *Verbal* and *implied* contracts are also accepted in courts of law. The courts hold that as long as two actions have taken place, a contract exists: first, an offer has to be made—"I will do this for you, if you will give me this in return." Second, there must be acceptance—"I accept your offer."

In the written and verbal contract, everything is spelled out in so many words. In an implied contract, no words of any kind may take place and yet it might be just as binding. An example of an implied contract is one in which an advertising director might send an artist an ad that needs illustrating. The artist prepares the illustrations and returns them to the advertising director. The ad is published. The art director, by sending the ad to the artist has implied, "If you will prepare the illustrations for this ad, I will pay you at the going rate." The artist, by holding onto the ad and preparing the illustrations, has responded, "I accept your offer." The fact that the advertising director published the illustrations answered, "Your work was acceptable and you are entitled to your money."

You must be careful to distinguish between negotiation and contract. *A binding contract does not exist until all the discussions about price and conditions are completed and a definite and final commitment has been made.*

SPECIFIC SALES ARRANGEMENTS

The simplest form of sales arrangement is the direct type, in which the artist sells a completed piece of work to the ultimate consumer, the person who is going to use it. The transaction here is the same as it would be for selling bananas or brooms: the customer gives the artist the cash and in return takes the artwork. There are two points of concern in such a transaction.

Return of Art.   The first practice that might give the artist some difficulty is that of allowing a customer to return artwork that does not fit into the decorative or social environment into which it is to be placed. This arrangement should not be entered into without a written agreement. The artist should indicate that the artwork cannot be returned if it is held beyond a certain length of time, or if it is defaced in any way. This can be a simple statement written on the artist's letterhead or bill form and signed by the artist and buyer.

Loan of Art. If an artist frequently loans out his/her artwork before purchase, (s)he should have a rental-purchase contract printed up similar to the "Artwork Loan-Purchase Agreement" that follows. The loan period commonly agreed upon is usually two months, with an equal time renewal option.

ARTWORK LOAN-PURCHASE AGREEMENT

Date: . . . .

Received this date from . . . .
                                                    (Artist)
a . . . . .with the understanding that I am to
          (art piece)
retain it for a period not to exceed . . . .
During this period it is understood that I am to determine whether or not I
will purchase the same at the price of . . . .
    Should at the end of that period I determine not to make this purchase,
to return the . . . .
                                        (art piece)
to . . . . in the same condition it was in at
          (Artist)
the time it was entrusted to my care.
    This undertaking on my part is in consideration of . . . .
                                                              (amount)
given possession of . . . .
                                (art piece)
for the aforesaid period of time. Should I choose to retain the . . . .
. . . . then the latter amount will be cred-
          (art piece)
ited toward the purchase price.

Buyer: . . . .

Artist: . . . .

Copyright Retention. A third concern that might be involved in a direct sales is that of copyright retention. The fact is, this may be a consideration of the artist any time (s)he sells a piece of work. Print reproduction sales can be substantial. Only the artist who has retained reproduction privileges can capitalize on this market. A simple contract such as the one following could take care of this situation.

RETENTION OF COPYRIGHT AGREEMENT

Agreement made this . . . . day of. . . . .
19 . . . . by and between. . . . . of . . . . ,
party of the first part, and. . . . . of
. . . . , party of the second part.
    WHEREAS, the party of the first part has agreed to sell to the party of
the second part a certain. . . . .

(art rendition)

and the party of the second part has agreed to purchase the same:

WITNESSETH

    NOW, THEREFORE, on consideration of the premises herein and other
good and valuable considerations, it is mutually agreed by and between the
parties hereto as follows:

    1. The party of the first part agrees to sell the . . . .
to the party of the second part for the sum of. . . . .
($. . . . .) dollars, upon delivery of the same.

    2. The parties here do covenant and agree that the party of the first
part, his/her heirs, personal representatives, and assigns are to retain all
copyrights and right of reproduction of said. . . . .
It is expressly understood that this reservation is to survive the passing of
the title contemplated herein and the party of the second part agrees to
permit reasonable access to the party of the first part his/her heirs, personal representative, and assigns to the . . . .
being sold under this agreement.

    IN WITNESS WHEREOF, the parties hereto have set their hands and
seals the day and year first above written . . . .

Buyer: . . . .

Artist: . . . .

New Art. When the artist is called upon to prepare a new piece
of work, the arrangements should be consummated in a written
form. Inexpensive pads of "conformation order" forms, which are
excellent for this use, may be purchased from the Artists Guild, Inc.
of New York, 129 East 10th Street, New York, N.Y. 10003. An
artist wishing to have a more comprehensive form of his/her own
may have one similar to the following printed up.

John Doe, Illustrator
Street number
City, State

Number ....
Date ....

Order Acknowledgment

This is to acknowledge that artwork of the following description will be prepared for:

Name ....
Address...................

....

Artwork Description:
This artwork will cost the buyers $..........................
payable in three payments as follows:

	Charge	Date Due
Rough sketches	....	....
Comprehensive sketches	....	....
Finished Artwork	....	....

The price indicated above *does/does not* include costs for:

models	consultations
props	typography
costumes	alterations
photostats	overtime

All expenses and additional work that cannot be accurately estimated in advance, and therefore not included in the above price, will be billed extra unless other arrangements have been agreed upon.

Use of Artwork:
It is agreed that all phases of this transaction will be in keeping with the intent and spirit stipulated in the Code of Fair Practice as adopted by the Joint Ethics Committee of the Society of Illustrators, the Art Directors Club, and the Artist Guild which appears on the reverse side of this form.

Terms: Ten days net.

....
For the Purchaser

....
For the Artist

Note: Please sign and return one copy of form. Retain second copy for your file.

The Code of Fair Practice referred to in the order acknowledgement can be found in Appendix pp. 264-266. If substantial changes are made in the original order, do not try to alter the original copy of the order acknowledgement—prepare a new one.

Changes on sketches submitted by the artist should be dated and initialed by the person making or suggesting the changes so it can be determined at whose expenses such changes are to be made. Whenever possible, have the changes indicated on a transparent overlay attached to the sketches and not on the sketches themselves. This, of course, is not always possible.

When the fine artist is commissioned to prepare an original work of art that does not as yet exist, (s)he is confronted by problems that differ from those faced by the commercial artist. The differences result primarily from their different methods of operation. The commercial artist usually submits rough visuals for the buyer's approval, then comprehensive sketches, and finally the finished work.

The fine artist, on the other hand, must usually wait until (s)he has completed a substantial part of the final artwork—and usually must wait until it is completed—before (s)he can get approval of the work. However, should the artist be able to segment his/her work so (s)he can ask for payment at different stages of development, this should most certainly be done.

The fine artist should insist on a written contract when (s)he is given a commission for a work such as a portrait, mural, civic sculpture, etc. The contract should be comprehensive enough to cover some of the more thorny problems that come up, such as the following:

1. *What obligations remain if the artist or buyer (patron) dies before the artwork is completed?* A fair arrangement is one that relieves the artist or his/her estate of any obligation if the preparation of the art piece is impossible by virtue of death, disabling illness, or insanity. Likewise, there should be no obligation to the buyer or his/her estate should (s)he die before there is any work done on the art piece. On the other hand, if the artist has completed sufficient work so that it can be satisfactorily completed without the presence of the buyer, then the buyer or his/her estate should be required to pay the agreed price. A complication could develop at this point if the payment was dependent on the "satisfying" of the person who died.

2. *To what degree should a completed art piece satisfy the buyer?* This is a problem that has many ramifications. A contract that contains a statement to the effect that the buyer must be satisfied before

(s)he pays for the work leaves the artist completely at the mercy of the buyer. If the contract requires that the artist produce a "satisfactory" art piece, the obligation may be entirely different than if the contract stipulates that the buyer "must be satisfied" before (s)he pays. "Satisfactory" can be an objective quality. In a court of law it may be interpreted to mean that the artwork must satisfy a reasonable person. In such a case, the expert opinion of a respected art dealer or fellow artist might be accepted.

Fig. 12.2　Olga de Amaral's "Fuchsia Flowers" is a 17-by 12-ft tapestry that hangs in the Fort Worth National Bank, Texas (Courtesy: The Fort Worth National Bank).

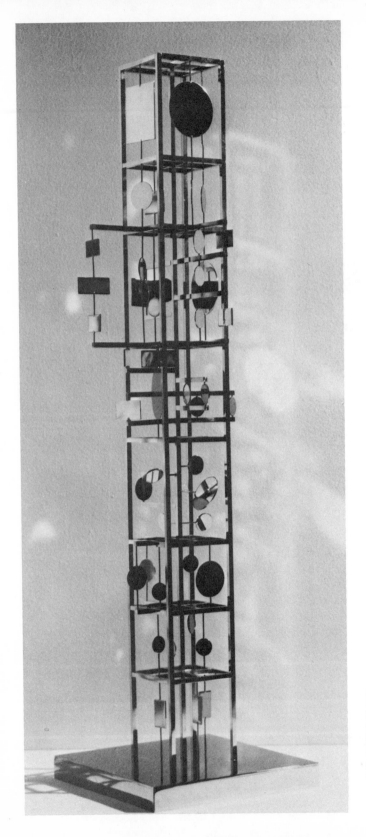

Fig. 12.3 This model of "Chronos XIV" by Nicholas Schoffer is located in the Embarcadero Center, San Francisco. It is mechanical and has lights reflecting multicolored light beams on its sixty-five silver discs. It stands approximately four stories high (Courtesy: John Portman).

If and when a buyer cancels a contract, the artist is free to dispose of the piece of art elsewhere. If the artwork involved is concerned with a subject of general interest, the artist may very well sell it to someone else. However, if the artwork involved is a mural, a portrait, or a statue of an individual, then additional complications may be involved.

Where the artwork is a mural affixed to the property of the buyer, a different condition is injected. There is a rule of law against *unjust enrichment.* In other words, the buyer cannot stipulate that (s)he is dissatisfied and refuse to pay. The law holds that the buyer was enriched and (s)he must pay an amount that adequately represents the value of the work performed. The amount is the point that must be negotiated. This usually falls somewhere between the contract price and the "open market price."

When a portrait or statue of the buyer or a person (s)he has designated is the artwork involved in a contract disagreement, then another complication must be considered. To sell such an object elsewhere may be considered an "invasion of privacy" by the person portrayed. If the person portrayed should consider the work so inferior as to portray him or her in a derogatory light, (s)he might sue the artist for libel if the work is exhibited without proper authorization. If the artist cannot possibly complete the artwork to the buyer's satisfaction, there are three alternatives. First, the contract may be renegotiated so that the work can go at a lower price. Second, the artist might try to get a written release from the person portrayed and perhaps sell the work elsewhere. Third, the work can be destroyed or kept hidden from view.

Whenever possible, the artist should have the buyer O.K. and initial any preliminary sketches that have satisfied him/her. Should the buyer express dissatisfaction with the final artwork, a collection of approved preliminary sketches may go a long way in helping the artist prove that a buyer's dissatisfaction is not genuine.

3. *Who should have reproduction rights?* If the artist feels that it is to his or her advantage to retain the reproduction right to the artwork, (s)he should have this indicated in the contract. If a contract involves a substantial sum of money, it would be wise to include a statement on how disputes are to be settled should they arise.

The artist may choose to have a second party sell his/her work. The commercial artist may have an agent or studio represent him/her. The fine artist may sell his/her work through a dealer or gallery. Every one of these financial arrangements could have dozens of variations and therefore should be covered by a written contract.

13 Legal Considerations

An art rendition, when completed and submitted to public scrutiny, is accepted as a statement of fact—much the same as a literary rendition prepared by an author. Like the literary work, it is subject to interpretation. Should an individual organization interpret the work to be detrimental, the artist can be subjected to a long and expensive legal involvement. This is an ever-present possibility.

The artist should be familiar with some of the many legal breaches (s)he might commit, knowingly or unknowingly. Knowing them, it is possible to take reasonable precautions to avoid them. And this is a case in which "an ounce of prevention is worth a pound of cure."

Many of the legal charges that can be brought against an artist as a result of his or her work are complex in nature. We cannot make a comprehensive presentation here, owing to a lack of space. But we can provide a brief definition. If the artist feels the need for more complete understanding, a lawyer should be consulted.

If there is any question at all of possible legal involvement, a
lawyer should be contacted *before* the artistic work is submitted to

public display. At such a time the lawyer can avoid trouble with little effort and expense. If the artist has not taken this precaution and, after displaying his or her work is charged with an offense, a competent lawyer should be engaged without delay.

Legal protection is not a one-way street. It is just as possible for the artist to be a victim of a wrong as it is to be the perpetrator. The artist should know his/her rights and the channels for retribution.

LIBEL

Any material—in picture, effigy, or written form—that tends to degrade a person in the eyes of a third party or jeopardize his/her means of livelihood may be judged libelous. The material may be considered to be defamatory, or just plain untrue. The jeopardy it will subject the defendant to will depend to a large extent on which state the suit is initiated in. The libel laws vary from state to state. There are, however, some general concepts that are accepted by most.

The basic consideration in libel is, "What injury has been done to the person's reputation and, in turn, how has (s)he been injured financially?" That the person's feelings have been hurt is of no consideration. In many states the injured person does not have to indicate any specific injury to collect damages, but merely the potential or possibility. In some states, however, the plaintiff must prove a specific injury to be awarded a judgment.

PLAGIARISM

The law of the land contends that a person should enjoy the benefits of his/her labors. That is why there are laws forbidding the theft of one person's ideas by another. These regulations apply in the art fields as well as in literature, drama, and music. One artist may *imitate* another, but (s)he may not make an exact copy and present it as his/her own.

The difficulty in proving a plagiarism charge lies in the fact that it is not easy to determine where copying ends and imitation begins. This gray area between the two is particularly hard to determine in the art fields. It is for this reason that there are so few plagiarism cases in the graphic arts.

INVASION OF PRIVACY

It can be safely estimated that most people in our society like publicity. The fact remains, however, there are people who want to avoid publicity—who want their privacy—and they have a right to it. To

Fig. 13.1 "The Big One," by Swiss artist Willi Gutmann, is located at the Peachtree Center in Atlanta. This two-ton, 35-ft-tall aluminum sculpture consists of two great discs cut in concentrical or circular pieces (Courtesy: John Portman).

deny them this right by exposing their picture, name, or details of their life without their consent is considered a personal injury and can be prosecuted as such.

It is not always easy to determine when the invasion of a person's privacy has taken place. The problem is not too complex when it involves the "average" person who cannot ordinarily be considered newsworthy. When such a person is pictorially presented, or his/her name is used in connection with an affiliation which (s)he does not approve, or details of his/her life are presented which (s)he considers derogatory, then the invasion is quite obvious. However, when people in the "public eye" are involved, such as politicians, theatrical people, sports stars, etc., they are considered newsworthy and permitted to be presented and viewed more intimately.

The artist must be particularly concerned about the invasion of privacy when his/her work appears in an advertisement or a similar commercial display that will allow that person to benefit financially. Unauthorized use of a person's, concern's, or organization's image, name, real or personal property, or copyright material in such a publication or on television may lead to a lawsuit. The wise thing to do, whenever possible, is to get a written release from all persons and organizations involved in your work. This should include friends and associates. Such a release gives you a positive form of protection that cannot be realized in any other way.

The artist must remember that when a minor is concerned, the release must be signed by the parent or guardian.

The release should clearly indicate who is concerned and the purpose to which the released material will be put. Following are suggested releases:

SUGGESTED RELEASE FORM

For good and valuable consideration, the receipt of which I hereby acknowledge, I hereby consent to the use by . . . .

(Artist's Name)

or by his/her legal representative or assigns, and all persons acting under his/her permission or authority, of my name and or a portrait, sculpture, or picture of me, or any reproduction of same in any form.

. . . .

(Signature of one portrayed)

. . . .

(Address)

. . . .

(Date)

SUGGESTED RELEASE WHEN MINOR IS INVOLVED

I, ... being the parent/guardian
(Name of parent or guardian)
of (minor's name) hereby consent and authorize (artist's name), his/her
successor, legal representative, and assign, to use and reproduce the portraits, sculptures, and pictures taken of (him/her) for any and all purposes,
including publication and advertising of every description. Value has been
received and no further claim of any kind will be made by me.

. . . .
(Signature of parent or guardian)
. . . .
(Address)
. . . .
(Date)

DISPARAGEMENT (DEFAMATION)

Broadly defined, disparagement is the act of expressing to a third
party an untrue written (illustrated) or spoken statement about a
person, his/her ability, work, or anything else that will destroy the
value of that person's property. It must be proven that the statement
in question was *directly responsible* for the injury inflicted on the
plaintiff.

The main point of concern, as relates to a charge of disparagement, is not whether the statement in question was true or untrue,
or whether it was delivered in malice or not, but whether it resulted
in financial loss to the injured. The person claiming the injury must
show a direct relationship between the statement and the resulting
loss.

OBSCENITY

An art presentation is considered to be obscene when it depicts
that which is lewd, indecent, and is calculated to shock the moral
sense of the beholder by a disregard of chastity or modesty, or incite lustful or immoral deeds. There are state, federal, and postal laws
and regulations that attempt to define what incites lust or depraves
and corrupts. In addition, there are self-appointed religious and
fraternal organizations that attempt to do the same. These cross-

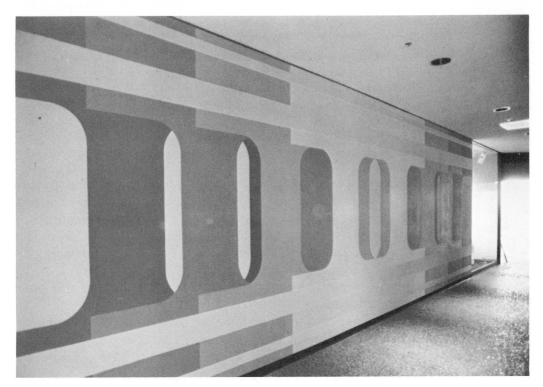

Fig. 13.2   Graphics by Bruce Dell of John Portman
& Associates. Located on the corridor wall of Rich's II
in the Peachtree Center Shopping Gallery, Atlanta
(Courtesy: John Portman).

currents of interpretation make the entire question of obscenity ambiguous and confusing for the artist.

The exposure of the nude body is not always permissible in art. If the nude should be positioned in the art rendition in such a way as to be excessively sexually suggestive or might incite impure thoughts in a "reasonable adult," then they can be declared obscene and the artist prosecuted if (s)he presents this work to public observation.

UNFAIR COMPETITION

Unfair competition concerns the illegal exploitation of the efforts and reputation of one person by another. This is not to say that every form of imitation can be prosecuted under this tort. It is an accepted fact in the field of art that every successful form or school of art invites imitation. In most cases such imitation flatters and enhances the original. However, when the imitation is employed to deny the originator his/her right and proper reward by deceiving the public, then it is proper grounds for legal action.

UNJUST ENRICHMENT

The painting of murals on commercial buildings and homes is becoming increasingly popular. The same is true of sculptures that are included as part of structures of all types. The question that confronts the artist is one of acceptance. "What could happen if I should paint a mural on the walls of a building and the owner should declare it as unacceptable? Can he refuse to pay for the work performed?" The answer is no, not entirely. This would be considered unjust enrichment; the patron would be gaining unreasonable benefits from the work of the artist.

It is assumed that the mural painted by the artist has some monetary value even though the patron may find it contrary to his/her liking. For practical purposes it is considered to have a value equal to that which it would bring on the open market. This is usually somewhat less than the original contract price.

CUSTOMS REGULATIONS

Single pieces of original, "customary" fine art are permitted entry duty-free. By customary is meant original oil paintings, water paintings, carved sculptures, etc. that are readily recognized and accepted as forms of fine art. In recognition of the fact that there are many new forms of experimental art being prepared, the customs regulations extends the duty-free classification to any type that can prove it represents "some school, kind, or medium of the free fine arts." In cases involving questionable artwork the collector of customs may demand verification from art experts.

There are some art renditions such as prints and cast sculptures which, by their very nature, permit mass production. In such cases the regulations permit the original model plus ten replicas to enter duty-free. The original sculpture model or master image from which the prints were made must be made by a recognized artist using customary methods. The sculptures and prints are to be used as fine art pieces.

BAILMENTS

Bailment is a legal relationship that is created when an artist leaves samples of his/her work with an agent, studio, auctioneer, or any similar second party. In this relationship the artist is known as the bailor, and the one to whom the artwork was delivered is the bailee.

Where there is no written contract between the bailor and the bailee, certain assumed conditions exist. First, the title to the artwork involved will always remain with the bailor (artist). Second, the bailee (the one who has received the artwork) is required to exercise reasonable care—care equal to that which a person would exercise over his own property.

WARRANTIES

There are a few considerations of warranty that might be involved in the sale of artwork. First and foremost there is an inferred warranty issued by the artist that the art piece will remain in good condition for a reasonable length of time—it will not fall apart, fade, or change its accepted character.

If the artist makes a written or verbal agreement to deliver an art piece at a future date in return for a previous payment, (s)he is bound by law to do so.

RIGHT OF FIRST REFUSAL

In some artist-agent (dealer) contracts there is a stipulation that the agent will have the "right of first refusal" on certain work produced by the artist. The artist is bound to submit his/her work as indicated in the contract. If the agent or dealer does not accept the work, the artist is then free to sell the work elsewhere. In a right of refusal arrangement it is wise for the artist to have the agent sign a simple statement of refusal when work is rejected by him/her.

ROYALTIES

The royalty contract, which is popularly used as a financial agreement, can give the artist a continuing return on reproductions of his/her artwork. In this contract, the artist is usually paid a specified amount for each reproduction, or ten, or hundred reproductions, depending on the use to which they are put.

Royalty contracts frequently have special provisions in them. One is an advance against royalties stipulation. In such an arrangement the artist is given a sum of money when the contract is signed. The royalties due the artist are charged off against the sum. The artist gets no return until the original sum is paid off. Another accepted procedure is to increase the artist's royalties after a specified number of reproductions have been sold. These increases do not usually start until the party producing the reproductions has covered his/her original investment. A regular scale of increases is sometimes worked out.

MEDIATION AND ARBITRATION

An artist experiencing difficulties in his or her contractual agreements with agent, dealer, gallery, customer, or patron may find need for these negotiating devices. Mediation is customarily the first step. In this arrangement a third party is invited to lend his/her good offices to help solve the difficulty. The recommendations made in mediation are not binding on the parties in a dispute.

When mediation fails to resolve the problem, the parties may, by mutual agreement, request that a third party arbitrate offering a decision after hearing both sides of the dispute. Such a decision is binding.

Those in the art field in need of mediation or arbitration may turn to two groups for assistance. One is an organization in New York City known as the Joint Ethics Committee. This is composed of members from four different art organizations. The other is the American Arbitration Association, which will supply panels of specialists for a nominal fee.

14 Keeping Good Records

To operate a successful art business, whether it is concerned with art or any other field of endeavor, requires an appropriate system for keeping record of its financial transactions. The two criteria for a good bookkeeping system are, first, that it include all necessary information but nothing more, and second, that it require a minimum amount of time and attention to maintain.

The artist who runs a one-person operation needs a very simple bookkeeping system. (S)he must keep track of the following as concerns his/her business:

1. Money owed for work created (customarily referred to as "accounts receivable").
2. Money owed to others for such things as supplies, materials, models, rent, light, fuel, etc. (customarily referred to as "accounts payable").

The system that is needed is one that will enable the artist to
know, in the space of a few minutes, how income (accounts receiv-

able) compares with expenses (accounts payable). Only by comparison of these two figures can you know how you stand financially.

Following are presented two very simple bookkeeping systems. Both accomplish the same things. They differ in the mechanics of their operation. Look them over and choose the one you feel will be easiest and most efficient for your needs. Neither of these systems requires more than a few moments of attention every two or three days for efficient operation. But they must be given the attention regularly or your system will deteriorate into uselessness in a short period of time.

Method 1: This sytem is based on the use of two notebooks. On one you write "Accounts Receivable." In this one, you record all the information concerning money due you. The pages in this book are laid out as follows and the entries made as illustrated:

ACCOUNTS RECEIVABLE

Description of work	Date Completed	Delivered to	Delivery Date	Price	Amount Received	Date Received	Remark
"Reflections" oil—20 x 30	7/1	Burns	8/17	$85	$57	10/5	Sold to J.T.
"Fall Fury" —oil—14 x 21	8/15	Burns	8/25	66	44	10/14	
Hotel rough visuals W.C.	9/5	C.T.	9/12	45	34	11/29	For Parker at Concord

The second notebook is labeled "Accounts Payable." In this book you enter all the money that must be paid out. The pages of this book should be laid out as follows and the entries made as illustrated:

ACCOUNTS PAYABLE

Item	Quantity	Cost	Date Billed	Amount Paid	Date Paid	Remarks
2 ¾" Oak Frames 16 x 20	2 ea.	$ 9.86	5/5	$ 9.86	6/1	Browns
Canvas 52" wide— smooth cotton	6 yds.	11.34	5/6	11.34	6/1	Tompkin Bill #1151
Letterheads	300 ea.	10.75	6/7			Chick Press
Envelopes to match	300 ea.	16.20	6/7			Chick Press

In addition to the two notebooks, you should have a file box in which you keep the copies of the original bills and statements.

Method 2: This method is even simpler than the first method. Here you keep no books. The bills you send out and receive serve as an entire record. This method is based on four filing folders, labeled as follows:

1. Accounts Receivable—Unpaid
2. Accounts Receivable—Paid
3. Payable Accounts—Unpaid
4. Payable Accounts—Paid

Fig. 14.1 "Red Banner" by John Portman & Associates Designs is located in the Embarcadero Center, San Francisco (Courtesy: John Portman).

The system operates as follows: For every bill you send out (and a bill should be prepared for every piece of work you do), make a duplicate. The duplicate is placed in folder 1 (Accounts Receivable—Unpaid). When the money is paid to you, the bill is removed from folder 1, marked paid and dated, and placed in folder 2 (Accounts Receivable—Paid).

Make sure to get a bill for *every* item purchased and every expense you have in connection with your artwork. The unpaid bill is placed in folder 3 (Payable Accounts—Unpaid). When the bill is paid, it is taken from folder 3, marked paid and dated, and put in folder 4 (Payable Accounts—Paid).

In addition to one of the bookkeeping systems mentioned above, you should also keep a separate checking system for your business needs alone. Such canceled checks not only help keep an accurate record of your finances but also serve as excellent evidence when your income tax return might be challenged.

Your file should have at least four additional folders: one for "letters received," a second for "letters sent," a third for "contracts," and a fourth for "publicity." These are the minimum. Clients for whom you do a great deal of work should have separate folders..

If in the course of your work you need the assistance of another individual, you must be careful of the manner in which you pay this person. If the work performed for you is completed in a short period of time, the individual can submit a bill for services. In such a case, the person submitting the bill has assumed the role of an independent contractor. Aside from paying the bill, you assume no additional obligations to this individual. This bill is entered in your accounts payable file and paid like any other.

On the other hand, if you employ an assistant on a regular basis and pay him/her a salary (usually weekly), you then must assume the responsibility of an employer. As an employer you are responsible for certain taxes and insurances to cover and protect the employee.

Information concerning employees should be kept separately. You should record the amount paid your worker each week. In addition, you must keep careful records of all tax withholdings and payments turned over to the government. At the end of the year, you must give your employee a summary statement of his/her earnings and withholdings.

The above bookkeeping recommendations will take care of the needs of most artists who have a limited operation. Should the artist expand his/her activities to the size of a studio, (s)he will need a more elaborate bookkeeping system.

15 Packing and Shipping Artwork

The safest procedure when you are transporting artwork in your own car is to box each individual piece to be transported in its own corrugated carton. Corrugated boxes of all sizes can be secured free of charge in every community. Secure a box or cut one to size so the art piece can be inserted and taken out without difficulty. In this way the carton can be reused many times. The art piece should fit snugly in the carton.

Unframed paintings can be packed a few to a box if they are stacked back to back and face to face with a corrugated cardboard separation sheet between the faces. Framed paintings can be packed back to back, two in a box. Never allow the hanging devices of the frame from any other work or any other projecting object to rest on or touch the painting.

When the time comes for your art piece to be shipped by a common carrier, then you must take elaborate precautions for its protection. The protective measures you should take in packing and shipping the art piece will depend on the fragility, size, weight, and value of the work involved plus the costs, its ultimate destination, and the time available for its shipment.

PACKING ARTWORK

There are two basic rules that must be followed in packing artwork: a strong, closed, waterproof container must be provided; the objects packed within the container must be protected against shock. Over the years the museums and galleries have developed certain packaging techniques that have become quite standardized. Necessity has dictated the acceptance of these techniques and it would be wise for the artist to do the same. The following general rules are based on the procedures recommended by experts in the trade:

1. Inspect the art object to be shipped to make sure it is sound and practical for shipment. Any painting that is more than seven feet in any one direction should not be shipped, because it will require special handling equipment that is not always available. Watercolors and drawings that are over 24 inches in any one direction should be framed under a plexiglas before shipping. Plexiglas is an unbreakable, transparent, plastic material with the appearance of plate glass.

2. When it is necessary to ship a work covered with glass, the glass should be protected with masking tape. The tape should be placed on the glass in parallel lines *not more than a quarter-inch* apart and as far as *but not overlapping* the frame. Never allow the tape to touch the frame (see Fig. 15.1). Tape requiring water must never be used. This is to guard against any possible water damage to a picture. Never

Fig. 15.1　Masking tape arrangement to protect glass (Courtesy: The American Federation of Arts).

tape plexiglas—it may disfigure the surface and besides, it does not shatter and therefore does not need this type of protection.

3. Pack artwork in wooden boxes. Carriers will not accept corrugated boxes (except for very small objects).

4. Enclose the art object in the waterproof package. Plastic bags of all sizes can be secured for this purpose. The entire box could be lined with waterproof paper instead of covering the individual piece. When this is done, use glue to hold the paper in place—*never* tacks!

5. Protect the contents of the box against vibration and shock. A resilient material such as excelsior, crumpled paper, or foam plastic should be used for this purpose. Foam plastic, one of the more modern packaging materials, can be secured in quantities free of charge from appliance stores. This plastic foam can be easily cut and shaped with a sharp knife or saw and can be glued together to make up larger pieces with liquid polyvinyl resin glue (such as Elmer's) or rubber cement (*not* Duco or model airplane cement). Whenever excelsior or cotton is used as a packing material around paintings, it should be wrapped in paper. Loose cotton or excelsior on the face of a picture may adhere to or scratch the varnish. Small, fragile objects should be wrapped in tissue, then in cotton to protect the surface, then floated in excelsior in a cardboard or corrugated box. This box is then floated in excelsior in a second outer packing box.

6. Do not pack heavy and light objects one on top of the other in the same container. If they must be shipped in the same container, partition the container and pack each piece in its own compartment.

7. The side of the box you wish to be opened should be screwed into place, never nailed. This permits the box to be used repeatedly without being injured or destroyed. Most museums, and some of the better-organized exhibits, have packers who very carefully note how an object is packed when received so the object can be repacked for return without difficulty.

8. Mark the box with appropriate cautions. Such as, "Fine Art: Fragile," "Use No Hooks," "This End Up" (with arrow), etc.

PACKING PICTURES

The following illustrations (Figs. 15.2 through 15.8) show the methods for packing paintings used by the Metropolitan Museum of Art, the Museum of Modern Art, and the American Federation of Arts, which furnished the illustrations and much of the following instructions. Most museums and galleries use the same techniques. There are a few variations that might be used by the artist, as mentioned in the following instructions.

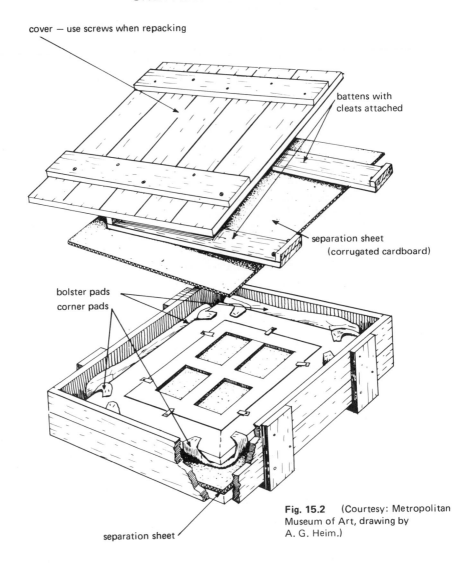

cover — use screws when repacking

battens with
cleats attached

separation sheet
(corrugated cardboard)

bolster pads
corner pads

Fig. 15.2 (Courtesy: Metropolitan
Museum of Art, drawing by
A. G. Heim.)

separation sheet

Packing case. The packing case can be made of ¾-inch or ⅞-inch
thick pine. For the top and bottom of the case ⅜-inch plywood can
be substituted for the thick wood shown. Nails are used to construct
the case except for its top or cover. The inside measurement of the
packing case should be at least 2¼ inches larger than the largest object to be enclosed.

Corner pads. These pads are individually fitted to each painting
to protect the frame and to provide a cushion within the box to

lessen shocks in transit. They are fitted diagonally around the front of the frame corners and stapled (never tacked) to the back of the frame, never to the stretcher of the painting. They are located, as far as possible, over solid portions of the frame—avoid fragile ornamentation areas. They must be thick enough to prevent contact between any free-standing ornament and separation sheet. Corner pads are usually made of cotton or excelsior wrapped in paper.

Bolster pads. These long, paper-wrapped pads are custom-made for the painting with which they are used. They are placed on either side and at the top and bottom of the painting between the frame and the sides of the box.

Separation sheets. These are made of corrugated cardboard.

Fig. 15.3 (Courtesy: Metropolitan Museum of Art, drawing by A. G. Heim.)

TWO (OR MORE) PAINTINGS IN A BOX

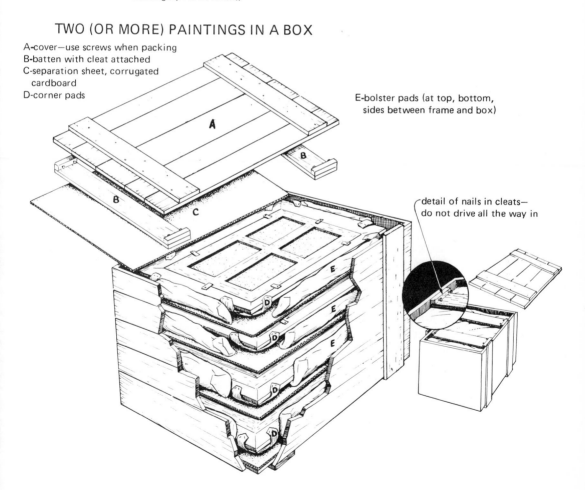

A-cover—use screws when packing
B-batten with cleat attached
C-separation sheet, corrugated
  cardboard
D-corner pads

E-bolster pads (at top, bottom,
  sides between frame and box)

detail of nails in cleats—
do not drive all the way in

TRAY UNIT FOR ONE PAINTING

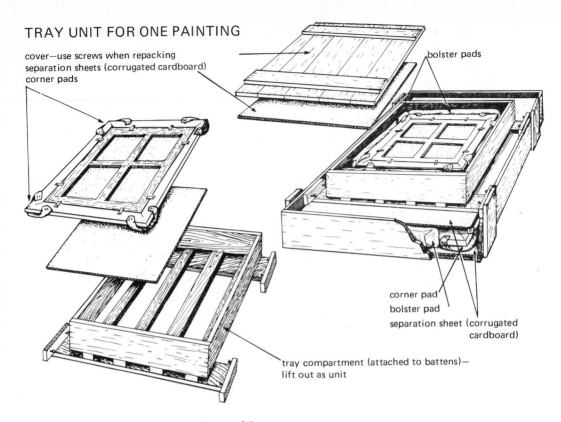

cover—use screws when repacking
separation sheets (corrugated cardboard)
corner pads

bolster pads

corner pad
bolster pad
separation sheet (corrugated
cardboard)

tray compartment (attached to battens)—
lift out as unit

Fig. 15.4　(Courtesy: Metropolitan Museum of Art,
drawing by A.. G. Heim.)

Battens.　Battens are used where there is extra space between the cover and the last painting in the box. They are gently but firmly forced into contact with the last separation sheet (which covers the last painting) in the box and held in place by cleats. The cleats are nailed to the sides of the box from the inside. Cleat nails are not driven all the way in—which makes removal of the battens easier when unpacking.

Unframed paintings of approximately the same sizes can be shipped in a reusable slide packing case (Figs. 15.7, 15.8). Strips of wood are nailed to the top and bottom of the case to form tracks and spacers. The tracks are fully covered with carpeting that has been glued into place. The tracks should be wide enough so the painting can slide freely in and out of the opening. The bottom board, to which the bottom tracks were nailed, should rest on rubber shims or washers inserted between it and the bottom of the case. Each painting should be numbered the same as its corresponding track so it **162** can be inserted in its proper place without delay.

TRAY UNIT FOR TWO PAINTINGS

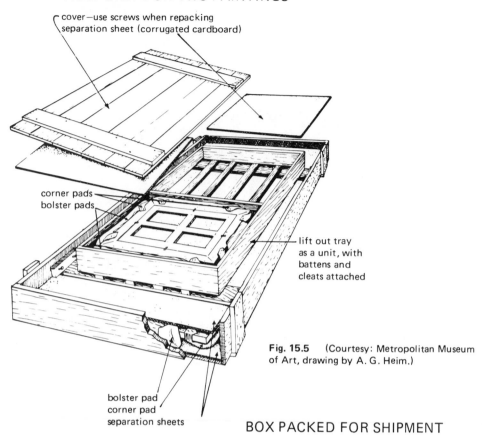

cover—use screws when repacking
separation sheet (corrugated cardboard)

corner pads
bolster pads

lift out tray
as a unit, with
battens and
cleats attached

Fig. 15.5   (Courtesy: Metropolitan Museum
of Art, drawing by A. G. Heim.)

bolster pad
corner pad
separation sheets

BOX PACKED FOR SHIPMENT

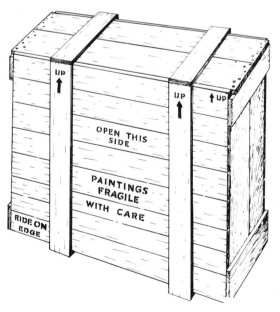

Fig. 15.6   (Courtesy: Metropolitan
Museum of Art, drawing
by A. G. Heim.)

UP

UP

UP

OPEN THIS
SIDE

PAINTINGS
FRAGILE
WITH CARE

RIDE ON
EDGE

163

Fig. 15.7 Unframed paintings of approximately the same size can be shipped in reusable slide packing case (Courtesy: American Federation of Arts).

Fig. 15.8 Mark shipping crate with appropriate cautions (Courtesy: American Federation of Arts).

Fig. 15.9 The odd and unusual shapes of sculpture require careful handling (Courtesy: American Federation of Arts).

PACKING SCULPTURES

The packing of sculpture is, in most cases, a much more complex operation than that of packing paintings. The odd and unusual shapes of sculpture require unusual handling techniques to protect them from injury. In almost all cases, each piece of sculpture work requires a custom-made crate that can be used for that piece of sculpture alone.

Before any sculpture work is packaged it must be *carefully inspected* for flaws. Stone, cast metals, and weldings frequently have defects in them that are not readily visible to the naked eye. These defects must be discovered and corrected before the sculpture is subjected to the rigorous ordeal of shipment.

Sculpture should be identified clearly, either by photographs on the inside of the box lid or by permanent, nondetachable labels. Clear packing instructions should be placed inside the lid of each box. These instructions should also say, *"When handling sculpture, lift it by its base."*

There are three basic methods of packaging sculpture: *wedging* (Fig. 15.9), *bracing* (Fig. 15.10), and *floating* (Fig. 15.11). The wedging method is used for sturdy sculptures that can withstand a fairly large amount of shock. The wedging material being put in place in Fig. 15.9 could be wood, with the surface against the sculpture covered with felt or carpeting, or the material could be plastic foam.

165

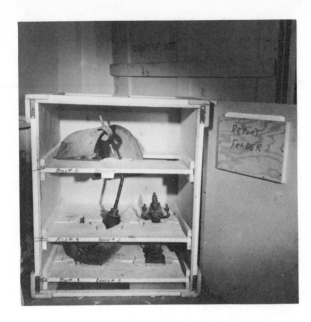

Fig. 15.10   A few sculptures can be packed in a single box (Courtesy: American Federation of Arts).

The wedging materials are held in place with temporary tacking; the nails are put in part-way so they can be easily removed. The temporary tackings must be so located that they will not injure the sculpture. The platform on which the sculpture rests in Fig. 15.9 can be separated from the base of the box with rubber washers.

Fig. 15.10 illustrates the brace method of holding sculptures. This method of packing is recommended for fairly flimsy types of sculp-

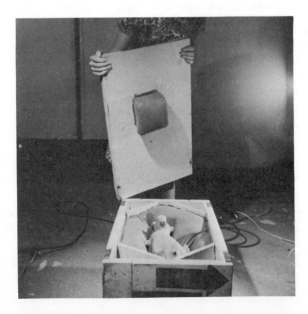

Fig. 15.11   Floating method for packing sculpture (Courtesy: American Federation of Arts).

ture. The braces are carefully fitted around the sculpture, and the openings that come up against the sculptures are padded. The braces fit into slots in the box; when the box is closed, the lid holds the braces in place. Note (in Figs. 15.9 and 15.10) how the bracings are carefully marked so that each piece can be reassembled without difficulty.

Small sculptures may be packaged in excelsior in corrugated cardboard boxes, or floated in excelsior in wooden crates. Large sculptures should be floated in fitted, custom-made felt padded wooden boxes as illustrated in Fig. 15.11.

PACKING PRINTS, DRAWINGS, AND WATERCOLORS

When prints, drawings, and watercolors are framed and covered with glass or plexiglas, they should be packaged in a wooden crate as described above. When they are merely matted or have no framing of any type, they can be more economically packed for shipping.

Whenever you are stacking prints, drawings, or watercolors for shipping, you should separate them from one another with tracing paper. If any hanging devices have been glued on the rear of the matting, then use a cardboard as a separater.

The stacked prints, drawings, or watercolors can be shipped in an envelope made up as follows: cut two pieces of corrugated cardboard or ³⁄₁₆-inch beaver board at least 1½ inches larger than the largest picture to be enclosed. Place the properly stacked pictures between the two cardboards and glue all around the edges with heavy gummed tape. Do not use masking or scotch tape; they are not strong enough. Mark the package "Fragile," "Do not bend," etc.

SHIPPING ARTWORK

There are five general methods available for anyone who wishes to ship an object—railway express, van moving, parcel post, air transportation, and motor freight. Of the five methods, only railway express is used extensively for the shipment of artwork. Van moving is used only for large, bulky shipments. Parcel post and air transportation are used to a very limited degree. Motor freight *should not* be used for shipping fine art.

Railway Express. Artwork shipped by railway express is usually given the kind of handling it deserves. Your art will be picked up at your studio and delivered directly to the receiver. The object must be packed in a wooden box, as described above. The rate scales should be requested from your local agent. These charges are standard and are published every time a change is made. The rates for shipments over 1,000 pounds are higher than van rates (under 1,000 pounds express rates are generally lower than van moving).

Express companies offer a special handling service for fragile and valuable shipments. For an additional fee your package can be given a "protective signature service," which means that every person who handles the shipment must sign for it. Arrangements for this service must be made at the time the shipment is accepted by the express company.

Van Moving. Large shipments (especially those weighing over 1,000 pounds) of low-average value are often less expensive sent by van than by railway express. There is very little handling (just into the van and out again); shipments can be padded by the carrier, and often do not need to be boxed. Indoor pick-ups and deliveries are guaranteed. Charges for shipping by van vary and should be checked before a decision is made.

Parcel Post. The objects that can be shipped by parcel post are limited as to size, weight, and value. For this reason, only fairly small objects of moderate value may be economically sent by this means. Small objects of great value can be sent by registered mail, which assures a person-to-person signature procedure. Complete information concerning parcel post shipments can be found in the "postal manual," which can be borrowed from the local postmaster or purchased from the Superintendent of Documents (U.S. Government Printing Office, Washington, D.C.).

Air Transportation. Where speed is a consideration in the shipping of a moderate size object, air transportation may be used. This is not as expensive as most people imagine and is increasing in popularity. Arrangement for domestic air express shipments may be made through the Railway Express Agency, a local post office that offers air parcel post, and air shipment companies. As for land shipments, there is air *express* and the less expensive air *freight*.

INSURING SHIPPED ARTWORK

Whenever a piece of artwork is shipped, there is an increased danger that it might be damaged or destroyed. This being the case, the artist should always carefully check to see that his/her shipped artwork is properly covered by insurance.

IV THE EDUCATION OF AN ARTIST

There are no legal requirements for certification to enter any of the art fields except for teaching and architecture. In other words, if you have some natural art ability, have the self-control to make yourself study and practice for long hours, and work at an art job at which you can receive some constructive criticism, you can become an artist without formal training. Several very successful artists have developed their art capabilities in just this way. However, most successful artists—in both the fine art and commercial art fields— have studied in formal art classes of some kind.

   The really important questions for the artist or would-be artist are, "What kind of training shall I have?" and "Where shall I get such training?" For practical purposes, the first question should be divided into two parts—between the fine arts and commercial art fields. Although both fields employ the same materials and more or less the same techniques, their intent, purpose, and approach are distinctly different, and therefore, each requires a unique type of training.

Sculpture class at the Art Students' League of New York.

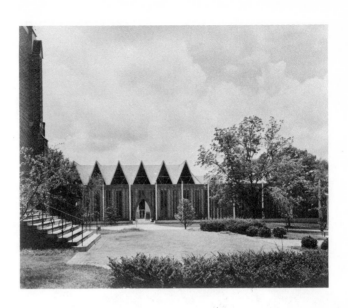

16 What Should I Study To Be a Fine Artist?

There is no cut-and-dried course of study for the fine artist. Even among the accepted authorities in the field there are widely divergent opinions.

If you have a "natural ability," or what might be called a "flair" for art, then your need for training in the basics may be substantially shortened or possibly, completely eliminated. If you are unfortunate not to have such a "flair," then you should spend long hours studying the basics. The art medium you choose as your ultimate form of expression will dictate, to a large extent, the kind and direction of your training. And finally, your financial status will determine which schools and private training opportunities will be available to you.

No matter what your ultimate field of art might be, your initial training should start with *drawing*. Some instructors will have you start by drawing duplicates of existing sketches. Following this, you will probably do still-lifes, outdoor sketching, sketches of sculptures, then the nude and clothed figures, and finally, experimentation in original concepts. The order in which you approach these will vary

Fig. 16.1 Inside the Dana Fine Arts Building at Agnes Scott College, a first-floor gallery opens to the skylight from the third-floor windows that light two levels of art studios on free-standing balconies.

from instructor to instructor. Many instructors object to copying at any time and will not permit it even for the beginner.

If you have chosen your ultimate field of specialization, then your courses can be chosen with little difficulty. You take as many courses as you can in your particular field. This is not to say that you do this to the exclusion of all other courses. On the contrary, often some work in other fields will help you to better understand and develop your ability in the field of your choice.

If you want to be a painter, you will take courses in such media as oil, watercolor, casein, pastel, tempera, gouache, the polymer media 172 (such as acrylic), and any new experimental materials of a related nature that may be on the market at the time. Work usually progresses from still-life to landscape to the human figure, then portraiture, and finally experimentation in abstracts. You will find value in an occasional course in the printmaking field—there is a close relationship between the two. Sculpture, on the other hand, offers the painter little that is of immediate value.

If sculpture is your interest, you, like the painter, will have quite a few materials and techniques at your disposal. You will start with a broad study of the field and then zero in on a medium and technique of specialization. The materials you will work with are clay, plaster, wood, stone, metal, plastic, wire, and any other material you can shape and form. These materials may be modeled, bent, carved, chipped, cut, and welded. In order to form and shape with skill and authority, you must thoroughly understand the very nature of the materials and tools. Such understanding must be a planned part

Fig. 16.2   The nationally acclaimed Dana Fine Arts Building at Agnes Scott College in suburban Atlanta, Georgia, houses the art and theatre departments, public galleries, and three levels of art studios that open to north-lit windows.

Fig. 16.3 The Dalton Galleries in the Dana Fine Arts
Building at Agnes Scott College are divided into intimate
spaces lit with adjustable lamps and furnished with lounge
chairs for leisurely viewing.

of your training. Drawing is an important asset to the sculptor.
Painting, on the other hand, is of little value.

If the "graphics" are your preference, then you will have a great
deal to learn about the printmaking media. Prints can be made with
many materials and by many techniques. Each requires specialized
understanding of related materials, equipment, tools, and procedures.
You should spend as much time as you can in the study of the
graphics before you choose your specialty. Understanding of the
basics in painting and sculpture are of value to you in printmaking
and should be a part of your training.

If photography is the art field you choose to pursue, you will have
need for some formal study augmented by practical training. In
school, take every course possible that will deepen your knowledge
of the photographic techniques. In most colleges, the photographic
courses are offered in different departments covering the subject
from various points of view. The art department would most likely

offer photographic design; the journalism school would have photo-journalism; in the medical school it would be medical photography; etc. Take every one of these courses you can, and, in addition, take every course you can possibly fit into your curriculum that is related to photography, such as picture editing, TV and motion picture production, audiovisual preparation, etc. During your spare time and vacations, work as an apprentice to the very best photographer who will have you. If paying jobs are not available, offer your services for the preparation of school and organization publications. In this way you gain the experience while someone else pays for the supplies.

Art history should be a part of your training whatever your art specialization. It gives you an insight and understanding of art that cannot be secured in any other way. It serves as an excellent way of measuring your development.

Fig. 16.4 Students viewing their project in the video class at Atlanta College of Art.

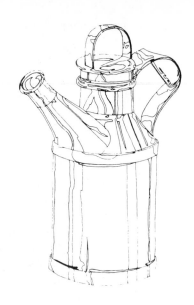

17 What Should I Study to Be a Commercial Artist?

The answer to this question depends entirely upon your present capabilities and the commercial art field you wish to enter. If you have developed an advanced degree of art skill and merely wish to apply this same skill to the commercial field, then your problem is quite simple. All you have to do is enroll in a few courses that will give you the latest procedures, practices, and concepts in the trade. For the really competent person this could possibly be accomplished with two or three courses. Exactly which two or three courses should you take? Here again, it depends entirely on one's individual needs.

The most worthwhile, efficient, and economical plan for study can be prepared if you have first made some positive determination. If you have made up your mind as to the exact commercial art field you want to enter, exactly what medium you want to work in, and exactly what type of material you want to prepare, you can plan a "tailor-made" program of study for yourself, or you can attend a school whose program is specially planned to prepare artists for

Fig. 17.1 Samples of artwork done by students at the Pels School of Art in New York City.

Fig. 17.2 Viewing a silk-screen project in the printmaking department at Atlanta College of Art.

the specific commercial art trade desired. If, for example, you have decided to become a cartoonist you could enroll in a program that has as its sole function the preparation of cartoonists.

If you plan to be a commercial artist but have not indicated a preference as to which field, or do not have any particular outstanding art skills, then it would be wise to enroll in a college that offers commercial art. The college program will usually start with a year of exploratory work. Here you will be given introductory courses in many different commercial art fields. This will give you the opportunity to sample different types of work and media and determine which you find most appealing.

The sooner you can make the final determination as to the kind of commercial artist you want to be, the more meaningful will be your college program. In your second, third, and fourth years you may be given "electives," courses of your own choice. If you have selected the ultimate field you wish to enter you can select electives that are directly related to your ultimate field.

Not all schools will give you a large selection of electives. In several schools you are merely given the opportunity to select a specific field of commercial art. Once you have made this designation you may be assigned to a very rigid program of study. This does not necessarily make the school undesirable. On the contrary, it may be best for you. If you have no background in commercial art nor any means for making a proper survey, then perhaps it is best *not* to have a wide and confusing choice of courses. If the school has had long experience in the commercial art field and has a good reputation, it probably knows what is needed and reflects this in its offerings.

Fig. 17.3   View of the sculpture studio at
the Atlanta College of Art.

18 Which Art School Should I Attend?

There are 2,000 different institutions and organizations in our country that offer art training in some form or other. They vary from one-teacher, one-room-in-the-attic-or-barn setup to the summer camp arrangement, to the correspondence courses, to the two-year community colleges, and ultimately to the four-year college and graduate school offerings.

No one school, no matter how elaborate and comprehensive its art curriculum and facilities may be, can be pointed to as *the* school for *all* art needs. This is true because there are so many different needs for study among the artists and potential artists. At one extreme are those who are looking to spend a short time brushing up on some art technique, while at the other end are those who want to make fine art or commercial art their lifetime profession and need at least a full college program of study. Between these extremes can be found literally hundreds of variations.

At best, choosing an art school is a precarious affair. Your only intelligent choice is to thoroughly investigate. Search out every bit of information you can. Your lifetime career and income may depend on it.

Start your search by answering a few pointed questions about yourself: What part do I want art to play in my life? What do I want to train for? How much time and money can I afford to spend? What are my special aptitudes and abilities? Am I willing to spend time in a general investigation of the art field before I specialize? Honest answers to these questions will point up your basic philosophy, purpose, and intentions. Once you have made these determinations, you are ready to select a school. Some of the important things to consider are the following:

1. *Curriculum Offerings:* Some schools will offer what might be called a general art course. In such a course you will be given an opportunity to work in many fields. Other schools offer separate programs in most of the major fields, such as fine art, sculpture, illustration, and industrial design. A third group of schools will offer only one field of specialization.

Which curriculum should you choose? It depends on how positive you are about what you want to do. If you are sure of what profession you want to enter, select a curriculum that concentrates on that particular profession. If you are not sure of the field you wish to enter, select a curriculum that offers you investigating opportunities.

2. *Caliber of the Faculty:* Checking on the faculty of an art school can be very confusing. The practice of using the names of prominent artists in advertisements and catalogs and then not having them participate in the actual teaching is rather common. If you are interested in working with a particular artist publicized by a school, ask the school point-blank just what part the artist will play in your education.

There is no hard and fast rule as to which type of person makes the best art teacher. In general, the successful artist turned teacher is usually superior to the teacher who has had no appreciable professional art experience. The artist-teacher who has had a few years of teaching experience is usually superior to the one that has newly entered the teaching field. Teaching in itself is a fine art and it takes time to develop.

3. *Type of Art Emphasis:* The emphasis results from the predominant attitude of the instructors and is frequently injected into the courses subconsciously. If more instructors have a fine arts background, the courses will have a fine arts orientation. If, on the other hand, most of the instructors are or have been professional commercial artists, the emphasis will most likely be partial to the professional point of view.

Fig. 18.1 The Atlanta Memorial Arts Center is a place, unique in the United States, in which all the visual and performing arts coexist under one roof. It houses the High Museum of Art, the Atlanta College of Art, the Atlanta Symphony Orchestra, the Alliance Theater Company, and the Atlanta Children's Theater (Courtesy: The Atlanta Arts Alliance, Inc.).

The difference in emphasis can make a great deal of difference to you, the student. If the emphasis is not in keeping with the type of training you desire, your education can be unsatisfactory. The best way to find information concerning the emphasis prevalent in an art school is to speak with some of the graduates. These people, who have completed their training and have tried to apply their learning, soon know their strong points and weak points, and usually know why they exist.

4. *School Standards:* Entrance requirements vary greatly among art schools. There are many that require a good-to-outstanding high school record, excellent references, and evidence of certain talents. At the other extreme are those that require nothing more than tuition. These latter schools may give you some superficial art "test," but in reality it's the tuition money that is the determining factor. In general, the stiffer the entrance requirements, the better the art offering. All things being equal, go to the school that has the highest entrance standards and will accept you.

In the better art schools it is just as hard to remain in the school as it is to enter. Such schools usually maintain very high standards of performance. Those students who do not maintain these standards are asked to leave. This may seem very severe to you, but it is actually the only fair procedure. A person must be very competent if (s)he is to succeed as a professional artist. For a school to "baby" you along, take your money, then send you out of the school a less than capable person would be unfair. It will not only waste your money, but also your valuable time.

5. *Degrees Granted:* The degree granted by a school is a secondary consideration. Many artists find it difficult to secure a satisfactory income from their artwork alone, and therefore turn to a second occupation as a supplement. It is in the process of qualifying for this second occupation that the degree can be an important consideration. All things being equal, select the school whose degree prepares you best for entrance into a secondary profession.

6. *Adequacy of School Facilities:* In looking over the school, first observe the equipment. Is there a sufficient amount to take care of all the students? Is the equipment of a type that is used professionally? Is it in good repair? Is the equipment conveniently located so that the students can use it without delay? How much of the equipment is furnished by the school and how much must be purchased by the student?

Check the availability of non-classroom equipment and facilities such as audiovisual equipment, library of filming equipment and publications, and art exhibiting provisions.

Fig. 18.2   Student among screen wire 3D projects from basic design class at Atlanta College of Art (Courtesy: Atlanta College of Art).

Notice whether or not there are sufficient materials available for the students' use. Check on the materials supplied by the school and those that you must furnish.

As for the classrooms, make sure they are large enough so that the activities scheduled in them can be carried on without difficulty and disturbance. Make sure the rooms are sufficiently lighted and satisfactorily ventilated. There should be lounges available for relaxing and activity rooms where the students can join in sports and social affairs.

If you plan to live on the school campus, then the dormitory or boarding facilities should be given the "once-over."

Do not let newness or old appearance affect your evaluation too severely; this has little effect on the quality of the art teaching that is done.

Fig. 18.3   Inside the Dana Fine Arts Building at Agnes Scott College, two levels of art studios are located on free-standing balconies. Below, on the first floor, one of five gallery areas opens to the skylight from the third-floor windows in the gabled roof.

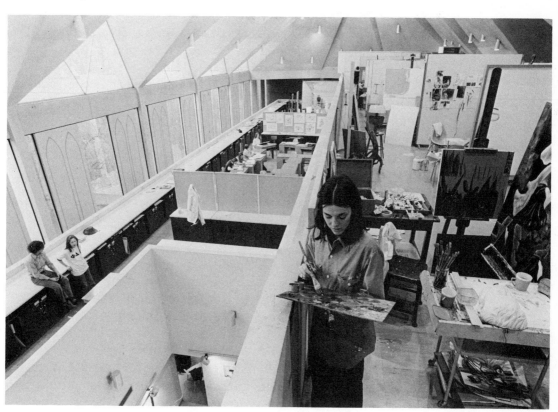

Unless you have had some experience in the art field, you will not find it easy to distinguish between the good and the poor concerning art facilities offered by schools. If you lack the necessary experience, it would be wise to take along a person experienced in the art field when you visit a school. The experienced person can, at a glance, see many of the minor features that might escape the inexperienced person.

7. *Reliability of Placement Service:* After graduation comes the big question, "Where can I get a job?" Securing this first job can be difficult. That is why you should first check to see if the school has a placement service; then, try to determine how successful the placement record has been. The more successful a school is in placing its students in desirable positions, the better the school.

Get as much assistance as you possibly can in your investigation of art schools. First of all, talk with people who are successful in the art fields. In most cases they will have rather strong opinions about art schools and will be happy to tell you how they feel. These people can give you an excellent insight into their own alma maters.

The guidance people in your local schools will also have a great deal of information for you.

Catalogs should be secured from all schools that interest you. The school catalog will include such basic information as costs, course offerings, and registration times.

Before you make a final selection about which school you are going to attend, make a strong effort to speak with some graduates of the schools that interest you. These people can tell you more about a school than anyone else.

EVENING, SATURDAY, AND SUMMER COURSES

There are two general types of art courses offered during "off-times" such as evenings, Saturdays, and summers. They are *credit courses* and *noncredit courses.* The credit courses are usually offered by colleges and universities that are normally offering full-time art programs during the day. The amount of credit granted for these off-time courses varies, depending on the amount of time devoted to them. If half as much time is spent in the off-time course as is required in a comparable daytime course, then a half-unit is granted. If the time is equal, a full unit is granted. Off-time credit courses are usually accepted for graduation and degrees on an equal basis with regular daytime program courses.

Fig. 18.4   Figure drawing class at Atlanta College of Art.

Noncredit evening, Saturday, and summer art courses are offered by colleges, special art schools, local adult education programs, YMCA's, art organizations and institutions, and individual artists. They are usually available to anyone who has the money to pay for them. Some of these are restricted to adults, others have ability requirements. In some cases the courses are available only to members of certain organizations and institutions.

No single quality standard can be drawn for the off-time noncredit art courses. These range all the way from some rather formalized college classes to the completely unrestricted classes conducted at some summer camp schools. Between these extremes you can find off-time noncredit art classes of every kind, form, and description being taught in communities across the country. Among the evening, Saturday, and summer art courses that are offered you can find one to meet your every art need.

HOME STUDY SCHOOLS

You must understand home study schools for what they are. Most of them are businesses organized to make money—nothing more and nothing less. And in this business, as in all businesses, there are honest, honorable people trying to give true value for the money they receive, and there are unscrupulous people whose only purpose is to separate you from your money. It is not always easy to recognize the honorable from the unscrupulous. Following are some guidelines you can use when considering home study schools:

1. Don't expect something for nothing. If you are asked to submit an insignificant line drawing for the possible opportunity of winning a scholarship, don't accept. This is nothing but a "come-on" to get your name.

2. Don't sign a contract for a home study course that you do not completely understand. If you have difficulty in understanding a contract, take it to a lawyer. *Don't have the representative from the school interpret the contract for you.* That person will tell you what is best for the business (s)he represents.

3. Don't enroll in a school that promises extraordinary results in a very short period of time. Education takes time and it cannot be accomplished in a few short weeks.

4. Don't sign a contract that requires you to purchase equipment and supplies along with your training. And don't believe a school that says it will give you equipment and supplies for nothing. You pay for everything you get. If a school gives you a special deal on equipment and supplies, have it give you complete specifications on each item. Then compare its prices with the price you may have to pay elsewhere.

5. Don't enroll in a school because it promises you a job on completion of the course. No school can honestly guarantee you a position.

6. If you seek a quality art course, you must expect to pay for it. Avoid "cut-rate" schools, or those that offer special financial inducements to get you to enroll. Avoid schools that pay commissions to students for obtaining enrollments.

A reputable home study school will furnish you with a catalog that will spell out in clear, concise detail just what you will receive and how much it will cost. Its contract will reflect what is stipulated in the catalog. Some of the better established schools are members of the National Home Study Council (located at 1601 Eighteenth Street, N.W., Washington, D.C. 20009).

Are home study courses really good for an artist? Only you can answer this. It depends on the kind of individual you are, the time you have available, and the amount of money you wish to spend.

Studying at home by yourself requires a very high degree of self-discipline, which most people lack. If you are convinced that you are emotionally oriented to home study, and that your time and finances are so limited that you cannot consider another type of school, then you are ready to enroll in a home study course. Your investigation of a home study school should be every bit as thorough as for any other type of school.

Following is a list of schools that offer home study courses in the art fields. The italicized numbers and letters following the schools correspond to the numbers and letters on the charts below, which indicate the courses available and other information about each school.

Course Offerings
1. Acrylic painting
2. Advertising art
3. Architecture
4. Art history & appreciation
5. Art teacher training
6. Basic design
7. Cartooning
8. Crafts
9. Drawing
10. Fashion illustrating
11. Filmmaking
12. Illustration
13. Interior design
14. Oil painting
15. Pastel painting
16. Pictorial composition
17. Photography
18. Textile design
19. Watercolor

Information about School
A. Certificates issued
B. Diplomas issued
C. Scholarships available

ALEXANDER SCHOOL OF PAINTING, 2720 Fifth Ave., San Diego, Cal. 92103, *2, 9, 12, 14, 15, 19; A.*

AMERICAN SCHOOL, Drexel Ave. at 58th St., Chicago, Ill. 60637, *3.*

AMERICAN SCHOOL OF PHOTOGRAPHY (div. of Career Institute), 1500 Cardinal Dr., Little Falls, N. J. 07424, *11, 17.*

ART INSTRUCTION SCHOOLS, 500 S. Fourth St., Minneapolis, Minn. 55415, *1, 2, 6, 7, 9, 10, 12, 14, 15, 16, 19; A.*

ART SCHOOL OF THE CRAFTS GUILD, 380 S. 168 Ave., R4., Holland, Mich. 49423, *6, 8, 9, 14; A.*

BUREAU OF CARTOONING, PO Box 7069, 1422 Hollyhock Dr., Colorado Springs, Colo. 80933 *2, 7, 9, 12; A.*

CAREER INSTITUTE, 1500 Cardinal Dr., Little Falls, N.J. 07424, *10, 13, 14; A.*

CARTOONISTS EXCHANGE, 15 N. Main St., Pleasant Hill, Ohio 45359, *7, 9; A.*

CHICAGO SCHOOL OF INTERIOR DECORATION (div. of Career Institute), 1500 Cardinal Dr., Little Falls, N.J. 07424, *13.*

CHICAGO TECHNICAL COLLEGE, 2000 South Michigan Ave., Chicago, Ill. 60616, *3.*

CONTINENTAL SCHOOLS, 1330 W. Olympic Blvd., Los Angeles, Cal. 90015, *2, 7, 9, 12; A.*

FAMOUS ARTISTS SCHOOL INC., 17 Riverside Ave., Westport, Conn. 06880, *1, 2, 6, 7, 9, 10, 12, 14, 16, 19; A, C.*

INTERNATIONAL CORRESPONDENCE SCHOOLS, Oak & Pawnee Sts., Scranton, Pa. 18515, *2, 3, 4, 6, 7, 9, 12, 13, 14, 15, 16, 18, 19; A.*

KACHINA SCHOOL OF ART, 3801 N. 30 St., Phoenix, Ariz. 85016, *4, 6, 9, 14, 16; A.*

LIFETIME CAREER SCHOOLS, 2251 Barry Ave., Los Angeles, Cal. 90064, *6, 8, 9, 12.*

MAWY ART SCHOOL, 909 Bergenline Ave., Union City, N.J. 07087, *2, 4, 7, 9, 10, 12, 13, 14, 16, 19; A, C.*

MERLIN ENABNIT, 2001 E. Solar Dr., Phoenix, Ariz. 85020, *6, 9, 12, 14, 16; A.*

NATIONAL ACADEMY OF WATERCOLOR, PO Box 1604, Janesville, Wisc. 53545; *9, 19.*

NATIONAL SCHOOL OF DRESS DESIGN (div. of Career Institute), 1500 Cardinal Dr., Little Falls, N.J. 07424, *10.*

NEW YORK INSTITUTE OF PHOTOGRAPHY, 263 Ninth Ave., New York, N.Y. 10001, *11, 17; A.*

NEW YORK SCHOOL OF INTERIOR DESIGN, 155 E. 56th St., New York, N.Y. 10022, *13; A.*

NORTH AMERICAN CORRESPONDENCE SCHOOLS, 4401 Birch St., Newport Beach, Cal. 92660, *2, 3.*

ROY KEISTER COLLEGE OF FINE ARTS, 15800 Highland Dr., San Jose, Cal. 95127, *9, 12, 14, 16.*

ROLAND PIERSON PRICKETT'S STUDIO & GALLERY OF THE FOUR WINDS, PO Box 182, Unionville, Conn. 06085, *14.*

SCHOOL OF MODERN PHOTOGRAPHY, 1500 Cardinal Dr., Little Falls, N.J. 07424, *17; B.*

VOICE OF FINE ARTS INSTRUCTION, PO Box 781, Vineland, N.J. 08360, *1, 4, 6, 9, 14, 19.*

WASHINGTON SCHOOL OF ART, 417 S. Dearborn St., Chicago, Ill. 60605, *6, 7, 9, 10, 12, 14, 15, 19; A.*

ART SCHOOL DIRECTORY

The following is a comprehensive listing of the many schools that offer art training. This is not a complete list of all art training facilities. The art training field fluctuates a great deal.

Schools add and drop courses, and in some cases whole programs in response to enrollment demands. These changes may take place from semester to semester or even quarter to quarter. Housing facilities may be changed as well as degree offerings, scholarships, and grant offerings. *The only way to really know what a school has to offer is to write or call directly to the registrar's office or public relations office of the school you are interested in at the time you are hoping to attend.* The information indicated after each of the schools in the following list was accurate at the time this book was compiled. It may or may not be correct at present.

The schools are arranged alphabetically first by states, then schools within the states. The italicized numbers and letters following the schools correspond to the numbers and letters on the charts below, which indicate the courses available and other information about the schools. The schools are co-educational unless indicated otherwise.

Course Offerings

1. Advertising art
2. Architecture
3. Art history
4. Art teacher training (Art Ed.)
5. Cartooning
6. Crafts
7. Drawing
8. Fashion illustrating
9. Illustration
10. Industrial design
11. Interior design
12. Painting
13. Photography
14. Printmaking (graphic arts)
15. Sculpture
16. Textile design
17. Watercolor

Information about School

A. Co-educational
B. Men only
C. Women only
D. Degrees
E. Scholarships & grants
F. Fall & spring term
G. Tri-semester
H. Evening classes
I. Summer classes
J. Home study courses
K. Housing facilities

Alabama

ALABAMA A & M UNIVERSITY, Normal Ala. 35762, *3, 4, 6, 7, 12, 14, 15; A, D, E.*

ALABAMA COLLEGE, Montevallo, Ala. 35115, *1, 3, 4, 6, 7, 12, 14, 15, 17; A, D, E, F, K.*

ALABAMA LUTHERAN ACADEMY & COLLEGE, 1804 Green St., Selma, Ala. 36701, *3, 4, 6, 7, 15, 17; F.*

ALABAMA POLYTECHNIC INSTITUTE, Auburn, Ala. 36830, *7, 10, 11, 12, 18; D, E.*

ALABAMA STATE COLLEGE, Jackson St., Montgomery, Ala. 36101, *3, 4, 6, 7, 12, 14, 15, 17; A, D, E, F, I, K.*

ATHENS COLLEGE, Athens, Ala. 35611, *1, 4, 6, 7, 12, 14, 15, 17; D.*

AUBURN UNIVERSITY, SCHOOL OF ARCHITECTURE & THE ARTS, Auburn, Ala. 36830, *1, 2, 3, 7, 9, 10, 11, 12, 14, 15, 17; A, D, E, F, I, K.*

AUBURN UNIVERSITY AT MONTGOMERY, Montgomery, Ala. 36109, *3, 4, 6, 7, 10, 12; A, D, E, F, H.*

BIRMINGHAM-SOUTHERN COLLEGE, 800 Eighth Ave. W., Birmingham, Ala. 35204, *4, 7, 12, 14, 15; D, E.*

FLORENCE STATE COLLEGE, College Station, Florence, Ala. 35603, *1, 3, 4, 6, 7, 9, 12, 13, 14, 15, 17; A, D, E, F, I, K.*

HUNTINGDON COLLEGE, Fairview Ave., Montgomery, Ala. 36106, *3, 4, 7, 12, 14, 15, 17; A, D, F, I, K.*

JACKSONVILLE STATE UNIVERSITY, Jacksonville, Ala. 36265, *1, 3, 4, 6, 7, 10, 12, 15; A, D, E, H, I, K.*

JEFFERSON DAVIS STATE JUNIOR COLLEGE, Alco Dr., Brewton, Ala. 36426, *3, 6, 7, 10, 12, 13; A, D, F, H, I.*

JUDSON COLLEGE, Marion, Ala. 36756, *1, 3, 4, 6, 7, 11, 12, 16, 17; C, D, E, G, K.*

LIVINGSTON UNIVERSITY, Livingston, Ala. 35470, *4, 6, 7, 9, 12, 17; D, E, H.*

MILES COLLEGE, Birmingham, Ala. 35208, *1, 4, 7, 9, 12, 14, 15, 16, 17; F.*

SACRED HEART COLLEGE, Cullman, Ala. 35055, *4, 6, 7, 12, 14; C, E, I, K.*

SAMFORD UNIVERSITY, 800 Lakeshore Dr., Birmingham, Ala. 35209, *1, 3, 4, 6, 7, 12, 14, 15, 17; D, E, I.*

SNEAD STATE JR. COLLEGE, Walnut St., Boaz, Ala. 35957, *3, 7, 12, 17; D, I.*

SOUTHERN UNION STATE JR. COLLEGE, Wadley, Ala. 36274, *1, 3, 7, 12, 14, 17; A, D, F, I, K.*

SPRING HILL COLLEGE, Mobile, Ala. 36608, *4, 7, 12, 13, 14, 15, 17.*

STILLMAN COLLEGE, PO Box 1430, Tuscaloosa, Ala. 35401, *3, 4, 6, 7, 12, 15; A, D, F, K.*

TROY STATE COLLEGE, Troy, Ala. 36081, *1, 3, 4, 6, 7, 12, 13, 15, 17; A, D, I, K.*

TUSKEGEE INSTITUTE, Tuskegee, Ala. 36088, *2, 3, 6, 7, 16; A, D, E, F, I, K.*

UNIVERSITY OF ALABAMA, PO Box 1249, University Dr., Huntsville, Ala. 35807, *1, 3, 4, 7, 9, 10, 11, 12, 15; A, D, E, H, I, K.*

UNIVERSITY OF ALABAMA, DEPARTMENT OF ART, Box F University, Montgomery, Ala. 35486, *1, 3, 4, 6, 7, 11, 12, 14, 15, 17; A, D, E, F, H, I, K, L.*

UNIVERSITY OF ALABAMA, 435 Bell St., Montgomery Center, Ala. 36104, *7, 12, 17; E, G, H, I.*

UNIVERSITY OF ALABAMA, Troy, Ala. 35486, *3, 4, 6, 7, 10, 12, 13, 14, 15; A, D, E, F.*

UNIVERSITY OF ALABAMA, Tuscaloosa, Ala. 35401, *4, 7, 10, 12, 14, 15, 18; A, D, E, H, I.*

UNIVERSITY OF MONTEVALLO, Montevallo, Ala. 35115, *1, 3, 6, 10, 12, 13, 14, 15; A, D, E, F, H, I, K.*

UNIVERSITY OF SOUTH ALABAMA, 307 Gaillard Dr., Mobile, Ala. 36608, *1, 3, 4, 7, 12, 14, 15; D, E, H, I.*

WALKER COLLEGE, Jasper, Ala. 35501, *3, 4, 7; A, E, F.*

Alaska

ALASKA METHODIST UNIVERSITY, Anchorage, Alaska 99504, *3, 4, 7, 9, 12; A, D, E, F, I.*

ANCHORAGE COMMUNITY COLLEGE, 1700 W. Hillcrest Dr., Anchorage, Alaska 99503, *3, 4, 6, 7, 10, 12, 13, 15, 16; A, G, H, I.*

SHELDON JACKSON JR. COLLEGE, Box 479, Sitka, Alaska 99835, *6, 7, 12; A, E, F, H, K.*

UNIVERSITY OF ALASKA, College, Alaska 99701, *4, 7, 12, 13, 14, 15; D, E.*

Arizona

ADVERTISING & MARKETING INSTITUTE OF ARIZONA, 3520 N. Seventh St., Phoenix, Ariz. 85014, *1, 8, 13.*

ARIZONA SCHOOL OF ART, Camelback Rd., Phoenix, Ariz. 85013, *1, 3, 7, 9, 11, 12, 17; A, F, I.*

ARIZONA STATE UNIVERSITY, Tempe, Ariz. 85281, *1, 3, 4, 6, 7, 9, 11, 12, 13, 14, 15, 17; A, D, E, F, H, I.*

ARIZONA WESTERN COLLEGE, Yuma, Ariz. 85364, *7, 12, 13, 15, 17; A, H, K.*

COCHISE COLLEGE, Douglas, Ariz. 85607, *1, 3, 6, 7, 9, 12, 15, 16, 17; A, D, E, F, H, I, K.*

EASTERN ARIZONA COLLEGE, Thatcher, Ariz. 85552, *3, 4, 6, 7, 12, 17; A, D, E, F, K.*

GRAND CANYON COLLEGE, 3300 W. Camelback Rd., PO Box 11097, Phoenix, Ariz. 85061, *1, 3, 4, 6, 7, 8, 10, 12, 14, 15; A, D, F, H, I, K.*

KACHINA SCHOOL OF ART, 3801 N. 30 Street, Phoenix, Ariz. 85016, *1, 2, 3, 5, 7; A, G, H.*

MESA COMMUNITY COLLEGE, 1833 W. Southern Ave., Mesa, Ariz. 85202, *1, 3, 6, 7, 12, 15; A, D, F, H, I.*

NORTHERN ARIZONA UNIVERSITY, Flagstaff, Ariz. 86001, *1, 3, 4, 5, 6, 7, 9, 12, 15, 17; A, D, E, F, H, I, K.*

PHOENIX COLLEGE, 1202 W. Thomas Rd., Phoenix, Ariz. 85013, *1, 2, 3, 5, 6, 7, 9, 11, 12, 13, 15, 17; A, D, E, F, H, I.*

TUCSON MUSEUM OF ART SCHOOL, 179 N. Main Ave., Tucson, Ariz. 85705, *3, 6, 7, 10, 12, 13, 15; A, H.*

UNIVERSITY OF ARIZONA, Tucson, Ariz., 85721, *3, 4, 6, 7, 9, 12, 14, 15; A, D, E, F,*

Arkansas

ARKANSAS A&M COLLEGE, College Heights, Ark. 71655, *4, 7, 12, 14, 17; D, F.*

ARKANSAS ARTS CENTER, MacArthur Park, Little Rock, Ark. 72203, *6, 7, 12, 13, 14, 15, 17; A, H, I.*

ARKANSAS POLYTECHNIC COLLEGE, Russellville, Ark. 72801, *1, 3, 4, 7, 9, 10, 12, 17; A, D, F, I, K.*

ARKANSAS STATE UNIVERSITY, State University, Ark. 72467, *1, 3, 4, 6, 7, 8, 10, 12, 13, 15; A, D, E, F, H, I, K.*

COLLEGE OF THE OZARKS, Clarksville, Ark. 72830, *3, 4, 7, 12; A, D, F, I, K.*

HARDING COLLEGE, Searcy, Ark. 72144, *1, 3, 4, 6, 7, 12, 14, 15; A, D, I.*

JOHN BROWN UNIVERSITY, Siloam Springs, Ark. 72761, *3, 4, 6, 7, 10, 12; A, E, F, K.*

OUACHITA BAPTIST UNIVERSITY, Arkadelphia, Ark. 71924, *1, 3, 4, 6, 7, 9, 12, 14, 15, 17; A, D, F, I, K.*

PHILANDER SMITH COLLEGE, Little Rock, Ark. 72203, *3, 7, 12, 15, 17; A, D, E, F, I, K.*

PHILLIPS COUNTY COMMUNITY COLLEGE, Box 785, Helena, Ark. 72342, *3, 6, 7, 12; A, D, F.*

SOUTHERN BAPTIST COLLEGE, College City, Walnut Ridge, Ark. 72476, *4, 7, 12, 13, 15, 17; D, F.*

SOUTHERN STATE COLLEGE, Magnolia, Ark. 71753, *3, 4, 6, 7, 12, 14, 15, 17; A, F, I.*

UNIVERSITY OF ARKANSAS AT FAYETTEVILLE, Fayetteville, Ark. 72707, *1, 3, 4, 7, 12, 13, 14, 15, 17; A, F, I.*

UNIVERSITY OF ARKANSAS AT LITTLE ROCK, University & 33, Little Rock, Ark. 72204, *1, 3, 4, 6, 7, 12, 14, 15, 17; D, E, I.*

UNIVERSITY OF CENTRAL ARKANSAS, Conway, Ark. 72032, *3, 4, 6, 7, 10, 12, 14, 15; A, D, F, I, K.*

WESTARK JR. COLLEGE, Grande Ave. & Waldron Rd., Fort Smith, Ark. 72901, *3, 4, 7, 12, 17; A, D, F, H, I.*

California

ACADEMY OF ART COLLEGE, 625 Sutter St., San Francisco, Cal. 94102, *1, 3, 5, 7, 9, 10, 12, 13, 15, 17; A, D, E, F, H, I, K.*

ALLAN HANCOCK COLLEGE, 800 S. College Dr., Santa Maria, Cal. 93454, *1, 3, 4, 6, 7, 8, 12, 13; A, D, H, I.*

AMERICAN RIVER COLLEGE, 4700 College Oak Ave., Sacramento, Cal. 95841, *1, 4, 6, 7, 11, 12, 14, 15; D, I.*

ART CENTER COLLEGE OF DESIGN, 1700 Lida St., Pasadena, Cal. 91103, *1, 8, 9, 10, 12, 13; A, D, E, G, H.*

ART CENTER SCHOOL, 5353 W. Third St., Los Angeles, Cal. 90005, *1, 3, 7, 9, 10, 11, 12, 13, 17; A, D, E, G, H.*

ART INSTITUTE OF OAKLAND, 339 15th St., Oakland, Cal. 94612, *1, 9.*

ART INSTITUTE OF ORANGE COUNTY, 706 West Katella Avenue, Orange, Cal. 92667, *1, 3, 4, 5, 7, 9, 12, 15, 17; A, D, E, G, H, I.*

BABCOCK'S BEAUX ARTS SCHOOL, 1500 Compromise Line Rd., Glendora, Cal. 91740, *12, 17; F, I, K.*

BAKERSFIELD COMMUNITY COLLEGE, Panorama Dr., Bakersfield, Cal. 93305, *1, 2, 3, 4, 7, 10, 11, 12, 13, 14, 15; D, E, I.*

BARSTOW COLLEGE, 2700 Barstow Road, Barstow, Cal. 92311, *1, 12.*

BRANDON ART SCHOOL, 2441 Balboa St., San Francisco, Cal. 94121, *12; H, I.*

BROOKS INSTITUTE, 2020 Alameda Padre Serra, Santa Barbara, Cal. 93103, *2, 7, 10, 12, 14, 15, 16, 17; D, E, G, I.*

BUONORA ART CENTER, 2039 Sawtelle Blvd., Los Angeles, Cal. 90025, *7, 12, 15; A, H, I.*

CABRILLO COLLEGE, 6500 Soquel Dr., Aptos, Cal. 95003, *6, 7, 12, 14, 15, 17; D, E, I.*

CALIFORNIA COLLEGE OF ARTS & CRAFTS, Broadway at College Ave., Oakland, Cal. 94618, *3, 4, 6, 7, 9, 12, 13, 14, 15; A, D, E, F, I.*

CALIFORNIA INSTITUTE OF THE ARTS, 2404 W. Seventh St., Los Angeles, Cal. 90057, *7, 12, 13, 14, 15; D, E, G.*

CALIFORNIA INSTITUTE OF TECHNOLOGY, 1201 E. California Ave., Pasadena, Cal. 91109, *3, 7, 14, 15; H, I.*

CALIFORNIA LUTHERAN COLLEGE, 60 Olsen Road, Thousand Oaks, Cal. 91360, *1, 2, 3, 4, 6, 7, 9, 12, 14, 15; A, D, E, G, H, I, K.*

CALIFORNIA POLYTECHNIC STATE UNIVERSITY AT SAN LUIS OBISPO, San Luis Obispo, Cal. 93407, *1, 3, 4, 6, 7, 8, 12, 15; A, D, E, H, I.*

CALIFORNIA SCHOOL OF FINE ARTS, 800 Chestnut Street, San Francisco, Cal. 94133, *4, 7, 10, 12, 14, 15, 18, 19, 21*

CALIFORNIA STATE COLLEGE, DOMINGUEZ HILLS, 1000 E. Victoria, Dominguez Hills, Cal. 90247, *4, 7; D, H.*

CALIFORNIA STATE COLLEGE, SONOMA, 1801 E. Cotati Ave., Rohnert Park, Cal. 94928, *3, 4, 5, 6, 7, 12, 13, 14, 15; A, D, E, F.*

CALIFORNIA STATE COLLEGE, STANISLAUS, 900 Monte Vista Blvd., Turlock, Cal. 95380, *3, 4, 6, 7, 12, 14, 15, 17; A, D, E, H, I, K.*

CALIFORNIA STATE UNIVERSITY, CHICO, W. First & Normals Sts., Chico, Cal. 95926, *3, 4, 6, 7; A, D, E, F, I.*

CALIFORNIA STATE UNIVERSITY, FRESNO, Shaw & Maple Ave., Fresno, Cal. 93740, *3, 6, 7, 8, 10, 11, 12, 15, 18, 19; A, D, E, F, H, I.*

CALIFORNIA STATE UNIVERSITY, FULLERTON, 800 N. State College Blvd., Fullerton, Cal. 92631, *1, 4, 6, 7, 9, 11, 12, 13, 14, 15, 16; D, E, H, I.*

CALIFORNIA STATE UNIVERSITY, HAYWARD, 25800 Hillary St., Hayward, Cal. 94542, *2, 3, 6, 7, 12, 13, 14, 15; A, D, E, H, I.*

CALIFORNIA STATE UNIVERSITY, LONG BEACH, 6101 E. 7th Street, Long Beach, Cal. 90804, *3, 4, 6, 7, 9, 10, 11, 12, 13, 14, 15, 16, 17; A, D, E, F, H, I, K.*

CALIFORNIA STATE UNIVERSITY, NORTHRIDGE, 1811 Nordhoff St., Northridge, Cal. 91324, *7, 12, 13, 14; A, D, E, F, H, I.*

CALIFORNIA STATE UNIVERSITY, SACRAMENTO, 600 Jay St., Sacramento, Cal. 95819, *1, 3, 4, 6, 7, 9, 12, 13, 14, 15, 17; A, D, E, F, I, K.*

CALIFORNIA STATE UNIVERSITY, SAN DIEGO, 5402 College Ave., San Diego, Cal. 92182, *1, 3, 4, 6, 7, 8, 9, 10, 11, 12, 13, 14, 15, 16; A, D, F, H, I, K.*

CARMEL ART INSTITUTE, PO Box 9, Carmel, Cal. 93921, *7, 12, 14.*

CERRITOS COLLEGE, 11110 E. Alondia Blvd., Norwalk, Cal. 90651, *1, 6, 7, 12, 13, 14, 15, 17; D, I.*

CHABOT COLLEGE, 25555 Hesperion Blvd., Hayward, Cal. 94545, *1, 5, 7, 12, 15; D, H, I.*

CHAFFEY JR. COLLEGE, 5885 Haven Avenue, Alta Loma, Cal. 91701, *1, 2, 3, 6, 7, 11, 12, 17; A, F, H, I.*

CHAPMAN COLLEGE, 333 N. Glassell, Orange, Cal. 92666, *3, 7, 12, 14, 15; A, D, F, H, I, K.*

CHOUINARD ART INSTITUTE, 743 South Grandview St., Los Angeles, Cal. 90057, *4, 7, 8, 10, 11, 12, 18, 21; D, E.*

CITRUS COLLEGE (COMMUNITY COLLEGE), 18824 Foothill Blvd., Azusa, Cal. 91702, *3, 6, 7, 12, 13, 17; A, D, F, H, I.*

CLAREMONT GRADUATE SCHOOL & UNIVERSITY CENTER, Claremont, Cal. 91711, *1, 3, 7, 9, 10, 11, 12, 14, 16.*

COALINGA COLLEGE, 300 Cherry La., Coalinga, Cal. 93210, *1, 3, 7, 9, 12, 17; A, F, H, K.*

COLLEGE OF MARIN, Kentfield, Cal. 94904, *1, 2, 3, 4, 5, 6, 8, 12, 13, 14; A, D, E, H, I.*

COLLEGE OF NOTRE DAME, Belmont, Cal. 94002, *3, 4, 7, 11, 12, 13, 14, 15, 16, 17; A, D, E, F, H, I, K.*

COLLEGE OF SEQUOIAS, Mooney Blvd., Visalia, Cal. 93277, *2, 3, 6, 7, 12, 13, 14, 17; A, D, E, F, H.*

COLLEGE OF THE DESERT, 43-500 Monterey Ave., Palm Desert, Cal. 92260, *1, 3, 7, 12, 14, 15, 17; A, F, H.*

COLLEGE OF THE HOLY NAMES, Oakland, Cal. 94619, *4, 6, 7, 12, 13, 14, 17; C, D.*

COLLEGE OF THE REDWOODS, Eureka, Cal. 95501, *1, 7, 12, 13, 14, 15, 17; D, E, H, I.*

COLLEGE OF THE SISKIYOUS, Rt. 1, Box 1025, Weed, Cal. 96094, *3, 4, 6, 7, 11, 12, 17; A, D, F, H, I, K.*

COMPTON COLLEGE, 1111 Artesia Blvd., Compton, Cal. 90221, *2, 6, 7, 9, 13; D, I.*

CORONADO SCHOOL OF FINE ARTS, 176 C. Avenue, PO Box 156, Coronado, Cal. 92118, *1, 3, 4, 5, 7, 9, 12, 14, 17; A, F, G, H, I.*

CUESTA COLLEGE, PO Box J, San Luis Obispo, Cal. 93401, *7, 12, 15; D, I.*

CYPRESS COLLEGE, 9200 Valley View St., Cypress, Cal. 90630, *1, 6, 7, 9, 12, 14, 15; A, D, F, H, I.*

DIABLO VALLEY COLLEGE, Golf Club Road, Pleasant Hill, Cal. 94523, *2, 3, 7, 12, 13, 15, 17; A, D, E, F, H, I.*

EAST LOS ANGELES COLLEGE, 5357 East Brooklyn Ave., Los Angeles, Cal. 90022, *1, 2, 3, 6, 7, 9, 10, 11, 12, 13, 14, 15, 17; A, D, F, H, I.*

EL CAMINO COLLEGE, Crenshaw & Redondo Beach Blvd., Torrance, Cal. 90506, *1, 3, 4, 6, 7, 9, 10, 12, 15, 17; A, D, F, H, I.*

FULLERTON JR. COLLEGE, 321 E. Chapman Ave., Fullerton, Cal. 92634, *1, 3, 4, 6, 7, 9, 11, 12, 14, 16; D, I.*

GAVILAN COLLEGE, 5055 Santa Teresa, Gilroy, Cal. 95023, *3, 4, 6, 7, 12, 13, 14, 15, 17; D, H, I, E.*

GLENDALE COLLEGE, 1500 N. Verdugo Rd., Glendale, Cal. 91208, *1, 2, 3, 6, 7, 10, 12, 13, 14, 15; A, D, E, H, I.*

GOLDEN WEST COLLEGE, 15744 Golden West St., Huntington Beach, Cal. 92647, *1, 3, 5, 6, 7, 8, 10, 12, 13, 14, 15, 16; A, D, H, I.*

GROSSMONT COLLEGE, 8800 Grossmont College Dr., El Cajon, Cal. 92020, *1, 4, 7, 12, 13, 15, 17; D, E, I.*

HARTNELL COLLEGE, 156 Homestead Ave., Salinas, Cal. 93901, *1, 3, 4, 7, 12, 13, 14, 15, 17; D, I.*

HOLLYWOOD ART CENTER, 2025 & 2027 N. Highland Ave., Hollywood, Cal. 90028, *1, 3, 5, 7, 9, 11, 12, 15, 16, 17; A, F, H, I.*

HOLY NAMES COLLEGE, 3500 Mountain Blvd., Oakland, Cal. 94619, *3, 4, 6, 7, 12, 13, 14; D, H, K.*

HUMBOLDT STATE UNIVERSITY, Arcata, Cal. 95521, *3, 4, 7, 12, 13, 14, 15, 17; A, D, F, H, I, K.*

IMMACULATE HEART COLLEGE, 5515 Franklin, Los Angeles, Cal. 90028, *4, 6, 13; D, H.*

IMPERIAL VALLEY COLLEGE, PO Box 158, Imperial, Cal. 92251, *3, 7; A, D, F, H, I.*

LA SIERRA COLLEGE, La Sierra, Cal. 92505, *2, 3, 6, 7, 10, 11, 12, 15, 18, 21.*

LAGUNA BEACH SCHOOL OF ART & DESIGN, 630 Broadway, Laguna Beach, Cal. 92651, *1, 3, 4, 9, 12, 16; A, C, F, G, I.*

LANEY COLLEGE, 1001 3rd Ave., Oakland, Cal. 94606, *1, 2, 3, 6, 7, 11, 12, 13, 14, 15; A, D, E, F, H, I, K.*

LA VERNE COLLEGE, 1950 Third St., La Verne, Cal. 91750, *3, 6, 7, 12, 13, 15; D, E, H, K.*

LOMA LINDA UNIVERSITY, Riverside, Cal. 92505, *3, 4, 6, 7, 12, 14, 15; A, D, E, H, K.*

LONE MOUNTAIN COLLEGE, 2800 Turk Blvd., San Francisco, Cal. 94118, *1, 3, 4, 6, 7, 8, 12, 13, 15; C, D, E, F, H, I, K.*

LONG BEACH CITY COLLEGE, 4901 East Carson Blvd., Long Beach, Cal. 90808, *1, 3, 6, 7, 9, 12, 14, 17; D, F, H, I.*

LOS ANGELES CITY COLLEGE, 855 N. Vermont, Los Angeles, Cal. 90029, *1, 3, 6, 7, 12, 14, 15, 17; D, I.*

LOS ANGELES HARBOR COLLEGE, 1111 Figueroa Pl., Wilmington, Cal. 90744, *1, 2, 3, 6, 7, 9, 11, 12, 13, 14, 17; A, D, F, H, I.*

LOS ANGELES PIERCE COLLEGE, 6201 Winnetka, Woodland Hills, Cal. 91364, *1, 3, 6, 7, 11, 12, 15; D, I.*

LOS ANGELES STATE COLLEGE, Los Angeles, Cal. 90015, *7, 12; D, E.*

LOS ANGELES TRADE TECHNICAL COLLEGE, 400 W. Washington Blvd., Los Angeles, Cal. 90015, *1, 2, 3, 7, 9, 13; A, D, E, F, H, I.*

LOS ANGELES VALLEY COLLEGE, 5800 Fulton Avenue, Van Nuys, Cal. 91401, *1, 3, 4, 6, 7, 9, 10, 12, 13, 14, 15, 17; A, D, E, F, H, I.*

LOYOLA UNIVERSITY OF LOS ANGELES, Loyola Blvd. at W. 80 St., Los Angeles, Cal. 90045, *3, 7, 12, 17; B, F, I.*

MARYMOUNT COLLEGE, LOYOLA UNIVERSITY, 7750 Fordham Rd., Los Angeles, Cal. 90045, *4, 7, 11, 12, 13, 15, 17; D, H.*

MENDOCINO ART CENTER, 540 Little Lake St., PO Box 36, Mendocino, Cal. 95460, *3, 6, 7, 12, 13, 14, 15; A, I, K.*

MERCED COLLEGE, Merced, Cal. 90340, *1, 3, 7, 11, 12, 13, 15, 17; A, D, E, F, H, I.*

MERRITT COLLEGE, 5714 Grove St., Oakland, Cal. 94609, *1, 3, 6, 7, 11, 12, 14, 16, 17; A, D, E, F, H, I.*

MESA COLLEGE, Mesa College Dr., San Diego, Cal. 92111, *3, 6, 7, 12, 13; A, D, H, I.*

MILLS COLLEGE, Oakland, Cal. 94613, *2, 7, 11, 12, 14, 15, 19; D, E.*

MIRA COSTA COLLEGE, Oceanside, Cal. 92054, *1, 7, 12, 15, 17; D, E, I.*

MODESTO JR. COLLEGE, College Ave., Modesto, Cal. 95350, *1, 3, 6, 7, 12, 15, 17; A, D, E, F, H, I.*

MONTEREY PENINSULA COLLEGE, 980 Fremont St., Monterey, Cal. 93940, *2, 3, 7, 12, 13, 15; A, D, E, F, H, I.*

MOUNT ST. MARY'S COLLEGE, 12001 Chalon Rd., Los Angeles, Cal. 90049, *3, 4, 7, 12, 14, 15, 17; C, D, E, H.*

MOUNT SAN ANTONIO COLLEGE, 1100 N. Grand Ave., Walnut, Cal. 91789, *1, 3, 7, 12, 14, 15; D, I.*

MOUNT SAN JACINTO COLLEGE, Box 248, Gilman Springs, Cal. 94558, *3, 12, 13, 15, 17; D, I.*

NAPA COLLEGE, 2277 Napa-Vallejo Hwy., Napa, Cal. 94558, *3, 7, 12, 13, 15, 17; D, H, I.*

OCCIDENTAL COLLEGE, 1600 Campus Rd., Los Angeles, Cal. 90041, *3, 4, 7, 12, 14, 15; A, E, G, K.*

ORANGE COAST COLLEGE, 2706 Fairview Rd., Costa Mesa, Cal. 92626, *1, 3, 7, 12, 13, 14, 15, 17; A, D, F, H, I.*

OTIS ART INSTITUTE OF LOS ANGELES COUNTY, 2401 Wilshire Blvd., Los Angeles, Cal. 90057, *3, 6, 7, 12, 15, 18, 21; D, E.*

PACIFIC UNION COLLEGE, Angwin, Cal. 94508, *1, 3, 4, 6, 7, 9, 12, 13, 17; D, H.*

PALO VERDE COLLEGE, Hobson Way, Blythe, Cal. 92225, *3, 6, 7, 12, 17; A, F, H.*

PALOMAR COMMUNITY COLLEGE, Hwy. 78, San Marcos, Cal. 92069, *1, 3, 6, 7, 9, 12, 13, 14, 15, 17; D, E, I.*

PARIS ART SCHOOL, 31014 Coast Blvd., South Laguna, Cal. 92677, *7, 12, 17.*

PASADENA CITY COLLEGE, 1570 E. Colorado Blvd., Pasadena, Cal. 91106, *1, 3, 4, 6, 7, 9, 10, 11, 12, 13, 14, 15, 17; A, D, E, F, H, I.*

PASADENA SCHOOL OF FINE ARTS, 314 S. Mentor Ave., Pasadena, Cal. 91106, *6, 7, 12, 13, 14, 15, 17; I.*

PEPPERDINE UNIVERSITY, 24255 Pacific Coast Hwy., Los Angeles, Cal. 90044, *3, 4, 6, 7, 11, 12, 14, 15, 17; A, D, E, G, K.*

PITZER COLLEGE, Claremont, Cal. 91711, *3, 6, 7, 12, 13, 15; A, D, E, F, K.*

POMONA COLLEGE, Claremont, Cal. 91711, *2, 7, 12, 15; D, E.*

PORTERVILLE COLLEGE, PO Box 952, Porterville, Cal. 93257, *3, 6, 7, 8, 12.*

REEDLEY COLLEGE, Reed & Manning Ave., Reedley, Cal. 93654, *1, 3, 6, 7, 9, 11, 17; A, D, E, F, H.*

RIO HONDO JR. COLLEGE, 3600 Workman Mill Rd., Whittier, Cal. 90601, *1, 3, 6, 7, 10, 11, 12, 14, 15; A, D, E, F, H, I.*

RIVERSIDE CITY COLLEGE, 3650 Fairfax Rd., Riverside, Cal. 92506, *1, 3, 4, 7, 9, 12, 14, 15, 17; A, D, E, F, H, I.*

RUDOLPH SCHAEFFER SCHOOL OF DESIGN, 2255 Mariposa St., San Francisco, Cal. 94110, *3, 4, 7, 11; A, E, H, I.*

SACRAMENTO CITY COLLEGE, 3835 Freeport Blvd., Sacramento, Cal. 95822, *1, 3, 6, 7, 11, 12, 14, 15, 17; D, E, I.*

SAN BERNARDINO VALLEY COLLEGE, 701 S. Mt. Vernon Ave., San Bernardino, Cal. 92403, *1, 2, 3, 4, 6, 7, 13, 15; A, D, E, H, I, K.*

SAN DIEGO CITY COLLEGE, 1425 Russ Blvd., San Diego, Cal. 92101, *6, 7, 12; D, I.*

SAN DIEGO MESA COLLEGE, 7250 Artillery Dr., San Diego, Cal. 92111, *3, 6, 7, 11, 12, 15; A, D, F, H, I.*

SAN FERNANDO VALLEY STATE COLLEGE, 18111 Nordhoff St., Northridge, Cal. 91324, *1, 3, 4, 6, 7, 12, 13, 14, 15, 17; A, D, F, H, I.*

SAN FRANCISCO ACADEMY OF ART COLLEGE, 625 Sutter St., San Francisco, Cal. 94102, *1, 5, 7, 8, 9, 10, 12, 13, 14, 15; D, E, I.*

SAN FRANCISCO ART INSTITUTE, 800 Chestnut St., San Francisco, Cal. 94133, *7, 12, 13, 14, 15; A, D, E, F, H, I.*

SAN FRANCISCO COMMUNITY COLLEGE, 50 Phelan Ave., San Francisco, Cal. 94112, *1, 2, 3, 4, 6, 7, 8, 10, 11, 12, 13; A, E, F, H, I.*

SAN FRANCISCO STATE UNIVERSITY, San Francisco, Cal. 94132, *4, 7, 8, 11, 12, 14, 15, 18, 19; A, D, E.*

SAN JOAQUIN DELTA COLLEGE, Kensington & Alpine, Stockton, Cal. 95204, *1, 3, 6, 7, 12, 13, 14, 15, 17; A, E, F, H, I, L.*

SAN JOSE CITY COLLEGE, 2100 Moorpark Ave., San Jose, Cal. 95128, *3, 6, 7, 10, 12, 14, 15; A, D, E, F, H.*

SAN JOSE STATE UNIVERSITY, Washington Sq., San Jose, Cal. 95112, *1, 3, 4, 6, 7, 9, 12, 14, 15, 16; A, D, E, F, I.*

SANTA ANA COLLEGE, 17 & Bristol, Santa Ana, Cal. 92706, *1, 3, 7, 9, 11, 12, 13, 14, 15; D, E.*

SANTA BARBARA CITY COLLEGE, 721 Cliff Dr., Santa Barbara, Cal. 93105, *3, 7, 12, 13, 15, 17; D, F.*

SANTA MONICA CITY COLLEGE, 1815 Pearl St., Santa Monica, Cal. 90405, *1, 3, 6, 7, 12, 13, 15; A, D, F, H, I, L.*

SANTA ROSA JUNIOR COLLEGE, 1501 Mendocino Ave., Santa Rosa, Cal. 95401, *1, 3, 6, 7, 8, 10, 12, 13, 14, 15, 16; A, D, E, I.*

SCRIPPS COLLEGE, Claremont, Cal. 91711, *2, 3, 4, 7, 12, 14, 15; A, D, E, F, I, K.*

SHASTA COLLEGE, Old Oregon Trail, Redding, Cal. 96001, *3, 6, 7, 12, 13, 14, 15, 17; A, D, F, H, K.*

SIERRA COLLEGE, 5000 Rocklin Rd., Rocklin, Cal. 95677, *3, 4, 6, 7, 12, 17; A, D, F, H, I, K.*

SOLANO COMMUNITY COLLEGE, Suisun Valley Rd., PO Box 246, Suisun City, Cal. 94585, *3, 6, 7, 10, 12, 14, 15; A, D, H.*

SONOMA STATE COLLEGE, 1801 E. Cotati Blvd., Rohnert Park, Cal. 94952, *3, 4, 7, 12, 14, 15; D.*

STANFORD UNIVERSITY, Stanford, Cal. 94305, *2, 4, 7, 12, 14, 15, 16, 17; D, E, H.*

UNITED STATES INTERNATIONAL UNIVERSITY, California Western Campus, 3902, Lomaland Dr., San Diego, Cal. 92106, *4, 6, 7, 12, 15, 17; D, H.*

UNIVERSITY OF CALIFORNIA, BERKELEY, 238 Kroebey Hall, Berkeley, Cal. 94705, *4, 7, 12, 14, 15, 17; D, H, J.*

UNIVERSITY OF CALIFORNIA, DAVIS, Davis, Cal. 95616, *2, 3, 4, 7, 12, 13, 14, 15, 17; D, H.*

UNIVERSITY OF CALIFORNIA, IRVINE, Irvine, Cal. 92717, *3, 6, 7, 12, 15; A, D, E, F, H, I.*

UNIVERSITY OF CALIFORNIA, LOS ANGELES, 405 Helgard Ave., Los Angeles, Cal. 90024, *1, 2, 7, 9, 10, 12, 13, 14, 15, 16; D, E, H, J.*

UNIVERSITY OF CALIFORNIA, RIVERSIDE, Riverside, Cal. 92507, *7, 12, 14; D, E, H.*

UNIVERSITY OF CALIFORNIA, SAN DIEGO, La Jolla, Cal. 92093, *3, 7, 12, 13; A, D, E, H, I, K.*

UNIVERSITY OF CALIFORNIA, SANTA BARBARA, Santa Barbara, Cal. 93106, *3, 4, 7, 12, 13, 14, 15, 17; A, D, E, G, I, K.*

UNIVERSITY OF CALIFORNIA, SANTA CRUZ, Santa Cruz, Cal. 95060, *3, 6, 7, 13, 14, 15; A, D, E, I.*

UNIVERSITY OF JUDAISM, 6525 Sunset Blvd., Los Angeles, Cal. 90028, *3, 4, 6, 7, 12, 13, 14, 15, 17; D, E.*

UNIVERSITY OF REDLANDS, Colton Ave., Redlands, Cal. 92373, *4, 6, 7, 12, 14, 15, 16; D, G, I.*

UNIVERSITY OF SAN DIEGO, Alcala Park, San Diego, Cal. 92110, *1, 3, 6, 7, 8, 12, 14, 15, 17; D, I.*

UNIVERSITY OF SOUTHERN CALIFORNIA—IDYLLWILD, School of Music and the Arts, Box 380, Idyllwild, Cal. 92349, *6, 7, 12, 14, 15, 17; A, I, K.*

UNIVERSITY OF SOUTHERN CALIFORNIA, University Park, Los Angeles, Cal. 90007, *1, 3, 4, 7, 12, 14, 15, 17; A, D, E, F, H, I, K.*

UNIVERSITY OF THE PACIFIC, Dept. of Art, Stockton, Cal. 95204, *1, 3, 4, 7, 12, 13, 14, 15, 17; A, D, F, I, K.*

VENTURA COLLEGE, 4667 Telegraph Road, Ventura, Cal. 93003, *3, 7, 10, 12, 18, 19, 21.*

WEST VALLEY COLLEGE, 14000 Fruitvale Ave., Saratoga, Cal. 95050, *2, 3, 6, 7, 8, 10, 12, 13, 15, 16; A, H, I.*

WHITTIER COLLEGE, Whittier, Cal. 90608, *3, 4, 6, 7, 12, 13, 14, 15; A, D, E, H, I, K.*

WOODBURY COLLEGE, 1027 Wilshire Blvd., Los Angeles, Cal. 90017, *1, 3, 4, 7, 8, 9, 10, 11, 12, 13, 14, 15, 16, 17; D, E, H, I.*

YUBA COLLEGE, Marysville, Cal. 95901, *3, 7, 12, 15, 17; A, D, E, F, H, I, K.*

Colorado

ALAMOSA STATE COLLEGE, Marysville, Colo. 95901, *3, 4, 6, 7, 12, 14, 15, 17; A, D, E, F, I, K.*

BLACK HAWK MOUNTAIN SCHOOL OF ART, 251 Main St., Black Hawk, Colo. 80422, *3, 6, 7, 9, 12, 13, 14, 15; summer only, K.*

COLORADO COLLEGE, Colorado Springs, Colo. 80903, *3, 4, 7, 12, 14, 15; A, E, F, I, K.*

COLORADO INSTITUTE OF ART, 16 W. 13th Ave., Denver, Colo. 80204, *3, 7, 9, 12; A, F, I.*

COLORADO STATE UNIVERSITY, Dept. of Art, Fort Collins, Colo. 80521, *1, 3, 4, 6, 7, 9, 11, 12, 14, 15, 16, 17; A, D, E, F, H, I, K.*

COLORADO WOMEN'S COLLEGE, Montview Blvd. & Quebec, Denver, Colo. 80220, *3, 4, 6, 7, 10, 12, 14, 15; C, D, E, K.*

ESTES PARK SCHOOL OF ART, PO Box 837, Estes Park, Colo. 80517, *7, 12; A, I.*

LORETTO HEIGHTS COLLEGE, 3001 S. Federal Blvd., Denver, Colo. 80236, *4, 7, 12, 13, 15, 16; D, F.*

MESA COLLEGE, 1120 N Ave., Grand Junction, Colo. 81501, *1, 3, 7, 9, 12, 14, 15, 17; A, D, H, K.*

NORTHEASTERN JR. COLLEGE, Sterling, Colo. 80751, *3, 7, 12, 14, 15, 17; A, H, I.*

ORTERO JR. COLLEGE, La Junta, Colo. 81050, *6, 7, 12, 16, 17; A, G, H.*

PUEBLO COLLEGE, 900 W. Orman, Pueblo, Colo. 81005, *3, 6, 7, 10, 11, 12, 15, 18, 21.*

REGIS COLLEGE, W. 50 & Lowell Blvd., Denver, Colo. 80221, *3, 7, 12; F.*

ROCKY MOUNTAIN SCHOOL OF ART, 1550 Downing, Denver, Colo. 80218, *1, 3, 5, 7, 9, 12, 17; A, E, F, H, I.*

SOUTHERN COLORADO STATE COLLEGE, Pueblo, Colo. 81005, *1, 4, 6, 7, 12, 14, 15, 17; D, E, H, I.*

UNIVERSITY OF COLORADO, Boulder, Col. 80302, *7, 11, 12, 14.*

UNIVERSITY OF COLORADO, 1400 Arapahoe, Denver, Colo. 80202, *7, 11, 12, 14, 15, 17; A, D, F, H, I.*

UNIVERSITY OF DENVER, School of Art, University Park, Denver, Colo. 80210, *1, 3, 4, 6, 7, 9, 11, 12, 14, 15, 16, 17; A, D, E, G, H, I, K.*

UNIVERSITY OF NORTHERN COLORADO, Greeley, Colo. 80639, *3, 6, 7, 12, 14, 15; A, D, E, I, K.*

UNIVERSITY OF SOUTHERN COLORADO, BELMONT CAMPUS, 2200 Bonforte Ave., Pueblo, Colo. 81005; *1, 3, 4, 6, 7, 12, 13, 14, 15, 17; A, D, E, I, K.*

WAGNER SCHOOL OF DRAWING & PAINTING, PO Box 456, Telluride, Colo. 81436, *7, 12, 17; A, I.*

WESTERN STATE COLLEGE OF COLORADO, Dept. of the Arts, Gunnison, Colo. 81230, *1, 3, 4, 6, 7, 12, 14, 15; A, D, F, I, K.*

Connecticut

ALBERTUS MAGNUS COLLEGE, New Haven, Conn. 06511, *7, 12, 14, 15, 17; C, D, E, F.*

ANNHURST COLLEGE, RR 1, Woodstock, Conn. 06281, *3, 4, 6, 7, 11, 12, 13, 15; A, D, E, I, K.*

CENTRAL CONNECTICUT STATE COLLEGE, 1615 Stanley St., New Britain, Conn. 06050, *3, 4, 6, 7, 12, 14, 15, 17; A, D, F, H, I, K.*

CONNECTICUT COLLEGE, ART DEPT., Mohegan Ave., New London, Conn. 06320, *3, 6, 7, 9, 12, 14, 15; C, D, F.*

EASTERN CONNECTICUT STATE COLLEGE, Windham St., Willimantic, Conn. 06226, *3, 6, 7, 12, 14, 15; A, D, E, H, I, K.*

FAIRFIELD UNIVERSITY, Fairfield, Conn. 06430, *3, 7, 12, 17; A, I.*

FOSTER CADDELL'S ART SCHOOL, Rt. 49, Voluntown, Conn. 06384, *3, 7, 9, 12, 17; H, I, J, K.*

HARTFORD ART SCHOOL, 200 Bloomfield Ave., West Hartford, Conn. 06117, *1, 3, 4, 6, 7, 9, 12, 14, 15, 17; A, D, E, F, H, I.*

HOUSATONIC COMMUNITY COLLEGE, Bridgeport, Conn. 06608, *3, 4, 6, 7, 10, 12, 15; A, D, H.*

JUNIOR COLLEGE OF CONNECTICUT, Bridgeport, Conn. 06602, *1, 3, 4, 6, 7, 10, 11, 12, 13, 14, 15; A, D, E, H, I.*

KENT SCHOOL, Box 401, Kent, Conn. 06757, *3, 6, 7, 9, 12, 15.*

MITCHELL COLLEGE, 437 Pequot Ave., New London, Conn. 06320, *3, 7, 9, 12, 14, 15; A, C, D.*

NEW ENGLAND ART ACADEMY, 59 Elm St., Bridgeport, Conn. 06880, *12; A, F, H, I.*

THE NORWICH ART SCHOOL, 108 Crescent St., Norwich, Conn. 06360, *3, 6, 7, 8, 12, 13, 14, 15, 17; A, H.*

PAIER SCHOOL OF ART, INC., 6 Prospect Ct., Hamden, Conn. 06511, *1, 3, 5, 7, 9, 11, 12, 13, 14, 17; I.*

SACRED HEART UNIVERSITY, 5229 Park Ave., Bridgeport, Conn. 06604, *4, 7, 9, 10, 12, 17; D, I.*

SILVERMINE COLLEGE OF ART, Silvermine Rd., New Canaan, Conn. 06840, *3, 6, 7, 12, 14, 15, 17; A, D, F, H, I.*

SOUTHERN CONNECTICUT STATE COLLEGE, 501 Crescent St., New Haven, Conn. 06515, *3, 4, 6, 7, 12, 14, 15, 17; A, D, E, F, H, I, K.*

TRINITY COLLEGE, Hartford, Conn. 06106, *3, 7, 12, 14, 15, 17; B, D, E, F, I, K.*

UNIVERSITY OF BRIDGEPORT, 219 Park Avenue, Bridgeport, Conn. 06602, *1, 3, 4, 6, 7, 9, 12, 13, 14, 15, 17; A, D, E, F, H, I, K.*

UNIVERSITY OF CONNECTICUT, School of Fine Arts, Storrs, Conn. 06268, *1, 3, 7, 12, 14, 15, 17; A, D, F, I, K.*

UNIVERSITY OF CONNECTICUT, Waterbury Branch, 32 Hillside Ave., Waterbury, Conn. 06710, *3, 7; E, I.*

UNIVERSITY OF NEW HAVEN, 300 Orange Ave., West Haven, Conn. 06505, *1, 3, 6, 9, 12, 13, 15; A, D, E, H, I, K.*

WESLEYAN UNIVERSITY, Middletown, Conn. 06457, *2, 3, 5, 6, 7, 12, 13, 14; A, D, E, I, K.*

YALE UNIVERSITY SCHOOL OF ART & ARCHITECTURE, 101 Chapel St., New Haven, Conn. 06513, *6, 7, 9, 12, 14, 15; A, D, E, F, I, K.*

Delaware

DELAWARE STATE COLLEGE, Dover, Del. 19901, *1, 3, 4, 6, 7, 9, 11, 12, 14, 15, 16, 17; D.*

REHOBOTH ART LEAGUE, INC., PO Box 84, Rehoboth Beach, Del. 19971, *6, 7, 12, 15.*

UNIVERSITY OF DELAWARE, Dept. of Art & Art History, Newark, Del. 19711, *3, 4, 6, 7, 9, 11, 12, 14, 15, 16; A, D, F, I.*

WESLEY COLLEGE, College Sq., Denver, Del. *1, 3, 4, 7, 9, 12, 16, 17; A, D, F, H, K.*

District of Columbia

AMERICAN UNIVERSITY, Massachusetts & Nebraska Ave. N.W., Washington, D.C. 20016, *1, 3, 4, 7, 11, 12, 13, 14, 15; A, D, E, F, H, I.*

CATHOLIC UNIVERSITY OF AMERICA, Art Dept., 620 Michigan Ave. N.E., Washington, D.C. 20017, *3, 4, 6, 7, 9, 12, 14, 15; A, D, F, I.*

CORCORAN SCHOOL OF ART, 17 St. at New York Ave. N.W., Washington, D.C. 20006, *1, 3, 7, 9, 12, 13, 14, 15, 17; A, D, E, F, H, I.*

CUPOLI SCHOOL OF ART, 930 F St. N.W., Washington, D.C. 20004, *7, 12, 17; G, I.*

DE BURGOS SCHOOL OF ART, 1303 Wisconsin Ave. N.W., Washington, D.C. 20007, *3, 4, 7, 12, 17; A, F, H, I.*

DUNBARTON COLLEGE OF HOLY CROSS, 2935 Upton St. N.W., Washington, D.C. 20008, *3, 7, 9, 12, 15, 17; C, D, E, H, K.*

GALLAUDET COLLEGE, Kendall Green N.E., Washington, D.C. 20002, *1, 3, 6, 7, 9, 12, 14, 15, 17; A, D, F, K.*

GEORGETOWN UNIVERSITY, 37 & O Sts. N.W., Washington, D.C. 20007, *3, 7, 12, 13; D, E, F, H, I.*

GEORGE WASHINGTON UNIVERSITY, Washington, D.C. 20006, *4, 7, 10, 12, 15, 18.*

HOWARD UNIVERSITY, Washington, D.C. 20001, *2, 4, 6, 7, 10, 12, 14, 15; A, D, H, K.*

IMMACULATA COLLEGE OF WASHINGTON, 4300 Nebraska Ave., Washington, D.C. 20016, *3, 4, 6, 7, 12, 17; C, D, F.*

MAJORIE WEBSTER JR. COLLEGE, 7775 17th St. N.W., Washington, D.C. 20012, *1, 3, 4, 7, 12, 17; C, D, E, F, K.*

MOUNT VERNON JR. COLLEGE, 2100 Foxhall Rd. N.W., Washington, D.C. 20007, *7, 11, 12, 13, 14, 15, 17; C, D, G.*

NATIONAL ART ACADEMY, 1763 R. St. N.W., Washington, D.C. 20009, *1, 3, 7, 9, 11, 12; A, D, F.*

TRINITY COLLEGE, Michigan Ave. at Franklin N.E., Washington, D.C. 20017, *3, 4, 6, 7, 12, 13, 14, 15; A, D, E, H, I.*

Florida

ART INSTITUTE OF FORT LAUDERDALE, 3000 E. Las Olas Blvd., Fort Lauderdale, Fla. 33316, *5, 9, 11, 12, 13, 17; H.*

ART INSTITUTE OF MIAMI INC., 7808 N.E. Second Ave., Miami, Fla, 33138, *1, 4, 6, 7, 9, 12, 13, 14, 15; E, I.*

ART LEAGUE OF MANATEE COUNTY, 209 Ninth Street West, Bradenton, Fla. 33505, *6, 7, 12, 13, 14, 15, 17; A, F, H, I.*

BARRY COLLEGE, 11300 N.E. Second Ave., Miami, Fla. 33161, *1, 3, 4, 6, 7, 9, 12, 14, 15, 16, 17; C, D, F, H, I, K.*

BAUDER FASHION COLLEGE, The Dupont Plaza Center, 300 Biscayne Blvd. Way, Miami, Fla. 33131, *1, 8, 9, 11; C, D, G.*

BREVARD JR. COLLEGE, Clearlake Rd., Cocoa, Fla. 32924, *3, 7, 12, 14, 17; A, D, E, G, H, I.*

CENTRAL FLORIDA COMMUNITY COLLEGE, PO Box 1388, Ocala, Fla. 32670, *3, 7, 12; A, F, I, H.*

CHASE SCHOOL OF ART, 1310 Bay Rd., Sarasota, Fla. 33479, *4, 6, 7, 12, 17; A, F.*

CHIPOLA JR. COLLEGE, Marianna, Fla. 32446, *3, 6, 7, 11, 12, 15; A, D, F, K.*

COLLEGE OF BOCA RATON, Boca Raton, Fla. 33431, *1, 3, 6, 7, 8, 10, 11, 12, 13, 14, 15; A, D, E, F, H.*

COLLEGE OF ORLANDO, 901 N. Highland Ave., Orlando, Fla. 32803, *3, 7, 12, 17; D, F.*

CONNI GORDON ART SCHOOL, 530 Lincoln Road, Miami Beach, Fla. 33139, *4, 7, 12, 15, 17; K.*

EDISON JR. COLLEGE, Cypress Lake Dr., Ft. Myers, Fla. 33901, *1, 3, 7, 11, 12, 17; A, D, F, I.*

ELIOT MC MURROUGH SCHOOL OF ART, 306 Fifth Ave., Indialantic, Fla. 32901, *7, 12, 15, 17; H, I.*

ELISE FRANK SCHOOL OF ART, Florida Institute of Technology, PO Box 2027, Tampa, Fla. 33602, *2, 10, 11.*

FARNSWORTH SCHOOL OF ART, 4823 Higel Ave., Sarasota, Fla. 33581, *7, 12, 17.*

FLORIDA A&M UNIVERSITY, Tallahassee, Fla. 32307, *1, 4, 6, 7, 12, 14, 15, 16, 17; D, H, I.*

FLORIDA ATLANTIC UNIVERSITY, Boca Raton, Fla. 33432, *3, 4, 6, 7, 9, 11, 12, 13, 14, 15, 17; A, D, H, I, K.*

FLORIDA COLLEGE, Temple Terrace, Fla. 33617, *3, 6, 7, 11, 15, 16; A, F, G, K.*

FLORIDA GULF COAST ART CENTER, INC., 111 Manatee Rd., Clearwater, Fla. 33516, *3, 5, 6, 7, 11, 12, 15, 17; I.*

FLORIDA JR. COLLEGE AT JACKSONVILLE, 2445 San Diego Rd., San Diego Campus, Jacksonville, Fla. 32216, *3, 7, 12, 14; D, E, I.*

FLORIDA MEMORIAL COLLEGE, 15800 N.W. 42 Ave., Miami, Fla. 33054, *3, 4, 6, 7, 12, 15, 17.*

FLORIDA SOUTHERN COLLEGE, Lakeland, Fla. 33802, *3, 4, 6, 7, 12, 14, 15; D, E, G.*

FLORIDA STATE UNIVERSITY, Dept. of Art, Tallahassee, Fla. 32306, *1, 2, 3, 4, 5, 9, 10, 12, 13, 14, 16, 17; A, B, C, I.*

FORT LAUDERDALE MUSEUM OF THE ARTS, 426 E. Las Olas Blvd., Fort Lauderdale, Fla. 33301.

HILTON LEACH ART SCHOOL, 4433 Riverwood Ave., Sarasota, Fla. 33581, *7, 12, 14, 17; A, F, I.*

INDIAN RIVER COMMUNITY COLLEGE, Fort Pierce, Fla. 33450, *3, 7; D.*

JACKSONVILLE UNIVERSITY, Jacksonville, Fla. 32211, *4, 7, 12, 14, 15; D, E, G, J.*

LAKE CITY COMMUNITY COLLEGE, Lake City, Fla. 32055, *3, 7, 12; A, D, F, G, H, I.*

LAKE-SUMPTER JR. COLLEGE, Leesburg, Fla. 32748, *2, 6, 7, 10, 12, 14, 17; D, H, I.*

MANATEE JUNIOR COLLEGE, 26th St. W, Bradenton, Fla. 33507, *2, 3, 6, 7, 8, 9, 12, 13, 15; A, D, F, H, I.*

MIAMI DADE COMMUNITY COLLEGE, 11380 N.W. 27th Ave., Miami, Fla. 33167, *1, 3, 6, 7, 11, 12, 14, 15; A, D, E, G, H.*

NEW COLLEGE, Sarasota, Fla. 33578, *3, 12, 14, 17; A, E, G, K.*

NORTH FLORIDA JR. COLLEGE, Madison, Fla. 32340, *1, 3, 7, 12, 14, 15, 17; A, D, G, H, K.*

NORTON SCHOOL OF ART, 1451 S. Olive Ave., West Palm Beach, Fla. 33401, *3, 4, 6, 7, 12, 14, 15.*

PALM BEACH JUNIOR COLLEGE, 4200 Congress Ave., Lake Worth, Fla. 33460, *1, 2, 3, 6, 7, 8, 9, 10, 12, 13, 15; A, D, H, I.*

PENSACOLA JR. COLLEGE, 1000 College Blvd., Pensacola, Fla. 32504, *1, 3, 7, 12, 14, 15, 17; A, D, E, G, H, I.*

POLK COMMUNITY COLLEGE, 999 Ave.H N.E., Winter Haven, Fla. 33880, *1, 3, 4, 7, 12, 14; D, E, G, I.*

RINGLING SCHOOL OF ART, Sarasota, Fla. 33580, *1, 3, 7, 9, 11, 12, 17; D, F, K.*

ROLLINS COLLEGE, ART DEPT., Winter Park, Fla. 32789, *1, 3, 4, 6, 12, 15; A, D.*

ST. JOSEPH COLLEGE, 720 S. Indian River Dr., Jensen Beach, Fla. 33457, *3, 4, 6, 14; A, D, F, H, I.*

SAINT LEO COLLEGE, PO Drawer F, St. Leo, Fla. 33574, *1, 4, 6, 7, 8, 12, 14, 15; D, E.*

ST. PETERSBURG JUNIOR COLLEGE, 6605 Fifth Ave. N., St. Petersburg, Fla. 33733, *1, 3, 6, 7, 12, 13, 14, 15; A, D, F, H, I.*

STETSON UNIVERSITY ART DEPT., Deland, Fla. 32720, *3, 4, 6, 7, 12, 14, 15, 17; A, D, F, G, H, I, K.*

TALLAHASSEE COMMUNITY COLLEGE, 444 Appleyard Dr., Tallahassee, Fla. 32303, *3, 7, 12, 13; A, D, H.*

UNIVERSITY OF FLORIDA, Gainesville, Fla. 32611, *1, 3, 6, 7, 9, 12, 13, 14, 15; A, D, E, G, I.*

UNIVERSITY OF MIAMI, Coral Gables, Fla. 33146, *2, 3, 4, 6, 7, 12, 13, 14, 15, 17; A, D, E, F, H, I, K.*

UNIVERSITY OF SOUTH FLORIDA, 4200 Fowler Ave., Tampa, Fla. 33620, *3, 4, 6, 7, 12, 13, 14, 15; D, E, H.*

UNIVERSITY OF TAMPA, Tampa, Fla. 33606, *1, 3, 4, 7, 12, 14, 15; A, D, E, F, H, I, K.*

UNIVERSITY OF WEST FLORIDA, Pensacola, Fla. 32504, *4, 6, 7, 8, 9, 12, 13, 14; A, D, H, I.*

WAGNER SCHOOL OF DRAWING & PAINTING, 1262 Third St. S., Suite F., Naples, Fla. 33940, *7, 12, 17; A, F, H.*

Georgia

AGNES SCOTT COLLEGE, Decatur, Ga. 30030, *3, 7, 12, 14, 15, 17; C, D, G.*

ATLANTA BAPTIST COLLEGE, 3000 Flowers Road, Atlanta, Ga. 30005, *3, 4, 6, 7, 12, 14, 15, 16; D, E, H, I.*

ATLANTA COLLEGE OF ART, 1280 Peachtree St. N.E., Atlanta, Ga. 30309, *1, 3, 7, 12, 14, 15, 17; A, D, E, F, H, I.*

ATLANTA UNIVERSITY CENTER COLLEGES, 350 Leonard St. S.W., Atlanta, Ga. 30314, *1, 4, 6, 7, 12, 13, 14, 15; D, F.*

AUGUSTA COLLEGE, 2500 Walton Way, Augusta, Ga. 30904, *3, 4, 6, 7, 12, 13; A, D, E, F, H.*

BERRY COLLEGE, Mt. Berry, Ga. 30149, *3, 4, 6, 7, 10, 11, 12, 14, 15, 16, 17; A, D, F, G, I, K.*

BRENAU COLLEGE FOR WOMEN, Gainesville, Ga. 30501, *4, 6, 7, 12, 17; C, D, F, H, I, K.*

BIRDWOOD JR. COLLEGE, Millpond Rd., Thomasville, Ga. 31792, *4, 7, 12, 17; D, H.*

BRUNSWICK JR. COLLEGE, Brunswich, Glynn, Ga. 31520, *3, 7, 12, 14, 17; A, D, E, F, H.*

CLARK COLLEGE, 240 Chestnut St. S.W., Atlanta, Ga. 30314, *1, 8, 9, 13, 14; A, D.*

COLUMBUS COLLEGE, Algonquin Dr., Columbus, Ga. 31907, *3, 4, 6, 7, 12, 13, 14, 15; D, E, H, J.*

COLUMBUS SCHOOL OF ART, 1601 12 St., Columbus, Ga. 31906, *1, 3, 5, 7, 9, 12, 16, 17; I.*

DALTON JR. COLLEGE, Dalton, Ga. 30720, *3; H.*

DEKALB COLLEGE, 555 N. Indian Creek Dr., Clarkston, Ga. 30021, *3, 7, 12, 17; H.*

EMORY UNIVERSITY, Atlanta, Ga. 30322, *3, 4, 12; A, C, D, E, I, K.*

GEORGIA INSTITUTE OF TECHNOLOGY, Atlanta, Ga. 30332, *2, 10; A, D, E, H.*

GEORGIA SOUTHERN COLLEGE, DEPT. OF VISUAL ARTS, Statesboro, Ga. 30458, *3, 4, 6, 7, 12, 14, 15, 16, 17; A, D, F, G, I, K.*

GEORGIA SOUTHWESTERN COLLEGE, Americus, Ga. 31709, *3, 4, 6, 7, 12, 15, 17; A, D, E, F, H, K.*

GEORGIA STATE UNIVERSITY, 33 Gilmer St. S.E., Atlanta, Ga. 30303, *1, 3, 4, 6, 7, 9, 11, 12, 13; A, D, E, F, H, I, K.*

LA GRANGE COLLEGE, La Grange, Ga. 30240, *3, 6, 7, 12, 13, 14, 17; A, D, E, G, I, K.*

MERCER UNIVERSITY, Macon, Ga. 31207, *3, 4, 7, 12, 14, 15; A, D, F, G, H, I, K.*

MIDDLE GEORGIA COLLEGE, Cochran, Ga. 31014, *3, 7, 9, 12; A, D, F, H, I, K.*

MORRIS BROWN COLLEGE, 604 Hunter St. N.W., Atlanta, Ga. 30314, *3, 4, 6, 7, 9; D, H.*

PIEDMONT COLLEGE, Demorest, Ga. 30535, *3, 4, 6, 7, 12, 13, 15; A, D, E, F, I, K.*

REINHARDT COLLEGE, Walaiska, Ga. 30183, *3, 4, 7, 12, 14, 17; D, H.*

SAVANNAH STATE COLLEGE, PO Box 183, Savannah, Ga. 31404, *3, 4, 6, 7, 12, 14, 15, 17; A, D, E, G, H, I, K.*

SHORTER COLLEGE, Rome, Ga. 30161, *2, 3, 4, 6, 7, 10, 11, 12, 14, 15, 16, 17; A, D, E, F, I, K.*

SOUTH GEORGIA COLLEGE, Douglas, Ga. 31533, *4, 7, 12, 14; D, H.*

TIFT COLLEGE, Forsyth, Ga. 31029, *2, 3, 4, 7, 12, 15; C, D, H.*

TRUETT-MCCONNELL COLLEGE, Cleveland, Ga. 30528, *3, 5, 6, 12, 14; A, D, H.*

UNIVERSITY OF GEORGIA, DEPT. OF ART, Athens, Ga. 30601, *1, 3, 4, 6, 7, 9, 11, 12, 13, 14, 15, 16; A, D, E, F, H, I.*

VALDOSTA STATE COLLEGE, DEPT. OF ART, Valdosta, Ga. 31601, *1, 3, 4, 5, 6, 7, 9, 12, 14, 15, 17; A, D, E, G, I, K.*

WESLEYAN COLLEGE, Macon, Ga. 31201, *1, 3, 4, 7, 12, 14, 15; C, D, E, F, K.*

WEST GEORGIA COLLEGE, Carrollton, Ga. 30117, *3, 7, 12; A, D, H, I, K.*

WOMAN'S COLLEGE OF GEORGIA, DEPT. OF ART, Milledgeville, Ga. 31061, *4, 6, 7, 11, 12, 16, 17; C, D, E, F, I, K.*

Hawaii

CHURCH COLLEGE OF HAWAII, Laie, Hawaii 96762, *1, 4, 6, 7, 9, 12, 14, 15, 17; D, E.*

FOUNDRY ART CENTER, 899 Waimanu St., Honolulu, Hawaii 96813, *3, 6, 7, 12, 14, 15; A, I.*

HONOLULU ACADEMY OF ARTS, 900 S. Beretania St., Honolulu, Hawaii 96814, *1, 7, 12; A, F, H, I.*

KAPIOLANI COMMUNITY COLLEGE, 620 Pensacola St., Honolulu, Hawaii 96814, *3, 6, 7, 12; A, D, E, H, I.*

KAUAI COMMUNITY COLLEGE, RR 1, Box 216, Lihne, Hawaii 96766, *3, 6, 7, 12, 13, 14, 17; A, D, H, I.*

MAUI COMMUNITY COLLEGE, 310 Kaahumanu Ave., Kahului Maui, Hawaii 96732, *2, 3, 5, 6, 7, 8, 10, 12, 13, 15, 16, 17; D, I.*

UNIVERSITY OF HAWAII, DEPT. OF ART, 2560 Campus Rd., Honolulu, Hawaii 96822, *1, 2, 3, 7, 9, 12, 13, 14, 15, 16, 17; A, D, F, H, I.*

Idaho

BOISE STATE UNIVERSITY, 1910 College Blvd., Boise, Idaho 83725, *3, 4, 6, 7, 11, 12, 13, 14, 15, 17; A, D, E, F, H, I, K.*

COLLEGE OF SOUTHERN IDAHO, PO Box 1238, Twin Falls, Idaho 83301, *3, 4, 6, 7, 10, 12, 15; A, D, E, H, I.*

COLLEGE OF ST. GERTRUDE, Cottonwood, Idaho 83522, *6, 12; C, D, F, H, I.*

IDAHO STATE UNIVERSITY, FINE ARTS BLDG., Pocatello, Idaho 83201, *3, 4, 6, 7, 12, 14, 15, 17; A, D, E, F, H, I, K.*

LEWIS-CLARK STATE COLLEGE, Lewiston, Idaho 83501, *3, 4, 7, 15, 17; D, E, F, H.*

NORTHWEST NAZARENE COLLEGE, Dewey & Holly Sts., Nampa, Idaho 83651, *3, 4, 7, 11, 12, 14, 15, 17; A, D, E, G, H, K.*

RICKS COLLEGE, College Ave., Rexburg, Idaho 83440, *3, 7, 12, 15, 17; D.*

UNIVERSITY OF IDAHO DEPT. OF ART & ARCHITECTURE, Moscow, Idaho 83843, *1, 2, 3, 4, 5, 7, 9, 11, 12, 14, 15, 17; A, D, E, F, H, I, K.*

Illinois

AMERICAN ACADEMY OF ART, 220 S. State St., Chicago, Ill. 60604, *1, 4, 5, 7, 9, 12, 17; A, E, F, H, I, K.*

ART INSTITUTE OF CHICAGO, Michigan Ave. at Adams St., Chicago, Ill. 60603, *1, 3, 4, 7, 9, 10, 11, 12, 13, 14, 15, 16, 17; A, D, E, F, I.*

AUGUSTANA COLLEGE, 3700 7th Ave., Rock Island, Ill. 61201, *3, 4, 6, 7, 12, 14, 15; A, D, E, F, H, I, K.*

BARAT COLLEGE, Lake Forest, Ill. 60045, *1, 3, 4, 7, 12, 14, 15, 17; C, D, E, F, K.*

BELLEVILLE AREA COLLEGE, 2500 Carlyle Rd., Belleville, Ill. 62221, *3, 6, 7, 9, 12, 14, 15, 17; A, D, H, I.*

BLACK HAWK COLLEGE, 6600-34th Ave., Moline, Ill. 61265, *1, 6, 7, 12, 15; A, D, F, H, I.*

BLACKBURN COLLEGE, Carlinville, Ill. 62626, *3, 7, 12, 15, 21.*

BLOOM COMMUNITY COLLEGE, 10th & Dixie Hwy., Chicago Heights, Ill. 60411, *3, 7, 12, 15; A, D, E, F, H, I.*

BRADLEY UNIVERSITY, Peoria, Ill. 61606, *1, 3, 4, 7, 9, 12, 14, 15, 16, 17; A, D, E, F, H, I, K.*

CANTON COMMUNITY COLLEGE, 102 E. Elm, Canton, Ill. 61520, *1, 3, 4, 7, 9, 12, 15, 17; A, D, F, H, I.*

CHICAGO ACADEMY OF FINE ARTS, 65 E. South Water St., Chicago, Ill. 60601, *1, 3, 5, 7, 9, 11, 12, 13, 14, 16, 17; A, D, E, F, I, K.*

203

CITY COLLEGE OF CHICAGO, KENNEDY-KING COLLEGE, 6800 S. Wentworth Ave., Chicago, Ill. 60601, *3, 4, 6, 7, 10, 12, 13; A, D, E, H.*

CITY COLLEGE OF CHICAGO, LOOP COLLEGE, 64 E. Lake St., Chicago, Ill. 60601, *3, 4, 6, 7, 10, 12, 15; A, D, E, H.*

CITY COLLEGE OF CHICAGO, MALCOLM X COLLEGE, 1900 W. Van Buren St., Chicago, Ill. 60612, *3, 4, 6, 7, 10, 12, 15; A, D, E, H.*

CITY COLLEGE OF CHICAGO, MAYFAIR COLLEGE, 4626 N. Knox Ave., Chicago, Ill. 60630, *3, 4, 7, 10, 12, 13.*

CITY COLLEGE OF CHICAGO, OLIVE-HARVEY COLLEGE, 10001 S. Woodlawn Ave., Chicago, Ill. 60628, *3, 4, 6, 7, 10, 12; A, D, F, H.*

CITY COLLEGE OF CHICAGO, SOUTHWEST COLLEGE, 7500 S. Pulaski Rd., Chicago, Ill. 60652, *3, 4, 6, 7, 12, 13, 15; A, D, E, H.*

CITY COLLEGE OF CHICAGO, WRIGHT COLLEGE, 3400 N. Austin Ave., Chicago, Ill. 60634, *1, 2, 3, 4, 6, 7, 8, 9, 12, 15; A, D, E, H, I.*

COLLEGE OF DU PAGE, Lambert Rd. & 22 St., Glen Ellyn, Ill. 60137, *2, 3, 6, 7, 8, 9, 11, 12, 13, 15, 16, 17; D, E, H, I.*

COLLEGE OF ST. FRANCIS, 500 N. Wilcox St., Joliet, Ill. 60435, *3, 4, 7, 12, 14, 15, 17; A, D, E, F, I.*

COLUMBIA COLLEGE CHICAGO, 540 N. Lake Shore Dr., Chicago, Ill. 60611, *1, 3, 7, 9, 12, 13, 14, 17; D, E, I.*

DE PAUL UNIVERSITY, 2323 N. Seminary, Chicago, Ill. 60614, *3, 7, 12, 14, 17; A, D, F, G, H, I.*

EASTERN ILLINOIS UNIVERSITY, Charleston, Ill. 61920, *1, 3, 4, 6, 7, 12, 14, 15, 17; A, D, E, F, I, K.*

ELGIN COMMUNITY COLLEGE, 373 E. Chicago St., Elgin, Ill. 60120, *3, 6, 7; F, H.*

ELMHURST COLLEGE, 190 Prospect, Elmhurst, Ill. 60126, *3, 4, 6, 7, 12, 13, 14, 15; A, D, E, H.*

EVANGELICAL THEOLOGICAL SEMINARY, Naperville, Ill. 60540, *13; I.*

FELICIAN COLLEGE, 3800 W. Peterson Ave., Chicago, Ill. 60645, *3, 4, 7, 17; C, F, I.*

FREEPORT COMMUNITY COLLEGE, 511 W. Stephenson St., Freeport, Ill. 61032, *7, 12; A, F.*

GREENVILLE COLLEGE, Greenville, Ill. 62246, *1, 4, 6, 7, 12, 15, 17.*

HARRINGTON INSTITUTE OF INTERIOR DESIGN, 410 S. Michigan Ave., Chicago, Ill. 60605, *3, 7, 9, 11, 13, 17; D, F, I.*

HIGHLAND COMMUNITY COLLEGE, RFD 2, Pearl City Rd., Freeport, Ill. 61032, *3, 6, 7, 12, 14; A, D, H, I.*

ILLINOIS INSTITUTE OF TECHNOLOGY, INSTITUTE OF DESIGN, 3360 S. State St., Technology Center, Chicago, Ill. 60616, *1, 3, 4, 7, 10, 13, 14, 15; A, D, E, F, H, I, K.*

ILLINOIS STATE UNIVERSITY, Normal, Ill. 61761, *3, 4, 6, 7, 12, 14, 15, 17; D, E, F, H, I.*

ILLINOIS TEACHERS COLLEGE, Chicago-North, 5500 N. St. Louis Ave., Chicago, Ill. 60625, *3, 4, 7, 12, 14, 15; A, D, E, G, H, I.*

ILLINOIS VALLEY COMMUNITY COLLEGE, Oglesby, Ill. 61348, *3, 4, 7, 12, 15, 17; D, I.*

ILLINOIS WESLEYAN UNIVERSITY, 210 E. University, Bloomington, Ill. 61701, *3, 4, 7, 10, 11, 12, 13, 14, 15, 16, 17; A, D, E, F.*

J. S. MORTON HIGH SCHOOL EAST & JR. COLLEGE, 2423 S. Austin Blvd., Cicero, Ill. 60650, *3, 7, 12, 15, 17; A, F, H, I.*

JUDSON COLLEGE, 1151 N. State St., Elgin, Ill. 60120, *1, 3, 7, 12, 14, 17; A, D, E, G, H, K.*

KENDALL COLLEGE, 2408 Orrington, Evanston, Ill. 60204, *3, 7, 12, 14, 17; A, D, E, F, H, I, K.*

LAKE FOREST COLLEGE, Sheridan Rd., Lake Forest, Ill. 60045, *2, 3, 4, 6, 7, 12, 13, 14, 15; A, D, E.*

LEWIS & CLARK COMMUNITY COLLEGE, Godfrey Rd., Godfrey, Ill. 62035, *3, 7, 12, 14, 15, 17; D, E, I.*

MACMURRAY COLLEGE, Jacksonville, Ill. 62650, *1, 4, 6, 7, 10, 11, 12; D.*

MALLINCKRODT JR. COLLEGE, 1041 Ridge Rd., Wilmette, Ill. 60091, *2, 3, 4, 7, 10, 12, 13, 14, 15, 16, 17; C, D, E, I, K.*

MILLIKIN UNIVERSITY, Decatur, Ill. 62522, *1, 3, 4, 7, 12, 14, 17; A, D, E, F, H, I, K.*

MONMOUTH COLLEGE, MONMOUTH ART CENTER, Monmouth, Ill. 61462, *3, 4, 7, 12, 14, 15; A, D, E, G, I, K.*

MUNDELEIN COLLEGE, 6363 Sheridan Rd., Chicago, Ill. 60626, *1, 3, 4, 6, 7, 11, 12, 13, 14, 15, 16, 17; D, E, G, I, K.*

NORTH PARK COLLEGE, 5125 N. Spaulding, Chicago, Ill. 60625, *1, 3, 4, 6, 7, 8, 9, 10, 11, 12, 13, 14, 15; A, D, E, H, I.*

NORTHEASTERN ILLINOIS UNIVERSITY, Bryn Mawr at St. Louis Ave., Chicago, Ill. 60625, *2, 3, 4, 7, 10, 12, 14, 15, 16; D, E, G, I.*

NORTHERN ILLINOIS UNIVERSITY, DEPT. OF ART, Fine Arts Bldg., Dekalb, Ill. 60115, *1, 3, 4, 6, 7, 9, 10, 11, 12, 13, 14, 15, 16, 17; A, E, F, H, I, K.*

NORTHWESTERN UNIVERSITY, Evanston, Ill. 60201, *3, 4, 7, 9, 11, 12, 14, 15; A, D, E, F, I.*

OLIVET NAZARENE COLLEGE, Kankakee, Ill. 60901, *3, 4, 6, 7, 12, 17; D, F, K.*

PRAIRIE STATE COLLEGE, PO Box 487, Chicago Heights, Ill. 60461, *1, 2, 3, 7, 11; D, I.*

QUINCY COLLEGE, Quincy, Ill. 62301, *3, 7, 12, 13, 15; A, D, F, K.*

ROCK VALLEY COLLEGE, 3301 N. Mulford Rd., Rockford, Ill. 61101, *3, 5, 6, 12; A, D, E, H, I.*

ROCKFORD COLLEGE, 5050 E. State St., Rockford, Ill. 61101, *3, 4, 6, 7, 12, 14, 15, 16, 17; A, D, E, F, H, I, K.*

ROOSEVELT UNIVERSITY, 430 S. Michigan, Chicago, Ill. 60605, *2, 3, 4, 6, 7, 12, 14; D, E, F, H, I.*

ROY-VOGUE SCHOOLS, 750 N. Michigan Ave., Chicago, Ill. 60611, *3, 5, 7, 9, 11, 13, 17; A, F, H, I, K.*

ST. DOMINIC COLLEGE, 1405 N. Fifth Ave., St. Charles, Ill. 60174, *3, 6, 7, 12, 13, 14, 15, 17; A, D, F, H.*

ST. XAVIER COLLEGE, 103rd St. at S. Central Pk. Ave., Chicago, Ill. 60655, *3, 4, 6, 7, 11, 12, 15, 16; C, D, F, K.*

SCHOOL OF THE ART INSTITUTE OF CHICAGO, Michigan at Adams, Chicago, Ill. 60603, *1, 3, 4, 6, 7, 8, 9, 12, 13, 14, 15, 16, 17; D, E, I.*

SHIMER COLLEGE, College & Seminary Sts., Mt. Carroll, Ill. 61053, *3, 7, 12, 17; A, F.*

SOUTHERN ILLINOIS UNIVERSITY, Carbondale, Ill. 62901, *1, 2, 3, 4, 6, 7, 9, 10, 11, 12, 13, 14, 16, 17; A, B, C, F, I.*

SOUTHERN ILLINOIS UNIVERSITY AT EDWARDSVILLE, Edwardsville, Ill. 62025, *1, 3, 4, 6, 7, 12, 14, 15, 16, 17; D, E, H, I.*

SPOON RIVER COLLEGE, 102 E. Elm, Canton, Ill. 61520, *1, 3, 4, 7, 9, 12, 15, 17; D, I.*

SPRINGFIELD COLLEGE IN ILLINOIS, 1500 N. Fifth St., Springfield, Ill. 62702, *4, 6, 7, 12, 15; D.*

THORNTON COMMUNITY COLLEGE, 15800 State St., South Holland, Ill. 60473, *1, 3, 4, 7, 12, 13, 14, 15; D, E, I.*

TRITON COLLEGE, 2000 Fifth ave., River Grove, Ill. 60171, *1, 3, 4, 6, 7, 8, 9, 10, 12, 14, 15; A, D, H, I.*

UNIVERSITY OF CHICAGO, Chicago, Ill. 60637, *3, 4, 7, 12, 14, 15, 17; A, D, E, F, I, K.*

UNIVERSITY OF ILLINOIS, DEPT. OF ART, 143 Fine Arts Bldg., Champaign, Ill. 61820, *1, 3, 4, 6, 7, 9, 10, 12, 13, 14, 15, 17; A, D, E, F, H, I, K.*

UNIVERSITY OF ILLINOIS, DEPT. OF ART, Chicago Circle Campus, 601 South Morgan, Chicago, Ill. 60680, *1, 3, 4, 5, 7, 9, 10, 12, 13, 16; A, B, I.*

UNIVERSITY OF ILLINOIS, Urbana, Ill. 61801, *2, 4, 7, 10, 12, 14, 15.*

WABASH VALLEY COLLEGE, College Drive, Mt. Carmel, Ill. 62863, *3, 4, 6, 7, 12, 15, 17; I, K.*

WESTERN ILLINOIS UNIVERSITY, Macomb, Ill. 61455, *1, 3, 4, 6, 7, 11, 12, 14, 15, 16, 17; A, D, E, G, H, I, K.*

WHEATON COLLEGE, Wheaton, Ill. 60187, *3, 4, 6, 7, 12, 14, 15, 17; D, H.*

WRIGHT COLLEGE, 3400 N. Austin Ave., Chicago, Ill. 60634, *2, 6, 7, 12, 15, 17; F, H, I.*

Indiana

ANCILLA DOMINI COLLEGE, Donaldson, Ind. 46513, *3, 6, 12, 14, 17; F, H.*

ANDERSON COLLEGE, Anderson, Ind. 46011, *4, 6, 7, 12, 13; D, F, I, J.*

BALL STATE UNIVERSITY, Muncie, Ind. 47306, *4, 6, 7, 12, 14, 19.*

DE PAUW UNIVERSITY, ART CENTER, Greencastle, Ind. 46135, *1, 3, 4, 5, 6, 7, 9, 10, 12, 13, 14, 15, 16, 17; A, D, F, H, K.*

EARLHAM COLLEGE, Richmond, Ind. 47374, *3, 4, 6, 7, 12, 13, 14, 15; A, D, E.*

FRANKLIN COLLEGE, Franklin, Ind. 46131, *4, 6, 7, 12, 13; A, D, K.*

FT. WAYNE ART INSTITUTE, 1026 W. Berry St., Ft. Wayne, Ind. 46804, *1, 3, 4, 6, 7, 9, 12, 13, 14, 15, 17; A, D, E, F, H, I.*

GOSHEN COLLEGE, 1700 S. Main St., Goshen, Ind. 46525, *3, 4, 6, 7, 12, 13, 14; A, D, H, I, K.*

GRACE COLLEGE, Winona Lake, Ind. 46590, *3, 4, 6, 7, 12, 13, 15; D.*

HANOVER COLLEGE, Hanover, Ind. 47243, *1, 3, 4, 7, 12, 13, 14, 15; D, E, F.*

HERRON SCHOOL OF ART, 1701 N. Pennsylvania St., Indianapolis, Ind. 46202, *1, 3, 4, 7, 9, 12, 13, 14, 15, 17; A, D, E, F, H, I.*

INDIANA CENTRAL UNIVERSITY, University Heights, Indianapolis, Ind. 46227, *1, 2, 3, 4, 6, 7, 12, 14, 15, 17; E, I.*

INDIANA NORTHERN UNIVERSITY, Box 1000, University Park, Gas City, Ind. 46933, *1, 8; D, H, I.*

INDIANA UNIVERSITY, Bloomington, Ind. 47401, *1, 3, 4, 5, 7, 9, 10, 11, 12, 14, 15, 16; B, I.*

INDIANA UNIVERSITY, FORT WAYNE, Coliseum Blvd. E., Fort Wayne, Ind. 46805, *4, 7; D, I.*

INDIANA UNIVERSITY, Indianapolis Downtown Campus, 518 N. Delaware St., Indianapolis, Ind. 46204, *3, 4, 6, 7, 12; A, F, H, I.*

INDIANA UNIVERSITY, South Bend Campus, North Side Blvd. at Greenlawn, South Bend, Ind. 46615, *3, 4, 9, 11, 12, 16; A, I.*

INDIANA UNIVERSITY, Terre Haute, Ind. 47809, *1, 3, 4, 6, 7, 11, 12, 13, 14, 15, 17; A, D, E, F, H, I, K.*

INDIANA-PURDUE REGIONAL CAMPUS, California Rd., Ft. Wayne, Ind. 46804, *2, 3, 4, 6, 7, 11, 13, 14, 15, 16, 17; A, D, E, F, H, I.*

INDIANA STATE UNIVERSITY, EVANSVILLE, 8600 University Blvd., Evansville, Ind. 47712, *3, 4, 6, 7, 8, 9, 10, 11, 12, 13, 15; A, D, E, H.*

INDIANA UNIVERSITY NORTHWEST, 3400 Broadway, Gary, Ind. 46408, *3, 6, 7.*

INDIANA UNIVERSITY SOUTHEAST, Warder Park, Jeffersonville, Ind. 47130, *3, 4, 6, 7, 12; I.*

MANCHESTER COLLEGE, College Ave., North Manchester, Ind. 46962, *1, 3, 4, 6, 7, 8, 9, 10, 11, 12, 14, 15; A, D, E, I, K.*

MARION COLLEGE, 3200 Cold Springs Rd., Indianapolis, Ind. 46222, *3, 4, 7, 11, 12, 14, 15, 17; A, D, F, H, I, K.*

OAKLAND CITY COLLEGE, Oakland City, Ind. 47660, *1, 3, 4, 6, 7, 12, 14, 15, 17; A, D, F, H, I, K.*

PURDUE UNIVERSITY, Barker Memorial Extension Center, Washington St., Michigan City, Ind. 46360, *3, 4; A, F, H, I.*

PURDUE UNIVERSITY, Dept. of Creative Arts, W. Lafayette, Ind. 47907, *1, 3, 4, 6, 7, 9, 10, 11, 12, 13, 14, 15; A, D, E, F, I, K.*

ST. BENEDICT COLLEGE, Ferdinand, Ind. 47532, *3, 4, 6, 7, 12, 15, 17; A, F, H, I, K.*

ST. FRANCIS COLLEGE, 2701 Spring, Ft. Wayne, Ind. 46808, *3, 4, 6, 7, 12, 14, 15, 17; A, D, E, F, H, I.*

ST. MARY-OF-THE-WOODS, St. Mary-of-the-Woods, Ind. 47876, *4, 6, 7, 12, 14, 15; C, D, E.*

ST. MARY'S COLLEGE, ART DEPARTMENT, Notre Dame, Ind. 46556, *1, 3, 6, 7, 12, 13, 14, 15, 17; C, D, F.*

ST. MEINARD COLLEGE, St. Meinard, Ind. 47577, *1, 3, 6, 7, 12, 14; H.*

TAYLOR UNIVERSITY, Upland, Indiana 46989, *3, 4, 7, 12, 14, 15, 17; D.*

UNIVERSITY OF EVANSVILLE, 1800 Lincoln Ave., Evansville, Ind. 47701, *3, 4, 6, 7, 12, 14, 15, 17; D, H, I.*

UNIVERSITY OF NOTRE DAME, DEPT. OF ART, Notre Dame, Ind. 46556, *1, 3, 6, 7, 10, 12, 14, 15; B, D, E, F, I.*

VALPARAISO UNIVERSITY, Valparaiso, Ind. 46383, *1, 3, 4, 6, 7, 9, 12, 13, 14, 15, 16, 17; E, I.*

VINCENNES UNIV. JR. COLLEGE, Second at College, Vincennes, Ind. 47591, *1, 3, 6, 7, 12, 14; D, I.*

WABASH COLLEGE, Crawfordsville, Ind. 47933, *3, 7, 12, 14; B, F, K.*

206

Iowa

BRIAR CLIFF COLLEGE, 3303 Rebecca St., Sioux City, Iowa 51104, *3, 4, 7, 9; A, D, H, K.*

BUENA VISTA COLLEGE, Storm Lake, Iowa 50588, *4, 7, 12, 14, 17; A, D, E, F, H, I, K.*

CARSONS COLLEGE, Fairfield, Iowa 52556, *3, 4, 7, 12, 13, 15; D, I.*

CENTRAL COLLEGE OF IOWA, Pella, Iowa 50219, *3, 4, 6, 7, 12, 14, 15; A, D, K.*

CLARKE COLLEGE, Dubuque, Iowa 52001, *3, 6, 7, 12, 14, 15, 17; A, C, D, E, F, H, I.*

COE COLLEGE, Cedar Rapids, Iowa 52402, *3, 6, 7, 12, 13, 14; A, D, F, I, K.*

CORNELL COLLEGE, Mount Vernon, Iowa 52314, *3, 6, 7, 12, 15; A, D.*

DRAKE UNIVERSITY, ART DEPT., University Ave., Des Moines, Iowa 50311, *1, 3, 4, 6, 7, 9, 11, 12, 14, 15, 17; A, D, E, F, H, I, K.*

EASTERN IOWA COMMUNITY COLLEGE, Clinton, Iowa 52732, *3; D.*

ELLSWORTH COLLEGE, 1100 College, Iowa Falls, Iowa 50126, *3, 6, 7, 12, 15; A, D, F, H, K.*

GRACE LAND COLLEGE, Lamoni, Iowa 50140, *1, 3, 4, 6, 7, 12, 14, 17; A, D, F, H, I, K.*

GRINNELL COLLEGE, Grinnell, Iowa 50112, *3, 7, 12, 14, 15, 17; D, F.*

INDIAN HILLS COMMUNITY COLLEGE, Centerville, Iowa 52544, *3, 7; D, I.*

IOWA CENTRAL COMMUNITY COLLEGE, Eagle Grove Center, Eagle Grove, Iowa 50533, *3, 7, 12, 17; A, F.*

IOWA CENTRAL COMMUNITY COLLEGE, 330 Ave. M, Fort Dodge, Iowa 50501, *7, 12; D, F.*

IOWA LAKES COMMUNITY COLLEGE, Rotunda Bldg., Estherville, Iowa 51334, *3, 7, 12, 17; D, E, H.*

IOWA STATE TEACHERS COLLEGE, Cedar Falls, Iowa 50613, *4, 7, 8, 10, 12, 14, 15, 18.*

IOWA STATE UNIVERSITY, Ames, Iowa 50010, *2, 7, 12.*

IOWA WESLEYAN COLLEGE, Mount Pleasant, Iowa 52641, *3, 4, 6, 7, 12, 13, 14; A, D.*

KIRKWOOD COMMUNITY COLLEGE, Kirkwood Blvd., Cedar Rapids, Iowa 52401, *3, 6, 7, 12, 13, 14; A, D, H, I.*

LORAS COLLEGE, Dubuque, Iowa 52001, 3, 4, 7, 12, 14, 15, 17; B, D, H.

LUTHER COLLEGE, Decorah, Iowa 52001, 4, 7, 12, 14, 15, 17; D, E.

MARYCREST COLLEGE, 1607 W. 12, Davenport, Iowa 52804, 1, 3, 4, 7, 9, 11, 12, 14, 15, 17; C, D, E, F, H, I, K.

MORNINGSIDE COLLEGE, Sioux City, Iowa 51106, 3, 4, 7, 12, 15, 17; A, D, E, F, H, I, K.

MOUNT MERCY COLLEGE, 1330 Elmhurst Dr. N.E., Cedar Rapids, Iowa 52402, 1, 3, 4, 7, 12, 14, 15, 17; D.

MOUNT ST. CLARE COLLEGE, 400 N. Bluff, Clinton, Iowa 52732, 3, 7, 12; D, F.

NORTH IOWA AREA COMMUNITY COLLEGE, 500 College Dr., Mason City, Iowa 50401, 3, 4, 9, 12; A, D, H, I.

NORTHWESTERN COLLEGE, 101 7th St., Orange City, Iowa 51041, 1, 2, 4, 6, 7, 11, 12, 14, 15; A, D, F, H, I, K.

OTTUMWA HEIGHTS COLLEGE, Grandview, Ottumwa, Iowa 52501, 3, 7, 12, 15; D, E, F.

ST. AMBROSE COLLEGE, Davenport, Iowa, 1, 3, 4, 7, 9, 12, 13, 14, 15, 17; D, E, I.

SIMPSON COLLEGE, Indianola, Iowa 50125, 3, 7, 12; F, I.

SOUTHWESTERN COMMUNITY COLLEGE, Cottonwood & Townline Rd., Creston, Iowa 50801, 3, 6, 7; F.

UNIVERSITY OF IOWA, SCHOOL OF ART, Iowa City, Iowa 52240, 1, 3, 4, 5, 6, 7, 9, 10, 11, 12, 13, 16, 17; A, B, C, I.

UNIVERSITY OF NORTHERN IOWA, Cedar Falls, Iowa 50613, 3, 4, 6, 7, 12, 14, 15, 16, 17; D, E.

UPPER IOWA COLLEGE, Fayette, Iowa 52142, 3, 4, 7, 12, 15; A, D, F, I, K.

WALDORF COLLEGE, Forest City, Iowa 50436, 7, 12; D.

WESTMAN COLLEGE, Le Mars, Iowa 51031, 3, 4, 6, 7, 12, 15, 17; A, D, E, F, I, K.

Kansas

BAKER UNIVERSITY, Baldwin, Kans. 66006, 3, 4, 7, 12, 14, 17; A, D, K.

BENEDICTINE COLLEGE, Atchison, Kans. 66002, 3, 4, 6, 7, 12, 13, 14, 15; A, D, E.

BETHANY COLLEGE, Lindsborg, Kans. 67456, 3, 4, 7, 12, 13, 14, 15, 17; D, E, F, I.

BETHEL COLLEGE, North Newton, Kans. 57117, 3, 4, 6, 7, 12, 14, 15; A, D, E, F, K.

BRESCIA COLLEGE, 120 W. Seventh St., Owensboro, Kans. 42301, 1, 2, 3, 4, 6, 7, 12, 13, 14; A, D, H, I, K.

BUTLER COUNTY COMMUNITY JR. COLLEGE, Towanda St. & Haver Hill Rd., El Dorado, Kans. 67042, 1, 12; A, D, E, F, H, K.

CLOUD COUNTY COMMUNITY COLLEGE, Concordia, Kans. 66901, 7, 12, 15; I.

COFFEYVILLE COMMUNITY JR. COLLEGE, 11 & Willow, Coffeyville, Kans. 67337, 3, 12, 17; D, F, I.

COLBY COMMUNITY COLLEGE, South Range, Colby, Kans. 67701, 1, 3, 6, 7, 8, 9, 12, 13, 14, 15, 17; D, E, I.

COLLEGE OF EMPORIA, Emporia, Kans. 66801, 3, 4, 6, 7, 12, 14, 15; A, D, E, I, K.

DODGE CITY COMMUNITY JR. COLLEGE, 1000 2nd Ave., Dodge City, Kans. 67801, 1, 4, 6, 7, 12, 14, 15, 17; A, D, E, F, H, I.

EMPORIA KANSAS STATE COLLEGE, Emporia, Kans. 66801, 3, 6, 7, 9, 10, 11, 12, 14, 15; A, D, I.

FORT HAYS KANSAS STATE COLLEGE, Hays, Kans. 67601, 4, 7, 12, 14, 15.

FRIENDS UNIVERSITY, Wichita, Kans. 67213, 1, 3, 4, 7, 12, 16, 17; A, D, E, F, H, I, K.

GARDEN CITY COMMUNITY JR. COLLEGE, 801 Campus Dr., Garden City, Kans. 67846, 1, 3, 7, 12, 15, 17; D, E, I.

HUTCHINSON COMMUNITY JR. COLLEGE, 1300 N. Clum St., Hutchinson, Kans. 67501, 7, 12, 15, 17; D, I.

INDEPENDENCE COMMUNITY JR. COLLEGE, Independence, Kans. 67301, 3, 4, 7; D, F.

KANSAS CITY KANSAS COMMUNITY JR. COLLEGE, 824 State, Kansas City, Kans. 66101, 3, 7; A, F, H.

KANSAS CITY STATE UNIVERSITY, Manhattan, Kans. 66502, 1, 2, 3, 4, 6, 7, 9, 10, 11, 12, 14; A, B, C, I.

KANSAS STATE COLLEGE OF PITTSBURG, 1701 S. Broadway, Pittsburg, Kans. 66762, 3, 4, 6, 7, 12, 14, 15; D, I.

KANSAS WESLEYAN UNIVERSITY, Salina, Kans. *3, 7, 9, 12; A, D, I, K.*

LABETTE COMMUNITY JR. COLLEGE, 200 S. 14th St., Parsons, Kans. 67357, *3, 4, 6, 7, 12, 17; A, F.*

MARYMOUNT COLLEGE, East Iron Ave. & Marymount Rd., Salina, Kans. 67401, *3, 6, 7, 12, 14, 15, 17; C, D, H, I.*

MC PHERSON COLLEGE, McPherson, Kans. 67460, *3, 4, 7, 12, 15, 17; A, D, E, F, H, I, K.*

MIDWAY COLLEGE, Stephens St., Midway, Kans. 40347, *3, 6, 7, 12.*

MT. ST. SCHOLASTICA COLLEGE, Atchison, Kans. 66002, *3, 4, 7, 12, 14, 15.*

NEOSHA COUNTY COMMUNITY JR. COLLEGE, Chanute, Kans. 66720, *3, 7, 9, 12, 15, 17; D, E, F.*

NORTHERN KENTUCKY STATE COLLEGE, 526 Johns Hill Rd., Highland Heights, Covington, Kans. 41076, *3, 4, 12, 13, 14, 15; A, D, I.*

OTTAWA UNIVERSITY, 10 & Cedar Sts., Ottawa, Kans. 66067, *3, 4, 6, 7, 12, 14, 15, 17; A, D, F, I, K.*

SACRED HEART COLLEGE, 3100 McCormick Ave., Wichita, Kans. 67213, *1, 3, 4, 7, 9, 12, 14, 15, 17; A, D, F, H, I, K.*

ST. BENEDICT'S COLLEGE, Atchison, Kans. 66002, *3, 7, 12, 15, 17; B, F, H, K.*

SCHOOL OF WICHITA ART ASSOCIATION, 9112 E. Central, Wichita, Kans. 67206, *6, 7, 12, 14, 17; A, E, F, H, I.*

SOUTHWESTERN COLLEGE, Winfield, Kans. *1, 4, 6, 7, 12, 14, 15, 17; D, E.*

STERLING COLLEGE, Sterling, Kans. 67579, *6, 7, 12, 14, 17; A, E, F, H, I.*

UNIVERSITY OF KANSAS, Dept. Design, Lawrence, Kans. 66044, *1, 3, 4, 5, 6, 7, 9, 10, 11, 12, 13, 14, 15, 16, 17; D, E, F, I, K.*

WASHBURN UNIVERSITY OF TOPEKA, 17th & Jewell Sts., Topeka, Kans. 66621, *3, 6, 7, 10, 12; A, D, E, K.*

WICHITA STATE UNIVERSITY, 1845 N. Fairmount, Wichita, Kans. 67208, *1, 3, 4, 6, 7, 9, 12, 14, 15, 17; A, D, E, F, H, I, K.*

Kentucky

ALICE LLOYD COLLEGE, Pippa Passes, Ky. 41844, *3, 7, 13, 15, 17; A, F, H, I.*

ART CENTER ASSOCIATION SCHOOL, 2111 S. First St., Louisville, Ky. 40208, *1, 3, 6, 7, 9, 12, 14, 15, 16, 17; A, E, F, H, I, K.*

ASHBURY COLLEGE, Wilmore, Ky. 40390, *3, 4, 6, 7, 12, 14, 17; A, D.*

BEREA COLLEGE, Art Department, Berea, Ky. 40403, *3, 4, 6, 7, 12, 14, 15, 17; A, D, E, F, K.*

CAMPBELLSVILLE COLLEGE, Campbellsville, Ky. 42718, *1, 3, 4, 6, 7, 12, 14, 15, 17; D, E, I.*

CENTRE COLLEGE OF KENTUCKY, Danville, Ky. 40422, *3, 7, 11, 12, 15, 17; D, H.*

CUMBERLAND COLLEGE, Williamsburg, Ky. 40769, *3, 4, 6, 7, 12, 14, 15, 17; A, D, E, F, I, K.*

EASTERN KENTUCKY UNIVERSITY, ART DEPT., Richmond, Ky. 40475, *4, 6, 7, 12, 14, 15; A, D, F, K.*

GEORGETOWN COLLEGE, Georgetown, Ky. 40324, *3, 4, 7, 12, 15; D, E.*

KENTUCKY STATE COLLEGE, E. Main, Frankfort, Ky. 40601, *3, 4, 7, 12; F, I.*

KENTUCKY WESLEYAN COLLEGE, 3000 Freserica St., Owensboro, Ky. 42301, *6, 7, 12, 21; A, D, K.*

LOUISVILLE SCHOOL OF ART, 100 Park Rd., Anchorage, Ky. 40223, *1, 6, 7, 8, 9, 10, 12, 13, 14, 15, 17; D, E, I.*

MOREHEAD STATE UNIVERSITY, Morehead, Ky. 40351, *1, 3, 4, 6, 7, 12, 15, 17; A, D, E, F, H, I, K.*

MURRAY STATE UNIVERSITY, ART DIVISION, Murray, Ky. 42072, *1, 3, 4, 5, 6, 7, 9, 12, 13, 14, 15, 16, 17; A, D, E, F, H, I, K.*

NAZARETH COLLEGE OF KENTUCKY, Nazareth, Ky. 40048, *1, 3, 4, 6, 7, 11, 12, 13, 14, 15, 16, 17; C, D, F, H, I, K.*

PADUCAH JR. COLLEGE, Blandville Rd., Paducah, Ky. 42001, *3, 7, 12, 14; A, F, I.*

SPALDING COLLEGE, P. O. Box 39, Nazareth, Ky. 40048, *1, 3, 4, 6, 7, 12, 13, 14, 15, 17; D, E, I.*

THOMAS MORE COLLEGE, Box 85, Covington, Ky. 41017; *1, 3, 4, 7, 12, 13, 14, 15; D, I.*

TRANSYLVANIA UNIVERSITY, Lexington, Ky. 40508, *3, 4, 12, 15; A, D, E, F, I, K.*

UNION COLLEGE, Barbourville, Ky. 40906, *3, 4, 6, 7, 12; A, F, I, K.*

UNIVERSITY OF KENTUCKY, Lexington, Ky. 40506, *2, 3, 5, 6, 7, 12, 13, 14, 15, 17; A, D, E, F, H, I, K.*

UNIVERSITY OF LOUISVILLE, Allen R. Hite Institute, Louisville, Ky. 40208, *3, 4, 6, 7, 12, 13, 14, 15; A, D, E, F, H, I, K.*

URSULINE COLLEGE, 3105 Lexington Rd., Louisville, Ky. 40206, *3, 4, 6, 7, 9, 12, 15, 16, 17; A, D, F, G, I, K.*

VILLA MADONNA COLLEGE, Covington, Ky. 41012, *1, 3, 4, 6, 7, 12, 14, 15, 17; A, D, E, F, H, I.*

WESTERN KENTUCKY UNIVERSITY, Bowling Green, Ky. 42101, *3, 4, 7, 12, 14, 15; A, D, F, H, I, K.*

Louisiana

CENTENARY COLLEGE OF LOUISIANA, Centenary Blvd., Shreveport, La. 71104, *3, 4, 6, 7, 12, 14; A, D, H, I, K.*

CLARKE COLLEGE, 1550 Clark Dr., Dubuque, La. *3, 6, 7, 8, 11, 12, 15, 21.*

DELGADO JUNIOR COLLEGE, 615 City Park Ave., New Orleans, La. 70119, *3, 7, 12; A, D, H.*

GRAMBLING COLLEGE, Grambling, La. 71245, *3, 4, 6, 7, 12, 14, 15, 17; A, D, F, I, K.*

LOUISIANA COLLEGE, Pineville, La. 71360, *1, 3, 4, 6, 7, 9, 12, 15, 17; A, D, E, F, H, I, K.*

LOUISIANA STATE UNIVERSITY, DEPT. OF FINE ARTS, Baton Rouge, La. 70803, *3, 4, 7, 11, 12, 14, 15; A, D, E, F, I.*

LOUISIANA TECH UNIVERSITY, Ruston, La. 71270, *1, 3, 4, 6, 7, 9, 11, 12, 14, 16, 17; A, D, E, F, I, K.*

LOYOLA UNIVERSITY OF THE SOUTH, New Orleans, La. 70118, *3, 4, 7, 12, 13, 14, 15, 17; A, D, E, F, H, I, K.*

THE JOHN McCRADY ART SCHOOL OF NEW ORLEANS, 910 Bourbon St., New Orleans, La. 70016, *1, 3, 6, 7, 8, 9, 10, 11, 12; A, H, I.*

McNEESE STATE UNIVERSITY, 4000 Ryan St., Lake Charles, La. 70601, *2, 3, 4, 6, 7, 12, 13, 15; A, D, H, I, K.*

NEW ORLEANS ART INSTITUTE, 2926 Canal St., New Orleans, La. 70119, *1, 3, 4, 6, 7, 8, 9, 10, 11, 12; A, H.*

NICHOLLS STATE UNIVERSITY, Thibodaux, La. 70301, *4, 6, 7, 12, 14, 15; A, D, F, H, I, K.*

NORTHEAST LOUISIANA STATE UNIVERSITY, 4001 De Siard Ave., Monroe, La. 71201, *1, 3, 4, 6, 7, 12, 13, 14, 15, 17; A, D, E, F, I, K.*

ST. MARY'S DOMINICAN COLLEGE, 7414 St. Charles Ave., New Orleans, La. 70118, *3, 4, 7, 12, 14, 15; C, D, E, F, K.*

SOUTHEASTERN LOUISIANA UNIVERSITY, University Sta., Hammond, La. 70401, *3, 4, 7, 9, 12, 14, 15, 17; A, D, E, F, I, K.*

SOUTHERN UNIVERSITY, NEW ORLEANS, New Orleans, La. 70118, *3, 4, 6, 7, 9, 10, 11, 12, 15; A, D, H.*

SOUTHWESTERN INSTITUTE OF ARTS, 657 Jordan St., Shreveport, La. 71101, *7, 12, 17; I.*

TULANE UNIVERSITY, NEWCOMB ART DEPT., New Orleans, La. 70118, *3, 7, 12, 14, 15; A, D, E, F, H, I.*

UNIVERSITY OF NEW ORLEANS, New Orleans, La. 70122, *3, 4, 7, 12, 14, 15; A, D, K.*

UNIVERSITY OF SOUTHWESTERN LOUISIANA, Lafayette, La. 70501, *2, 3, 7, 10, 11, 12, 15, 18.*

XAVIER UNIVERSITY OF LOUISIANA, 3817 Pine St., New Orleans, La. 70125, *1, 3, 4, 7, 12, 14, 15, 17; A, D, E, F, I, K.*

Maine

AROOSTOOK STATE COLLEGE, Presque Isle, Me. 04769, *3, 4, 6, 7, 9, 12, 13, 14, 15; A, F.*

BATES COLLEGE, Lewiston, Me. 04240, *7, 12, 14, 17; D, F.*

BOWDOIN COLLEGE, Brunswick, Me. 04011, *1, 3, 4, 9, 10, 12, 14, 16; B, C, I.*

COLBY COLLEGE, Waterville, Me. 04901, *1, 3, 4, 9, 11, 12, 14, 16; B, C, I.*

FARMINGTON STATE COLLEGE, Farmington, Me. 04938, *3, 6, 7, 12, 14, 16, 17; A, D, F, K.*

NASSON COLLEGE, Waterville, Me. 04901, *A, D.*

PORTLAND SCHOOL OF ART, 97 Spring St., Portland, Me. 04101, *6, 13, 14, 15; A, D, H, I.*

UNIVERSITY OF MAINE AT MACHIAS, Machias, Me. 04654, *3, 4, 6, 11, 12, 14, 15, 17; D, H.*

UNIVERSITY OF MAINE, Carnegie Hall, Orono, Me. 04473, *3, 4, 7, 9, 12, 14, 16; A, D, K.*

UNIVERSITY OF MAINE, PORTLAND, Gorham, Me. 04038, *3, 4, 6, 7, 15, 17; D, F, H, I, K.*

WASHINGTON STATE COLLEGE, O'Brien Ave., Machias, Me. 04654, *3, 4, 6, 7, 11, 12, 14, 17; A, D, E, F, K.*

Maryland

ALLEGHANY COMMUNITY COLLEGE, 340 Frederick St., Cumberland, Md. 21502, *1, 7; A, F, H, I.*

BOWIE STATE COLLEGE, Jericho Rd., Bowie, Md. 20715, *4, 6, 7, 12, 14, 15; D.*

CATONSVILLE COMMUNITY COLLEGE, 800 S. Rolling Rd., Catonsville, Md. 21228, *1, 3, 6, 7, 12, 15, 17; D, E, I.*

COLLEGE OF NOTRE DAME OF MARYLAND, 4701 N. Charles St., Baltimore, Md. 21210, *3, 4, 6, 7, 9, 12, 14, 15, 17; C, D, E, F, I.*

COLUMBIA UNION COLLEGE, Carroll & Flower, Takoma Park, Md. 20012, *3, 4, 12; A, G, H.*

COMMUNITY COLLEGE OF BALTIMORE, 2901 Liberty Heights Ave., Baltimore, Md. 21215, *1, 3, 6, 7, 10, 13, 15; A, D, H, I.*

COPPIN STATE COLLEGE, 2500 W. North Ave., Baltimore, Md. 21216, *3, 4, 7, 12, 15; D.*

FROSTBURG STATE COLLEGE, Frostburg, Md. 21532, *1, 3, 4, 5, 6, 7, 9, 12, 14, 15, 16, 17; A, D, F, H, I, K.*

GOUCHER COLLEGE, TOWSON, Towson, Md. 21204, *3, 7, 12, 14, 15, 17; C, D, E, G, K.*

HARTFORD COMMUNITY COLLEGE, 401 Thomas Run Rd., Bel Air, Md. 21014, *3, 7, 12, 13, 14, 15, 17; A, D, F, H.*

HOOD COLLEGE, Frederick, Md. 21701, *3, 12, 15; D.*

JOHNS HOPKINS UNIVERSITY, Charles & 34th Sts., Baltimore, Md. 21218, *3, 4; A, D, H, K.*

MARYLAND INSTITUTE, 1300 Mt. Royal Ave.. Baltimore, Md. 21217, *1, 2, 3, 4, 6, 7, 9, 10, 11, 12, 13, 14, 15, 17; A, D, E, F, H, I, K.*

MARYLAND SCHOOL OF ART & DESIGN, 932 Philadelphia Ave., Silver Spring, Md. 20910, *1, 7, 9, 12, 14, 15; A, F, I.*

MARYLAND STATE COLLEGE, Princess Anne, Md. 21853, *3, 4, 6, 7, 10, 11, 12, 13, 14, 15, 16, 17; A, D, E, F, H, K.*

MARYLAND UNIVERSITY, College Park, Md. 20740, *2, 3, 4, 7, 12, 14, 15, 17; A, D, E, F, H, I, K.*

MORGAN STATE UNIVERSITY, Coldspring Lane & Hillen Rd., Baltimore, Md. 21212, *3, 4, 6, 7, 12, 13, 14, 15, 17; A, D, F, H, I, K.*

PRINCE GEORGE'S COMMUNITY COLLEGE, 301 Largo Rd., Largo, Md. 20870, *1, 3, 7, 9, 12, 15, 17; D, E, I.*

ST. JOSEPH COLLEGE, Emmitsburg, Md. 21727, *4, 7, 8, 11, 12, 14, 15; D, I.*

ST. MARY'S COLLEGE OF MARYLAND, St. Mary's City, Md. 20686, *4, 6, 7, 12, 14, 15, 17; D.*

SALISBURY STATE COLLEGE, Camden Ave., Salisbury, Md. 21801, *3, 4, 6, 7, 12, 14; D, E, I.*

SCHULER SCHOOL OF FINE ARTS, 5 E. Lafayette Ave., Baltimore, Md. 21202, *7, 12, 15, 17; A, F, H, I.*

TOWSON STATE COLLEGE, York Rd., Towson, Md. 21204, *1, 2, 3, 4, 7, 12, 13, 14, 15, 16, 17; D, E, I.*

UNIVERSITY OF MARYLAND, College Park, Md. 20742, *3, 4, 7, 12, 15; A, D, E, I, K.*

WESTERN MARYLAND COLLEGE, Westminster, Md. 21157, *3, 4, 6, 7, 9, 12, 14, 15, 17; A, D, E, F, I, K.*

Massachusetts

AMHERST COLLEGE, Amherst, Mass. 01002, *3, 12, 13, 14, 15; D, E, K.*

ANNA MARIA COLLEGE, Sunset Lane, Paxton, Mass. 01612, *1, 3, 4, 6, 7, 12, 13, 15, 17; A, D, H, I, K.*

ART INSTITUTE OF BOSTON, 700 Beacon St., Boston, Mass. 02215, *1, 5, 7, 9, 11, 12, 13, 14, 15, 16, 17; E, I.*

ATLANTIC UNION COLLEGE, South Lancaster, Mass. 01561, *3, 4, 7, 11, 12, 14, 15, 17; D, E, I.*

BASSFORD NORTH TRURO SCHOOL OF ART, Box 63, Pond Rd., North Truro, Mass. 02652, *4, 7, 12, 17; A, I, K.*

BAY PATH JR. COLLEGE, Longmeadow, Mass. 01106, *6, 7, 12, 16; C, D, F, I.*

BEAUPRE (summer school), Stockbridge, Mass. 01262, *6, 7, 12; C.*

BERKSHIRE COMMUNITY COLLEGE, Second St., Pittsfield, Mass. 01201, *1, 3, 4, 7, 9, 12, 17; A, D, F, H, I.*

BOSTON CENTER FOR ADULT EDUCATION, 5 Commonwealth Ave., Boston, Mass. 02116, *2, 3, 6, 7, 8, 11, 12, 13, 14, 15, 17; E, H, I.*

BOSTON COLLEGE, Chestnut Hill, Boston, Mass. 02167, *3, 7, 12, 15, 17; A, F, H.*

BOSTON UNIVERSITY, SCHOOL OF FINE AND APPLIED ARTS, 855 Commonwealth Ave., Boston, Mass. 02215, *1, 3, 4, 6, 7, 11, 12, 14, 15; A, D, E, F, H, I, K.*

BRADFORD JR. COLLEGE, Bradford, Mass. 01830, *3, 12, 15; C, F.*

BRANDEIS UNIVERSITY, South Bend, Waltham, Mass. 02154, *1, 3, 9, 10, 11, 12, 15; A, D, E, I, K.*

BRIDGEWATER STATE COLLEGE, Bridgewater, Mass. 02324, *3, 4, 6, 7, 11, 12, 14, 15, 16; I.*

BROCKTON ART CENTER, Oak St., Brockton, Mass. 02401, *2, 3, 6, 7, 10, 11, 12, 13, 14, 15, 16; A, H, I.*

BUTERA SCHOOL OF ART, 111 Beacon St., Boston, Mass. 02116, *1, 3, 9; A, F, H.*

CAMBRIDGE CENTER FOR ADULT EDUCATION, Cambridge, Mass. 02165, *3, 6, 7, 8, 12, 13, 14, 15, 16, 17; E, H, I.*

CAPE SUMMER SCHOOL OF ART, Provincetown, Mass. 02657, *7, 12; A.*

CHAMERLAYNE JR. COLLEGE, 128 Commonwealth Ave., Boston, Mass. 02116, *2, 3, 7, 11, 12, 14, 16, 17; A, F.*

CLARK UNIVERSITY, Worcester, Mass. 01610, *1, 3, 4, 6, 7, 8, 9, 10, 11, 12, 13, 14, 15; A, D, H, I, K.*

COLLEGE OF OUR LADY OF THE ELMS, Springfield St., Chicopee, Mass. 01013, *4, 6, 7, 12, 14, 15, 17; C, D, E, F.*

COLLEGE OF THE HOLY CROSS, Worcester, Mass. 01610, *3, 4, 6, 7, 12, 14, 15; A, D, E, K.*

DEAN JR. COLLEGE, Franklin, Mass. 02038, *3, 7, 12, 14, 15; A, D, E, F, H, I, K.*

EMMANUEL COLLEGE, 400 The Fenway, Boston, Mass. 02115, *3, 4, 6, 7, 9, 12, 13, 15, 17; C, D, F.*

ENDICOTT COLLEGE, Hale St., Beverly, Mass. 01915, *1, 3, 6, 7, 9, 11, 12, 13, 17; B, D, E, F, K.*

FRAMINGHAM STATE COLLEGE, Framingham, Mass. 01701, *2, 3, 4, 6, 10, 11, 12, 13; A, D, K.*

GARLAND JR. COLLEGE, 409 Commonwealth Ave., Boston, Mass. 02215, *2, 3, 7, 8, 10, 11, 12, 18, 21.*

GREENFIELD COMMUNITY COLLEGE, Greenfield, Mass. 01301, *1, 3, 7, 9, 12, 17; A, D, F, H, I, K.*

HARVARD UNIVERSITY, Cambridge, Mass. 02138, *2, 7, 12, 13; B, D, E, H, I, K.*

HOLYOKE ACADEMY OF FINE ART, 225 High St., Holyoke, Mass. 01040, *1, 3, 5, 6, 7, 8, 9, 10, 11, 12; A.*

HOLYOKE COMMUNITY COLLEGE, 165 Sargent St., Holyoke, Mass. 01040, *4, 7, 12, 14, 17; D, E, I.*

LASELL JR. COLLEGE, Woodland Ave., Auburndale, Mass. 02166, *1, 3, 6, 7, 11, 12, 17; C, D, E, F, K.*

LEICESTER JR. COLLEGE, Leicester, Mass. 01524, *7; D, F.*

MASSACHUSETTS COLLEGE OF ART, 364 Brooklin Ave., Boston, Mass. 02215, *1, 2, 3, 4, 6, 7, 9, 10, 12, 13, 14, 15, 17; A, D, F, H, I.*

MASSACHUSETTS INSTITUTE OF TECHNOLOGY, Cambridge, Mass. 02138, *2.*

MODERN SCHOOL OF FASHION DESIGN, 323 Newbury St., Boston, Mass. 02115, *3; A, D, E, F, H, I, K.*

MORRIS DAVIDSON SUMMER SCHOOL OF MODERN PAINTING, Miller Hill Rd., Provincetown, Mass. 02657, *4, 12; A.*

MT. HOLYOKE COLLEGE, ART DEPT., South Hadley, Mass. 01075, *3, 7, 12, 14, 15, 17; C, D, E, F, K.*

MT. IDA JR. COLLEGE, 777 Dedham St., Newton Center, Mass. 02159, *1, 3, 7, 12, 15; C, F.*

NEW ENGLAND SCHOOL OF ART, 28 Newbury St., Boston, Mass. 02116, *1, 3, 7, 9, 11, 12, 17; A, E, F, H.*

NEWTON COLLEGE OF THE SACRED HEART, 885 Centre St., Newton, Mass. 02159, *2, 4, 6, 7, 12, 13, 14, 15; C, D, E.*

NORTHEASTERN UNIVERSITY, 360 Huntington Ave., Boston, Mass. 02115, *2, 3; A, D, G, H, I.*

PINE MANOR JR. COLLEGE, 400 Heath St., Chestnut Hill, Mass. 02167, *3, 7, 12, 13, 14, 15; C, D, E, G.*

PROVINCETOWN WORKSHOP, 492 Commercial St., Provincetown, Mass. 02657, *7, 12, 17; E, I.*

QUINCY JR. COLLEGE, 34 Coddington St., Quincy, Mass. 02169, *3; D.*

QUINSIGAMOND COMMUNITY COLLEGE, 241 Belmont St., Worcester, Mass. 01605, *3, 7; A, D, F, H, I.*

REGIS COLLEGE, 235 Wellesley St., Weston, Mass. 02193, *3, 4, 7, 12, 13, 14, 15, 17; C, D, I, K.*

SCHOOL OF FASHION DESIGN, 136 Newbury St., Boston, Mass. 02116, *3, 6, 7, 8, 9, 16; E, I.*

SCHOOL OF PRACTICAL ART, 718 Beacon St., Boston, Mass. 02215, *1, 3, 5, 7, 9, 12, 13, 14, 15, 17; A, E, F, H, I, K.*

SCHOOL OF THE MUSEUM OF FINE ARTS, 230 The Fenway, Boston, Mass. 02115, *1, 3, 4, 6, 7, 9, 11, 12, 13, 14, 15, 17; A, D, E, G, H.*

SIMON'S ROCK EARLY COLLEGE, Alford Rd., Barrington, Mass. 01230, *3, 6, 7, 12, 13, 14; A, K.*

SMITH COLLEGE, Northampton, Mass. 01060, *2, 3, 4, 7, 12, 14, 15; C, D, E, F, K.*

SOUTHEASTERN MASSACHUSETTS UNIVERSITY, North Dartmouth, Mass. 02747, *1, 3, 7, 9, 12, 13, 14, 16; A, D, E, F, H, I.*

SPRINGFIELD COLLEGE, 263 Alden St., Springfield, Mass. 01109, *3, 6, 7, 12, 14, 15; A, G, H, I, K.*

STATE COLLEGE AT LOWELL, Broadway, Lowell, Mass. 01844, *3, 6, 7, 12, 14, 15, 16, 17; A, D, F, H, I, K.*

SWAIN SCHOOL OF DESIGN, 19 Hawthorne St., New Bedford, Mass. 02740, *1, 3, 7, 9, 12, 14; A, E, F.*

TRURO CENTER FOR THE ARTS AT CASTLE HILL, INC. (summer school), Castle Rd., Truro, Mass. 02666, *6, 7, 12, 14, 15.*

TUFTS UNIVERSITY, Medford, Mass. 02155, *1, 2, 3, 4, 5, 6, 7, 9, 10, 11, 12, 13, 14, 15, 16, 17; A, D, E, F, H, I, K.*

UNIVERSITY OF MASSACHUSETTS, Amherst, Mass. 01002, *3, 4, 7, 12, 14, 15, 17; A, D, E, F, I.*

VESPER GEORGE SCHOOL OF ART, 44 St. Botolph St., Boston, Mass. 02116, *1, 3, 7, 9, 11, 12, 17; A, E, F, H, I.*

WELLESLEY COLLEGE ART DEPT., Wellesley, Mass. 02181, *3, 4, 5, 9, 10, 12; C, I.*

WESTFIELD STATE COLLEGE, Westfield, Mass. 01085, *4, 6, 7, 12, 14, 15, 17; D, I.*

WHEATON COLLEGE, Norton, Mass. 02766, *3, 7, 12, 14, 17; C, D, F, K.*

WHEELOCK COLLEGE, 200 The Riverway, Boston, Mass. 02215, *3, 4, 6, 7, 12, 13, 14; D, G, I.*

WILLIAMS COLLEGE ART DEPT., Williamstown, Mass. 01267, *1, 3, 9, 10, 12, 14; B, I.*

WM. SCHULTZ ART SCHOOL, 482 Pittsfield-Lenox Rd. (Rt. 7), Lenox, Mass. 01201, *7, 12; A, F, H, I, K.*

WORCESTER ART MUSEUM SCHOOL, Worcester, Mass. 01608, *4, 7, 10, 12, 14, 15.*

Michigan

ADRIAN COLLEGE, Adrian, Mich. 49221, *3, 4, 6, 7, 9, 12, 14, 15, 17; A, D, F, I, K.*

ALBION COLLEGE, DEPT. OF ART, Albion, Mich. 49224, *3, 6, 7, 12, 14, 15, 17; A, F.*

ALMA COLLEGE, Alma, Mich. 48801, *3, 4, 6, 7, 12, 14, 15, 17; A, D, E, G, K.*

ALPENA COMMUNITY COLLEGE, Johnson St., Alpena, Mich. 49707, *3, 4, 6, 7, 12, 14, 15; A, F, H, I, K.*

ANDREWS UNIVERSITY ART DEPT., Berrien Springs, Mich. 49104, *1, 3, 4, 6, 7, 9, 10, 12, 14, 15, 17; A, D, F, I.*

AQUINAS COLLEGE, 1607 Robinson Rd. S.E., Grand Rapids, Mich. 49506, *3, 4, 7, 12, 14, 15; A, D, F, H, I, K.*

ART SCHOOL OF CRAFTS GUILD, 380-168th Ave., Holland, Mich. 49423, *3, 6, 7, 12, 15, 21.*

ART SCHOOL OF THE SOCIETY OF ARTS & CRAFTS, 245 E. Kirby, Detroit, Mich. 48202, *1, 3, 6, 7, 9, 10, 11, 12, 13, 14, 15, 17; A, D, E, F, H, I.*

BIRMINGHAM-BLOOMFIELD ART ASSOCIATION, 1516 S. Cranbrook Rd., Birmingham, Mich. 48009, *1, 3, 6, 7, 8, 9, 12, 14, 15, 16; A.*

CALVIN COLLEGE, Grand Rapids, Mich. 49503, *3, 4, 7, 12, 14, 15, 17; A, D, E, F, H, I, K.*

CENTER FOR CREATIVE STUDIES—COLLEGE OF ART AND DESIGN, 245 E. Kirby St., Detroit, Mich. 48202, *1, 3, 4, 7, 8, 9, 10, 11, 12, 13, 14, 15, 16, 17; A, D, H, I, K.*

CENTRAL MICHIGAN UNIVERSITY, Mt. Pleasant, Mich. 48858, *3, 4, 6, 7, 12, 15, 16, 17; A, D, E, F, H, I, K.*

CHARLES STEWART MOTT COMMUNITY COLLEGE, 1401 E. Court St., Flint, Mich. 48503, *3, 4, 6, 7, 12, 15; A, D, H, I.*

CRANBROOK ACADEMY OF ART, 500 Lone Pine Rd., Bloomfield Hills, Mich. 48013, *2, 3, 7, 10, 11, 12, 14, 15, 16, 17; A, D, E, F, H, K.*

DELTA COLLEGE, University Center, Mich. 48710, *1, 2, 3, 4, 6, 7, 10, 12; A, G, H.*

DETROIT INSTITUTE OF ARTS, 5200 Woodward, Detroit, Mich. 48202, *3, 6, 7, 12, 15, 17; A.*

EASTERN MICHIGAN UNIVERSITY, Ypsilanti, Mich. 48197, *3, 4, 6, 7, 12, 14, 15, 17; A, D, E, F, H, I, K.*

FERRIS STATE COLLEGE, Big Rapids, Mich. 49307, *1, 2, 7, 9, 12, 13, 17; A, D, E, F, K.*

FLINT COMMUNITY JR. COLLEGE, 1401 E. Court St., Flint, Mich. 48503, *3, 4, 6, 7, 12, 15; A, E, F, I.*

FLINT INSTITUTE OF ARTS, De Waters Art Center, 1120 E. Kearsley St., Flint, Mich. 48503, *6, 7, 12, 15, 17.*

GENESEE COMMUNITY COLLEGE, 1401 E. Court, Flint, Mich. 48503, *4, 6, 7, 12, 15, 17; D, E, I.*

GOGEBIC COMMUNITY COLLEGE, Greenbush Ave., Ironwood, Mich. 49958, *4, 6, 7, 12, 14, 15, 17; I.*

GRAND RAPIDS JR. COLLEGE, 143 Bostwick N.E., Grand Rapids, Mich. 49502, *3, 4, 6, 7, 12, 14, 15; A, D, H, I.*

GRAND VALLEY STATE COLLEGE, College Landing, Allendale, Mich. 49401, *3, 4, 6; A, K.*

HENRY FORD COMMUNITY COLLEGE, 5101 Evergreen Rd., Dearborn, Mich. 48128, *1, 3, 4, 6, 7, 12, 14, 15, 17; A, D, F, H, I.*

HIGHLAND PARK COLLEGE, Glendale at Third, Highland Park, Mich. 48203, *3, 6, 7, 17.*

HILLSDALE COLLEGE, Hillsdale, Mich. 49242, *3, 4, 7, 11, 12, 15; D, E, I.*

HOPE COLLEGE, Holland, Mich. 49423, *3, 4, 6, 7, 12, 14, 15; A, D, E, F, I, K.*

JACKSON COMMUNITY COLLEGE, 51 Wildwood Ave., Jackson, Mich. 49201, *3, 4, 6, 7, 12, 17; A, E, F, H, I.*

KALAMAZOO COLLEGE, Academy St., Kalamazoo, Mich. 49001, *3, 4, 6, 7, 12, 14, 15; A, D, H, I, K.*

KALAMAZOO INSTITUTE OF ARTS, 314 S. Park St., Kalamazoo, Mich. 49006, *12, 13, 14, 15, 17; E.*

KELLOGG COMMUNITY COLLEGE, 450 N Ave., Battle Creek, Mich. 49016, *3, 4, 6, 7, 12, 14, 17; A, D, F, H, I.*

KENDALL SCHOOL OF DESIGN, 1110 College N.E., Grand Rapids, Mich. 49503, *1, 3, 7, 9, 11; A, F, I.*

LANSING COMMUNITY COLLEGE, 419 N. Capitol, Lansing, Mich. 48914, *1, 3, 7, 9, 12, 15, 17; D, H, I.*

MACOMB COUNTY COMMUNITY COLLEGE, 14500 Twelve Mile, Warren, Mich. 48093, *3, 7, 12, 15, 17; D, I.*

MADONNA COLLEGE, 36600 School Craft Rd., Livonia, Mich. 48150, *3, 4, 6, 7, 12, 14, 15, 17; D, F, H, I, K.*

MARYGROVE COLLEGE, 8425 W. McNichol Rd., Detroit, Mich. 48221, *1, 3, 4, 7, 9, 11, 12, 13, 14, 17; C, D, G, K.*

MERCY COLLEGE, 8200 W. Outer Dr., Detroit, Mich. 48219, *4, 6, 7, 15, 16; D.*

MICHIGAN STATE UNIVERSITY, Kresge Art Center, E. Lansing, Mich. 48823, *1, 3, 4, 6, 7, 10, 12, 14, 15; A, D, E, F, H, I, K.*

MUSKEGON COMMUNITY COLLEGE, 221 S. Quarterline Rd., Muskegon, Mich. 49442, *3, 4, 7, 12, 13, 14, 15, 17; D, E, I.*

NAZARETH COLLEGE, Nazareth P.O., Kalamazoo, Mich. 49704, *1, 3, 4, 6, 7, 11, 12, 13, 14, 15, 17; C, D, F, I, K.*

NORTH CENTRAL MICHIGAN COLLEGE, Petoskey, Mich. 49770, *3, 4, 7, 12, 17; D.*

NORTHERN MICHIGAN UNIVERSITY, Marquette, Mich. 49855, *1, 4, 6, 7, 9, 10, 11, 12, 13, 14, 15, 16, 17; A, D, E, F, I, K.*

NORTHWOOD INSTITUTE, Midland, Mich. 48640, *3, 7, 12, 15, 17; D, E, G.*

OAKLAND UNIVERSITY, Rochester, Mich. 48008, *7, 12, 14, 15, 17; D.*

OLIVET COLLEGE, Olivet, Mich. 49076, *3, 7, 12, 14, 15; A, D, E, F, I, K.*

PONTIAC CREATIVE ARTS CENTER, 47 Williams St., Pontiac, Mich. 48053, *3, 6, 7, 12, 13, 15; A, H.*

PORT HURON JR. COLLEGE, 323 Erie St., Port Huron, Mich. 48060, *1, 3, 7, 12, 14, 15, 17; A, E, F, H, I, K.*

SAGINAW VALLEY STATE COLLEGE, University Center, Mich. 48710, *1, 3, 4, 6, 7, 9, 12, 13, 15; A, D, H, I, K.*

ST. CLAIR COUNTY COMMUNITY COLLEGE, 323 Erie St., Port Huron, Mich. 48060, *1, 7, 12, 15, 17; D, E, I.*

SCHOOLCRAFT COLLEGE, Haggerty Rd., Livonia, Mich. 48154, *3, 4, 6, 7, 12, 14, 15, 17; A, D, E, G, H, I.*

SIENA HEIGHTS COLLEGE, Siena Heights Dr., Adrian, Mich. 49221, *4, 7, 12, 13, 14, 15, 16, 17; D, E.*

SUOMI COLLEGE, Hancock, Mich. 49930, *3, 6, 7, 9, 12, 17; A, D, E, F.*

UNIVERSITY OF DETROIT, McNichols Rd. at Livernois, Detroit, Mich. 48221, *1, 2, 3, 7, 9, 12, 14, 15, 17; A, D, G, H, I, K.*

UNIVERSITY OF MICHIGAN, Ann Arbor, Mich. 48104, *1, 2, 3, 4, 7, 9, 10, 11, 12, 13, 14, 15, 17; A, D, E, F, G, I, K.*

WAYNE STATE UNIVERSITY, 450 W. Kirby, Detroit, Mich. 48202, *3, 6, 7, 10, 11, 12, 15; D, H.*

WESTERN MICHIGAN UNIVERSITY, Kalamazoo, Mich. 49001, *1, 4, 6, 7, 12, 14, 15, 16, 17; A, D, F, I, K.*

Minnesota

ART INSTRUCTION SCHOOLS, 500 S. 4th St., Minneapolis, Minn. 55415, *1, 5, 12.*

AUGSBURG COLLEGE, 707 21 Ave. S., Minneapolis, Minn. 55404, *1, 3, 4, 7, 12, 13, 14, 15; D, H.*

BEMIDJI STATE UNIVERSITY, Bemidji, Minn. 56601, *3, 4, 6, 7, 12, 13, 14, 15, 16, 17; A, D, F, H, I, K.*

BETHANY LUTHERAN COLLEGE, 734 March St., Mankato, Minn. 56001, *3, 6, 7, 10, 11, 12; D, K.*

CARLETON COLLEGE, Northfield, Minn. 55057, *2, 3, 4, 6, 7, 12, 14, 15, 17; A, D, E, G, K.*

COLLEGE OF ST. BENEDICT, St. Joseph, Minn. 56374, *1, 3, 4, 7, 12, 13, 14, 15; A, D, E, F, H.*

COLLEGE OF ST. CATHERINE, 2004 Randolph Ave., St. Paul, Minn. 55105, *3, 4, 6, 7, 12, 13, 14, 15; A, D, E, I.*

COLLEGE OF ST. SCHOLASTICA, Kenwood Ave., Duluth, Minn. 55811, *3, 4, 6, 7, 12, 14, 15; C, D, F, I, K.*

COLLEGE OF ST. TERESA, Winona, Minn. 55987, *3, 4, 6, 7, 12, 14, 15; C, F, I.*

CONCORDIA COLLEGE, 820 So. Seventh Street, Moorhead, Minn. 56560, *3, 6, 7, 12, 15, 18, 21.*

CORBETT COLLEGE, Summit Ave., Crookston, Minn. 56716, *3, 6, 7, 12, 17; A, F, H, K.*

ELY JR. COLLEGE, Ely, Minn. 55731, *3, 6, 7, 12, 15, 18.*

GUSTAVUS ADOLPHUS COLLEGE, ART DEPT., St. Peter, Minn. 56082, *1, 3, 4, 6, 7, 12, 13, 14, 15, 17; A, D, E, F, I, K.*

HAMLINE UNIVERSITY, Taylor & Snelling, St. Paul, Minn. 55101, *3, 4, 7, 12, 13, 14, 15; D, H.*

HIBBING STATE JR. COLLEGE, Hibbing, Minn. 55746, *3, 7; E, H, I.*

ITASCA COMMUNITY COLLEGE, Grand Rapids, Minn. 55744, *7, 12, 17; D, H.*

LUTHERAN BRETHREN SCHOOLS, W. Vernon Ave., Fergus Falls, Minn. 56537, *1, 7, 9, 12, 17.*

MAC ALESTER COLLEGE, 1600 Grand Ave., St. Paul, Minn. 55101, *3, 4, 7, 12, 14, 15; D.*

MANKATO STATE UNIVERSITY, Mankato, Minn. 56001, *3, 4, 6, 7, 12, 14, 15, 17; A, D, E, F, H, I, K.*

MINNEAPOLIS COLLEGE OF ART AND DESIGN, 200 E. 25th St., Minneapolis, Minn. 55405, *3, 4, 6, 7, 12, 14, 15, 17; A, D, E, F, H, I, K.*

MINNESOTA MUSEUM ART SCHOOL, 30 E. 10 St., St. Paul, Minn. 55102, *1, 5, 6, 7, 9, 10, 12, 13, 14, 15, 16, 17; E, G, I, J.*

MINNETONKA CENTER OF ARTS & EDUCATION, Box 158, Crystal Bay, Minn. 55323, *7, 12, 15, 17; A, G, H.*

MOORHEAD STATE UNIVERSITY, Moorhead, Minn. 56560, *1, 3, 4, 7, 9, 12, 13, 14, 15, 17; D, G, I.*

NORTH HENNEPIN COMMUNITY COLLEGE, 7411 85th Ave. N., Minneapolis, Minn. 55445, *1, 2, 3, 6, 7, 8, 9, 10, 11, 12, 13, 14; A, D, E, H, I.*

ST. CLOUD STATE UNIVERSITY, St. Cloud, Minn. 56301, *1, 3, 4, 6, 7, 8, 9, 10, 11, 12, 13, 14, 15, 16; A, D, E, H, I.*

ST. JOHN'S UNIVERSITY, Collegeville, Minn. 56321, *1, 2, 3, 7, 12, 15; B, D, F.*

ST. MARY'S JR. COLLEGE, 2600 S. 6 St., Minneapolis, Minn. 55406, *1, 3, 6, 7, 9, 12, 14, 17; A, G.*

ST. OLAF COLLEGE, Northfield, Minn. 55057, *2, 3, 4, 6, 7, 12, 14, 15; D.*

SCHOOLS OF THE ASSOCIATED ARTS, 344 Summit Ave., St. Paul, Minn. 55102, *1, 3, 4, 6, 7, 9, 10, 11, 12, 13, 14, 15, 16; A, F, I.*

UNIVERSITY OF MINNESOTA, DULUTH, Duluth, Minn. 55812, *3, 4, 6, 7, 12, 14, 15, 17; A, D, E, G, H, I, K.*

UNIVERSITY OF MINNESOTA, MINNEAPOLIS, Studio Arts Dept., 208 West Bank Art Bldg., Minneapolis, Minn. 55455, *2, 7, 12, 14, 15, 19; D, E, H, I.*

UNIVERSITY OF MINNESOTA, MORRIS, Morris, Minn. 56267, *3, 4, 6, 7, 12, 13, 14, 15; A, D, E, H, K.*

UNIVERSITY OF MINNESOTA, ST. PAUL, St. Paul, Minn. 55108, *3, 4, 6, 7, 8, 9, 10, 11, 12, 13, 14, 15, 16; A, D, E, I, K.*

VERMILLION COMMUNITY COLLEGE, 1900 E. Camp, Ely, Minn. 55731, *1, 3, 7, 14, 15; D, H, I.*

WILLMAR STATE COMMUNITY COLLEGE, Willmar, Minn. 56201, *3, 4, 7, 12; A, D, G, K.*

WINONA STATE COLLEGE, Winona, Minn. 55987, *3, 4, 6, 7, 9, 10, 11, 12; A, D, I.*

WORTHINGTON STATE JR. COLLEGE, Worthington, Minn. 56187, *3, 4, 7, 11, 12, 13, 14, 15, 17; D, E, H, I.*

Mississippi

ALCORN STATE UNIVERSITY, Alcorn College Rural Sta., Lorman, Miss. 39096, *4, 6, 7, 12, 15; D, E.*

BELHAVEN COLLEGE, Peachtree St., Jacobson, Miss. 39202, *1, 3, 4, 6, 7, 11, 12, 14, 17; A, D, F, I, K.*

CLARKE MEMORIAL COLLEGE, Newton, Miss. 39345, *3, 7; D, E, I.*

DELTA STATE COLLEGE, Cleveland, Miss. 38732, *3, 4, 6, 7, 9, 11, 12, 14; A, D, E, F, I, K.*

EAST CENTRAL JR. COLLEGE, Decatur, Miss. 39327, *3, 4, 6, 7, 15, 16; A, D, F, K.*

EAST MISSISSIPPI JR. COLLEGE, Scoaba, Miss. 39358, *1, 4, 6, 7, 12, 14, 15, 17; D, E, F.*

GULF PARK COLLEGE, Long Beach, Miss. 39560, *1, 3, 6, 7, 9, 11, 12, 17; C, D, E, F, K.*

HINDS JUNIOR COLLEGE, Raymond, Miss. 39154, *1, 6, 7, 9, 10, 11, 12; A, D, E, H, I, K.*

HOLMES JR. COLLEGE, Goodman, Miss. 39079, *3, 7, 12, 14; D, F.*

JACKSON STATE COLLEGE, Lynch at Dalton St., Jackson, Miss. 39203, *1, 3, 4, 6, 7, 11, 12, 14, 16; A, D, E, F, I.*

JONES COUNTY COLLEGE, Ellisville, Miss. 39437, *1, 2, 3, 4, 6, 7, 9, 10, 11, 12, 14; A, D, I, K.*

MERIDIAN JR. COLLEGE, Meridian, Miss. 39301, *1, 4, 7, 9, 10, 12, 14, 15, 17; A, D, F, H, I.*

MILLSAPS COLLEGE, Jackson, Miss. 39210, *3, 4, 7, 12, 14, 17.*

MISSISSIPPI COLLEGE, Clinton, Miss. 39056, *1, 3, 4, 7, 12, 15, 17; A, D, F, H, I, K.*

MISSISSIPPI DELTA JR. COLLEGE, Moorhead, Miss. 38761, *3, 7, 12, 14, 17; D, I.*

MISSISSIPPI UNIVERSITY FOR WOMEN, Columbus, Miss. 39701, *1, 3, 4, 6, 7, 8, 9, 11, 12, 13, 15, 16, 17; C, D, E, I.*

MISSISSIPPI VALLEY STATE COLLEGE, Itta Bena, Miss. 38941, *3, 4, 6, 7, 12, 13; A, D, E, F, K.*

NORTHEAST MISSISSIPPI JR. COLLEGE, Cunningham Blvd., Booneville, Miss. 38829, *3, 6, 7, 12; A, F, K.*

NORTHWEST MISSISSIPPI JR. COLLEGE, Seratobia, Miss. 38668, *1, 7, 9, 12, 17; D, E, I.*

TOUGALOO COLLEGE, Tougaloo, Miss. 39174, *3, 6, 7, 12; A, D.*

UNIVERSITY OF MISSISSIPPI, University, Miss. 38677, *1, 3, 4, 7, 11, 12, 14, 15; A, D, F, H, I.*

UNIVERSITY OF SOUTHERN MISSISSIPPI, Hattiesburg, Miss. 39401, *1, 3, 4, 6, 7, 9, 12, 15, 17; D, H.*

WILLIAM CAREY COLLEGE, Tuscan Ave., Hattiesburg, Miss. 39401, *3, 4, 6, 7, 12, 17; D, E, I.*

Missouri

AVILA COLLEGE, 11901 Wornall Rd., Kansas City, Mo. 64145, *3, 4, 6, 7, 9, 12, 15, 17; C, D, E, F, H, I, K.*

CENTRAL METHODIST COLLEGE, Fayette, Mo. 65248, *4, 7, 12, 14, 15, 17; D.*

CENTRAL MISSOURI UNIVERSITY, Warrensburg, Mo. 64093, *1, 3, 4, 7, 9, 11, 12, 14, 15, 17; A, D, E, F, I, K.*

COLLEGE OF ST. TERESA, 5600 Main Street, Kansas City, Mo. 64118, *3, 7, 12, 15.*

COLLEGE OF THE SCHOOL OF THE OZARKS, Point Lookout, Mo. 65726, *1, 3, 7, 9, 12, 14, 15, 17; A, D, E, G, K.*

COLUMBIA COLLEGE, Columbia, Mo. 65201, *1, 6, 7, 12, 13, 14, 15, 17; D, E.*

COTTEY COLLEGE, Nevada, Mo. 64772, *1, 3, 7, 9, 12, 14, 15, 17; A, D, E, G, K.*

CROWDER COLLEGE, Neosho, Mo. 64850, *3, 7, 12, 13; D, E, F, I.*

CULVER-STOCKTON COLLEGE, Canton, Mo. 63435, *4, 6, 7, 12, 13, 14, 15, 17; D.*

DRURY COLLEGE, Springfield, Mo. 65802, *3, 4, 7, 12, 14, 15, 17; D, I.*

EAST CENTRAL JUNIOR COLLEGE, PO Box 529, Union, Mo. 63084, *3, 4, 6, 7, 9, 10, 11, 12, 14, 15; A, D, E, H, I.*

FLORISSANT VALLEY COMMUNITY COLLEGE, 3400 Pershall Rd., St. Louis, Mo. 63135, *1, 3, 7, 9, 12, 13, 14, 15; D, I.*

FONTBONNE COLLEGE, 6800 Wydown Blvd., St. Louis, Mo. 63105, *3, 4, 6, 7, 12, 13, 14, 15, 16, 17; D, E, G, I.*

HANNIBAL-LA GRANGE COLLEGE, College Heights, Hannibal, Mo. 63401, *1, 3, 4, 6, 7, 9, 12, 14, 15, 17; D, F, I, K.*

KANSAS CITY ART INSTITUTE, 4415 Warwick Blvd., Kansas City, Mo. 64111, *1, 3, 6, 7, 9, 10, 11, 12, 13, 15, 17; A, D, E, F, H, I, K.*

LINCOLN UNIVERSITY, Lafayette at Dunklin St., Jefferson City, Mo. 65101, *4, 6, 7, 12, 15, 17; D, E.*

LINDENWOOD COLLEGE, St. Charles, Mo. 63033, *3, 7, 12, 14, 15; C, E, F, I, K.*

MARYVILLE COLLEGE OF THE SACRED HEART, 13550 Conway Rd., St. Louis, Mo. 63141, *3, 7, 11, 12, 14, 15; C, D, E, F, I, K.*

MERAMAC COMMUNITY COLLEGE, 959 S. Geyer Rd., Kirkwood, Mo. 63122, *1, 3, 7, 9, 12, 14, 15; A, D, E, F, H, I.*

MINERAL AREA COLLEGE, 116 College Ave., Flat River, Mo., 63601, *3, 6, 7, 15, 17; A, F, H, I.*

MISSOURI SOUTHERN STATE COLLEGE, Newman & Duquesne Rds., Joplin, Mo. 64801, *3, 4, 6, 7, 9, 11, 12, 14, 15; A, D, E, H, I, K.*

MISSOURI WESTERN COLLEGE, 4525 Downs Dr., St. Joseph, Mo. 64506, *3, 4, 7, 12, 14, 15, 17; D, E, I.*

MOBERLY JR. COLLEGE, College & Rollins, Moberly, Mo. 65270, *7, 12, 17; I.*

NORTHEAST MISSOURI STATE UNIVERSITY, Kirksville, Mo. 63501, *1, 3, 4, 6, 7, 12, 14, 17; A, D, F, I, K.*

NORTHWEST MISSOURI STATE UNIVERSITY, Maryville, Mo. 64468, *3, 4, 7, 9, 12, 14, 15, 17; A, D, E, F, I, K.*

NOTRE DAME COLLEGE, 320 E. Rioa Ave., St. Louis, Mo. 63125, *3, 4, 7, 12, 14, 15, 17; C, D, G, I.*

SOUTHEAST MISSOURI STATE UNIVERSITY, Normal Ave., Cape Girardeau, Mo. 63701, *1, 3, 4, 5, 6, 7, 9, 12, 14, 15, 16, 17; A, D, E, F, H, I, K.*

SOUTHWEST BAPTIST COLLEGE, Bolivar, Mo. 65613, *3, 7, 12; A, F, I.*

SOUTHWEST MISSOURI STATE UNIVERSITY, 901 S. National, Springfield, Mo. 65802, *1, 3, 4, 7, 9, 12, 13, 14, 15, 17; D, E, I.*

TARKIO COLLEGE, Tarkio, Mo. 64491, *3, 4, 7, 12, 14, 15, 17; A, G.*

UNIVERSITY OF MISSOURI AT COLUMBIA, 126 Fine Arts Center, Columbia, Mo. 65201, *3, 4, 6, 7, 14, 15, 17; A, D, F, I, K.*

UNIVERSITY OF MISSOURI AT KANSAS CITY, 5100 Rockhill Rd., Kansas City, Mo. 64110, *1, 3, 4, 7, 12, 14, 17; A, D, E, F, H, I, K.*

WASHINGTON UNIVERSITY, School of Fine Arts, St. Louis, Mo. 63130, *1, 3, 4, 6, 7, 9, 12, 14, 15, 17; A, D, E, F, H, I, K.*

WEBSTER COLLEGE, 470 E. Lockwood, St. Louis, Mo. 63119, *3, 4, 6, 7, 12, 13, 14, 15; A, D, E, F, H, I, K.*

WILLIAM JEWELL COLLEGE, Liberty, Mo. 64068, *7, 12, 15, 17; A, F, K.*

WILLIAM WOOD COLLEGE, Westminster College, Fulton, Mo. 65251, *3, 4, 7, 11, 12, 14, 15, 17; D, E, F.*

Montana

CARROLL COLLEGE, Helena, Mont. 59601, *3, 4, 7, 12, 13, 14, 15, 17; A, D, F, I.*

COLLEGE OF GREAT FALLS, 1301 20th St. S., Great Falls, Mont. 59405, *4, 6, 7, 12, 13, 14, 15, 16; A, D, E, H, I.*

EASTERN MONTANA COLLEGE, Billings, Mont. 59101, *3, 4, 6, 7, 12, 14, 15, 17; D, H, I.*

MILES COMMUNITY COLLEGE, 2715 Dickenson St., Miles City, Mont. 59301, *3, 4, 6, 7, 12, 17; D, H, I.*

MONTANA STATE UNIVERSITY, Bozeman, Mont. 59715, *1, 4, 6, 7, 10, 11, 12, 13, 14, 15, 17; A, D, G, I, K.*

NORTHERN MONTANA COLLEGE, Havre, Mont. 59501, *1, 3, 4, 6, 7, 12, 14, 15, 17; A, D, E, F, H, I.*

ROCKY MT. COLLEGE, 1511 Poly Dr., Billings, Mont. 59102, *1, 3, 4, 7, 12, 14, 15, 17; A, D, E, F, K.*

UNIVERSITY OF MONTANA, Art Dept., Missoula, Mont. 59801, *3, 4, 6, 7, 12, 13, 14, 15, 17; A, D, E, I, K.*

WESTERN MONTANA COLLEGE, Dillon, Mont. 59725, *3, 4, 6, 7, 12, 13, 14, 15, 17; D, H.*

Nebraska

CHADRON STATE COLLEGE, Chadron, Nebr. 69337, *4, 6, 7, 12, 14, 15, 17; D, I.*

COLLEGE OF ST. MARY, 72 & Mercy Rd., Omaha, Nebr. 68124, *3, 4, 7, 11, 12, 13, 15; C, D, E, F, H, I, K.*

CONCORDIA TEACHERS' COLLEGE, 800 N. Columbia, Seward, Nebr. 68434, *4, 6, 7, 12, 14, 15; D, I.*

CREIGHTON UNIVERSITY, Fine Art Bldg., 304 N. 14th St., Omaha, Nebr. 68102, *1, 3, 4, 7, 12, 13, 14, 15; A, F, H, I, K.*

DANA COLLEGE, College Hill, Blair, Nebr. 68008, *3, 4, 6, 7, 12, 13, 14, 15, 17; D, E, I.*

DOANE COLLEGE, Crete, Nebr. 68333, *3, 4, 7, 12, 15, 17; A, D, E, F, I, K.*

FAIRBURY JR. COLLEGE, Fairbury, Nebr. 68352, *4; H.*

HASTINGS COLLEGE, 7 & Turner, Hastings, Nebr. 68901, *3, 4, 6, 7, 12, 14, 15, 17; A, D, E, F, I, K.*

JOHN F. KENNEDY COLLEGE, Wahoo, Nebr. 68066, *3, 4, 7, 12, 15; D, E, H.*

KEARNEY STATE COLLEGE, Kearney, Nebr. 68847, *3, 4, 7, 12, 14, 15, 17; D, I.*

NEBRASKA WESLEYAN UNIVERSITY, 50 & St. Paul Sts., Lincoln, Nebr. 68504, *3, 4, 7, 12, 14, 15, 17; A, D, F, I, K.*

NEBRASKA WESTERN COLLEGE, Scottsbluff, Nebr. 69361, *4, 7, 17; D, F, I.*

NORTHEASTERN NEBRASKA COLLEGE, 510 Philip, Norfolk, Nebr. 68701, *3, 6, 12, 17; D.*

UNION COLLEGE, 3800 S. 48, Lincoln, Nebr. 68506, *1, 3, 4, 6, 7, 12, 17; A, D, F, I.*

UNIVERSITY OF NEBRASKA, Lincoln, Nebr. 68508, *1, 4, 7, 10, 11, 12, 14, 15; D, I, K.*

UNIVERSITY OF NEBRASKA AT OMAHA, Box 688, Downtown Sta., Omaha, Nebr. 68101, *3, 4, 6, 7, 9, 12, 14, 15, 17; A, D, E, F, H, I.*

WAYNE STATE COLLEGE, Wayne, Nebr. 68787, *4, 6, 7, 12, 14, 15; D, E, G, I.*

YORK COLLEGE, York, Nebr. 68467, *4, 7, 12; A, D, E, F, K.*

Nevada

NEVADA SOUTHERN UNIVERSITY, 4504 Maryland Pkwy., Las Vegas, Nev. 89109, *1, 3, 4, 6, 7, 12, 13, 14, 15, 17; A, D, E, F, H, I, K.*

UNIVERSITY OF NEVADA, Reno, Nev. 89507, *4, 7, 12, 13, 14, 15, 16, 17; D, I.*

New Hampshire

BELKNAP COLLEGE, Center Harbor, N.H. 03226, *3, 7, 12, 17; D, I.*

COLBY SAWYER COLLEGE, New London, N.H. 03257, *3, 7, 12, 13, 14, 15; D, F.*

DARTMOUTH COLLEGE, Box 423, Hanover, N.H. 03755, *2, 3, 7, 12, 14, 15, 17; B, D, E, G, I, K.*

FRANCONIA COLLEGE, Franconia, N.H. 03580, *3, 7, 9, 12, 14, 15; A, D, F, G, H, I, K.*

FRANKLIN PIERCE COLLEGE, Rindge, N.H. 03461, *3, 7, 12, 14; A, D, E, F, G, I, K.*

LEAGUE OF N. H. ARTS & CRAFTS, 205 N. Main St., Concord, N.H. 03301, *6; A, H.*

MANCHESTER INSTITUTE OF ART AND SCIENCES, 148 Concord St., Manchester, N.H. 03104.

NATHANIEL HAWTHORNE COLLEGE, Fine Arts Dept., Antrim, N.H. 03440, *3, 7, 12, 15, 17; A, D, F, K.*

NOTRE DAME COLLEGE, 2321 Elm St., Manchester, N.H. 03104, *1, 3, 4, 6, 7, 12, 14, 15, 17; C, D, F, K.*

PLYMOUTH STATE COLLEGE OF THE UNIVERSITY OF NEW HAMPSHIRE, Plymouth, N.H. 03264, *3, 4, 6, 7, 9, 12, 14, 15, 17; A, D, E, F, H, I, K.*

PRINCETON UNIVERSITY DEPT. OF ART, Princeton, N.H., *3, 4, 9, 12; A, B, I.*

RIVIER COLLEGE, Nashua, N.H. 03060, *1, 3, 4, 6, 7, 8, 9, 10, 11, 12, 13, 14, 15, 16; C* (limited number of men), *D, E, H, I, K.*

ST. ANSELM'S COLLEGE, Manchester, N.H. 03102, *3, 7, 12, 13; A, D, H, I, K.*

SHARON ARTS CENTER, RFD 2, Box 361, Peterborough, N.H. 03458, *6, 7, 8, 9, 12, 16; A, H.*

UNIVERSITY OF NEW HAMPSHIRE, PAUL ARTS CENTER, Durham, N.H. 03824, *3, 4, 6, 7, 9, 12, 13, 14, 15, 17; A, D, E, F, H, I, K.*

New Jersey

BLOOMFIELD COLLEGE, Bloomfield, N.J. 07003, *3; D, E, I.*

CALDWELL COLLEGE, Caldwell, N.J. 07006, *1, 3, 4, 6, 7, 12, 14, 15, 17; C, D, E, F, I, K.*

CAPE MAY COUNTY ART CENTER, 1050 Washington St., Cape May, N.J. 08204, *6, 12, 14, 15, 17; A, E, I.*

CENTENARY COLLEGE FOR WOMEN, Hackettstown, N.J. 07840, *1, 6, 7, 12, 15, 17; C, D, K.*

COLLEGE OF ST. ELIZABETH, Convent Station, N.J. 07961, *3, 4, 7, 11, 12, 14, 15, 17; C, D, F, I, K.*

COUNTY COLLEGE OF MORRIS, Rt. 10, Center Grove Rd., Dover, N.J. 07801, *1, 3, 6, 7, 12, 13, 15; A, D, H.*

DREW UNIVERSITY, Madison, N.J. 07940, *3, 7, 12, 14, 15, 17; A, D, F, K.*

DU CRET SCHOOL OF THE ARTS, 559 Rt. 22, North Plainfield, N.J. 07060, *1, 3, 7, 9, 11, 12, 13, 15, 16, 17; E, I.*

ENGLEWOOD CLIFFS COLLEGE, Hudson Terr., Englewood Cliffs, N.J. 07632, *4, 6, 7, 11, 17; C, H, I.*

FAIRLEIGH DICKINSON UNIVERSITY, Rutherford, N.J., *3, 12, 15; A, F, H, I.*

GEORGIAN COURT COLLEGE, Lakewood Ave., Lakewood, N.J. 08701, *1, 2, 3, 4, 6, 7, 12, 13, 14, 15, 16; A, D, E, I, K.*

GUILD OF CREATIVE ART, 620 Broad St., Shrewsbury, N.J. 07701, *7, 12, 17; F, H, I.*

GLASSBORO STATE COLLEGE, Glassboro, N.J. 08028, *3, 4, 6, 7, 12, 14, 15, 17; A, D, F, H, I.*

IMMACULATE CONCEPTION JR. COLLEGE, S. Main St., Lodi, N.J. 07644, *3, 4, 6, 7, 12, 17; C, H.*

JERSEY CITY STATE COLLEGE, 2039 Kennedy Blvd., Jersey City, N.J. 07305, *1, 3, 4, 6, 7, 12, 13, 14, 15, 16, 17; A, D, F, H, I, K.*

KEAN COLLEGE OF NEW JERSEY, Morris Ave., Union, N.J. 07083, *1, 3, 4, 6, 7, 9, 10, 11, 12, 13, 14, 15, 16; A, D, E, H, I, K.*

LONG BEACH ISLAND FOUNDATION OF ARTS, Box 87, Harvey Cedars, N.J. 08040, *6, 7, 12, 14, 15, 17; A, E, H, I.*

MERCER COUNTY COMMUNITY COLLEGE, 101 W. State St., Trenton, N.J. 07305, *1, 2, 4, 7, 12, 13, 14, 15, 17; D, I.*

MONMOUTH COLLEGE, Cedar & Norwood Ave., West Long Branch, N.J. 07764, *2, 3, 4, 6, 7, 12, 13, 14, 15; A, D, H, I.*

MONTCLAIR MUSEUM ART SCHOOL, 3 S. Mt. Ave., Montclair, N.J. 07042, *7, 12, 17; F, H.*

MONTCLAIR STATE COLLEGE, Upper Montclair, N.J. 07043, *4, 7, 8, 11, 12, 14, 15; D, E, I.*

NEWARK SCHOOL OF FINE & INDUSTRIAL ART, 550 High St., Newark, N.J. 07102, *1, 3, 7, 9, 10, 11, 12, 13, 14, 15, 16, 17; A, H.*

NEWARK STATE COLLEGE, Union, N.J. 07083, *1, 3, 4, 6, 7, 10, 12, 13, 14, 15, 16, 17; A, D, E, F, H, I, K.*

OCEAN CITY SCHOOL OF ART, 409 Wesley Ave., Ocean City, N.J. 08826, *3, 6, 7, 12, 13, 14, 17; A, H, I.*

PATERSON STATE COLLEGE, Pompton Road, Wayne, N.J. 07470, *4; D.*

PRINCETON UNIVERSITY, Princeton, N.J. 08540, *7, 12, 13, 14, 15; F.*

RAYLYN ART CENTER, 316 Main St., Lakewood, N.J. 08701, *7, 12, 15; F, I.*

RIDER COLLEGE, Lawrence Rd., Trenton, N.J. 08638, *3, 7, 12, 14, 15, 17; D, I.*

RIDGEWOOD SCHOOL OF ART, 74 Oak St., Ridgewood, N.J. 07450, *1, 3, 7, 9, 12, 14, 15; G, I.*

RUTGERS STATE UNIVERSITY OF NEW JERSEY, New Brunswick, N.J. 08903, *3, 4, 6, 7, 9, 10, 11, 13, 14; A, D, E, H, I.*

RUTGERS UNIVERSITY, Newark Campus, 21 James St., Newark, N.J. 07102, *3, 4, 7, 12, 14, 15; A, D, E, F, H, I.*

ST. PETER'S COLLEGE, Kennedy Blvd., Jersey City, N.J. 07306, *7, 12; D, I.*

SETON HALL UNIVERSITY, S. Orange Ave., South Orange, N.J. 07079, *7, 12; D, I.*

TRENTON STATE COLLEGE, Trenton, N.J. 08625, *3, 6, 7, 14, 15, 17; A, D, F, H, I, K.*

UPSALA COLLEGE, East Orange, N.J. 07017, *3, 7, 12, 14, 17; A, D, F, H, I, K.*

New Mexico

AMERICAN CLASSICAL COLLEGE, 2640 Sixth St. N.W., Albuquerque, N.M. 87107, *1, 3, 4, 7, 12, 15, 17; D, E.*

COLLEGE OF ARTESIA, Rickey & 13 St., Artesia, N.M. 88210, *1, 3, 4, 5, 9, 12, 14, 15, 17; D, E, I.*

EASTERN NEW MEXICO UNIVERSITY, Portales, N.M. 88130, *1, 3, 4, 6, 7, 8, 12, 14, 15, 17; D, I.*

EL PORTAL INSTITUTE FOR FINE ARTS & CRAFTS, 745 N. Alameda Ave., Las Cruces, N.M. 88001, *6, 7, 12, 14, 15, 17; A, H.*

NEW MEXICO HIGHLANDS UNIVERSITY, Las Vegas, N.M. 87701, *3, 4, 6, 7, 12, 14, 15, 17; A, D, E, F, I, K.*

NEW MEXICO STATE UNIVERSITY, Box 3F, Las Cruces, N.M. 88001, *3, 4, 6, 7, 12, 13, 14, 15, 17; D, E, I.*

NEW MEXICO STATE UNIVERSITY, University Pk., N.M. 88070, *3, 4, 6, 7, 12, 14, 15, 17; A, D, E, F, H, I, K.*

UNIVERSITY OF ALBUQUERQUE, St. Joseph Pl. N.W., Albuquerque, N.M. 87105, *1, 3, 4, 6, 7, 12, 14, 15, 17; A, D, E, F, I, K.*

UNIVERSITY OF NEW MEXICO, Albuquerque, N.M. 87106, *2, 3, 4, 6, 7, 12, 13, 14, 15, 17; A, D, E, F, H, I, K.*

ABBE INSTITUTE INC., 100 Fifth Ave., New York, N.Y. 10011, *1, 7, 12; F, I.*

ADELPHI SUFFOLK COLLEGE, Oakdale, N.Y. 11769, *2, 3, 4, 6, 7, 12, 14, 15, 17; A, D, E, F, H, I, K.*

ADELPHI UNIVERSITY, Garden City, L.I., N.Y. 11530, *1, 3, 4, 6, 7, 11, 12, 14, 15, 17; F, H, I.*

ALBERT PEIS SCHOOL OF ART INC., 2109 Broadway, New York, N.Y. 10023, *1, 2, 7, 8, 9, 10, 11, 12, 17; B, E, I.*

AMERICAN ART SCHOOL, 152 W. 56th St., New York, N.Y. 10019, *1, 7, 12; A, F, H, I.*

ART CAREER SCHOOL, 175 Fifth Ave., New York, N.Y. 10010, *1, 3, 7, 9, 11, 16, 17; A, F, H, I.*

ART STUDENTS LEAGUE OF NEW YORK, 215 W. 57 St., New York, N.Y. 10019, *5, 7, 9, 12, 14, 15, 16, 17; E, I.*

BALLARD SCHOOL, 610 Lexington Ave., New York, N.Y. 10022, *3, 7, 12, 13, 17; A, G, H, I.*

BARD COLLEGE, DIVISION OF ART, Annandale-on-Hudson, New York, N.Y. 12504, *1, 3, 4, 10, 12; B, C, I.*

BENNETT COLLEGE, Millbrook, N.Y. 12545, *7, 10, 12, 15; C, D, E, F.*

BRIARCLIFF COLLEGE, Briarcliff Manor, N.Y. 10510, *3, 4, 7, 12, 13, 14, 15, 17; C, D, E, F.*

BRONX COMMUNITY COLLEGE, 120 E. 184th St., Bronx, N.Y. 10468, *1, 3, 7, 17; A, D, F, H, I.*

BROOKLYN COLLEGE, Brooklyn, N.Y. 11210, *1, 2, 3, 4, 6, 7, 11, 12, 13, 14, 15, 16, 17; A, D, E, F, H, I.*

BROOKLYN MUSEUM ART SCHOOL, Eastern Pkwy., Brooklyn, N.Y. 11238, *6, 7, 12, 15, 17; A, E, F, H, I.*

C. W. POST COLLEGE OF L. I. UNIVERSITY, Northern Blvd., Greenvale, N.Y. 11548, *1, 2, 3, 4, 7, 12, 13, 14, 15, 17; A, D, E, F, H, I, K.*

CATON-ROSE INSTITUTE OF ART, 86 - 19 150 St., Jamaica, L.I., N.Y. 11435, *1, 5, 6, 7, 9, 11, 12, 13, 14, 15, 17; E, I.*

CAZENOVIA COLLEGE, Cazenovia, N.Y. 13035, *3, 7, 10, 12.*

CHAUTAUQUA ART CENTER, Chautauqua, N.Y. 14722, *3, 6, 7, 12, 13, 15, 17; A, E, I, K.*

CITY COLLEGE OF THE CITY OF NEW YORK, Convent Ave. at 138th St., New York, N.Y. 10031, *3, 4, 5, 7, 9, 10, 11, 16; A, B, I.*

COLGATE UNIVERSITY, Dana Creative Arts Center, Hamilton, N.Y. 13347, *3, 7, 12, 15; B, D, F, I, K.*

COLLEGE OF MT. SAINT VINCENT, W. 263rd St. & Riverdale Ave., Bronx, N.Y. 10471, *1, 3, 4, 7, 11, 12, 14, 15, 17; C, D, E, F, H, K.*

COLLEGE OF NEW ROCHELLE, DEPT. OF FINE ARTS, Castle Pl., New Rochelle, N.Y. 10805, *1, 3, 4, 6, 7, 9, 10, 11, 12, 13, 14, 15, 16, 17; C, D, E, F, K.*

COLLEGE OF SAINT ROSE, Western Ave., Albany, N.Y. 12203, *1, 3, 4, 6, 7, 8, 9, 10, 11, 12, 13, 14, 15; D, E, H, K.*

COLUMBIA COLLEGE, Teachers College, 525 W. 120th St., New York, N.Y. 10027, *1, 4, 6, 7, 9, 11, 12, 14, 15, 16, 17; A, D, E, F, I, K.*

COLUMBIA UNIVERSITY SCHOOL OF THE ARTS, 440 W. 110th St., New York, N.Y. 10025, *7, 12, 13, 14, 15; A, D, E, H, I.*

COOPER UNION SCHOOL OF ART & ARCHITECTURE, Cooper Square, New York, N.Y. 10003, *1, 2, 7, 12, 13, 14, 15; D, E, F, I.*

CORNELL UNIVERSITY, DEPT. OF ART, College of Architecture, Ithaca, N.Y. 14850, *1, 3, 4, 9, 10, 12, 16; A, B, C, I.*

CORNING COMMUNITY COLLEGE, Corning, N.Y. 14830, *3, 6, 7, 12, 15; D, I.*

CRAFT STUDENTS LEAGUE OF THE YWCA, 610 Lexington Ave., New York, N.Y. 10022, *6, 7, 9, 12, 15; A, H.*

CREATIVE ART CENTER, 1442 3rd Ave., New York, N.Y. 10028, *7, 12, 14, 15; A, G, H, I.*

DOMINICAN COLLEGE OF BLAUVELT, Western Hwy., Blauvelt, N.Y. 10913, *3, 6, 7, 12, 17; C, F, H, I.*

DONALD PIERCE SCHOOL OF PAINTING, 463 West St., New York, N.Y. 10014, *7, 12, 17; A.*

DOWLING COLLEGE, Idle Hour Blvd., Oakdale, N.Y. 11769, *1, 2, 3, 4, 6, 7, 9, 10, 11, 12, 13, 14, 15; A, D, H, I, K.*

DOWNTOWN YMCA ADULT EDUCATION SCHOOL, 45 W. Mohawk St., Buffalo, N.Y. 14202, *12; A, F, H, I.*

DUTCHESS COMMUNITY COLLEGE, Poughkeepsie, N.Y. 12601, *1, 2, 3, 5, 6, 7, 9, 11, 12, 13, 14, 15, 17; A, D, E, F, H, I.*

D'YOUVILLE COLLEGE, 320 Porter Ave., Buffalo, N.Y. 14201, *3, 7, 12; C.*

EDUCATIONAL ALLIANCE ART SCHOOL, 197 E. Broadway, New York, N.Y. 10002, *6, 7, 12, 13, 15, 17; A, E, F, H, I.*

EISENHOWER COLLEGE, Seneca Falls, N.Y. 13148, *1, 3, 7, 12, 13, 14, 15, 17; D, E, F.*

ELIZABETH SETON COLLEGE, 1061 N. Broadway, Yonkers, N.Y. 10701, *1, 3, 6, 7, 12, 17; C, D, F, H, I, K.*

ELMIRA COLLEGE, Elmira, N.Y. 14901, *1, 3, 4, 6, 7, 9, 12, 13, 14, 15, 17; C, D, E, F, H, I, K.*

FASHION INSTITUTE OF TECHNOLOGY, 227 W. 27th St., New York, N.Y. 10001, *3, 11, 13, 16; A, D, E, F, H, I, K.*

FINCH COLLEGE, 52 E. 78 St., New York, N.Y. 10021, *1, 3, 7, 8, 12, 14, 15; C, D, E, F.*

FORDHAM UNIVERSITY, Bronx, N.Y. 10458, *D, F.*

FRANK REILLY SCHOOL OF ART, 111 W. 57th St., New York, N.Y. 10019, *7, 9, 12; A, G, H, I.*

GERMAIN SCHOOL OF PHOTOGRAPHY, 225 Broadway, New York, N.Y. 10007, *13; I.*

HARPUR COLLEGE, Endicott, N.Y. 13760, *7, 12; D, E.*

HARRIET LEBLAND'S ADVANCED PAINTERS WORKSHOP, Premium Point, New Rochelle, N.Y. 10801, *4, 6, 7, 9, 12, 14; A, H, I.*

HARTWICK COLLEGE, Oneonta, N.Y. 13820, *3, 6, 7, 12, 15, 17; F, K.*

HENRY STREET SETTLEMENT SCHOOL OF ART & POTTERY, 265 Henry St., New York, N.Y. 10002, *6, 7, 12, 13, 14; A, H, I.*

HERBERT H. LEHMAN COLLEGE, 2 Van Cortland Ave. E., Bronx, N.Y. 10468, *3, 6, 7, 12, 13, 14, 15; A, D, H, I.*

HILBERT COLLEGE, 5200 S. Park Ave., Hamburg, N.Y. 14075, *4, 7, 12; D, E, I.*

HOBART & WILLIAM SMITH COLLEGES, Geneva, N.Y. 14456, *2, 3, 6, 7, 12, 13, 14, 15; A, D, K.*

HOFSTRA UNIVERSITY, Hempstead, N.Y. 11550, *3, 4, 6, 7, 9, 12, 14, 15, 16, 17; A, D, E, F, H, I, K.*

HOUGHTON COLLEGE, Houghton, N.Y. 14744, *3, 4, 6, 7, 12, 14, 15, 17; A, D, F, H, I, K.*

HUDSON VALLEY COMMUNITY COLLEGE, Troy, N.Y. 12180, *7, 12; F, I.*

HUNTER COLLEGE, 695 Park Ave., New York, N.Y. 10001, *3, 4, 7, 8, 10, 11, 12, 15, 18, 21; A, D, I.*

INSTITUTE OF TECHNOLOGY, Wheatley Rd., Old Westbury, N.Y. 11568, *1, 3, 7, 9, 11, 12, 13, 14, 15, 16, 17; A, D, E, F.*

ITHACA COLLEGE, Ithaca, N.Y. 14850, *3, 7, 12, 13, 15; A, F.*

JAMESTOWN COMMUNITY COLLEGE, Jamestown, N.Y. 14701, *3, 7, 12, 15, 17; D, I.*

JEFFERSON COMMUNITY COLLEGE, PO Box 255, Watertown, N.Y. 13601, *15; F, I.*

JIRANEK SCHOOL OF FURNITURE DESIGN, 160 Lexington Ave., New York, N.Y. 10016, *7, 10; D, E, H, I.*

LADYCLIFF COLLEGE, Highland Falls, N.Y. 12440, *3, 7, 10, 11, 12, 15; C.*

LAKE PLACID SCHOOL OF ART, Saranac Ave., Lake Placid, N.Y. 12946, *3, 6, 7, 12, 13; A, H, I, K.*

LONG ISLAND UNIVERSITY, Zeckendorf Campus, Brooklyn, N.Y. 11201, *3, 4, 9, 11, 12, 16; B, I.*

MANHATTAN COLLEGE, Manhattan College Parkway, Bronx, N.Y. 10471, *4, 7, 11, 12, 15, 17; B, D, E, F.*

MANHATTAN COMMUNITY COLLEGE, 134 W. 51 St., New York, N.Y. 10020, *3, 7, 12, 15, 17; D, I.*

MANHATTANVILLE COLLEGE, Purchase, N.Y. 10523, *1, 7, 9, 12, 13, 14, 15, 16, 17; D.*

MARIA REGINA COLLEGE, 1024 Court St., Syracuse, N.Y. 13208, *4, 17.*

MARYMOUNT COLLEGE, Tarrytown, N.Y. 10591, *1, 3, 4, 5, 6, 9, 10, 12, 14; D, E.*

MASTER INSTITUTE OF UNITED ARTS INC., 310 Riverside Drive, New York, N.Y. 10025, *6, 7, 12, 15, 16, 17; E, I.*

MAYER SCHOOL OF FASHION DESIGN, 64 W. 36th St., New York, N.Y. 10018, *8; I.*

MOLLOY COLLEGE, 1000 Hempstead Ave., Rockville Centre, N.Y. 11570, *3, 6, 7, 10, 12; C, D, E.*

MUNSON-WILLIAMS-PROCTOR INSTITUTE, 310 Genesee St., Utica, N.Y. 13503, *6, 7, 12, 13, 14, 15; A, H, I.*

NASSAU COMMUNITY COLLEGE, Stewart Ave., Garden City, N.Y. 11530, *1, 3, 4, 6, 7, 9, 12, 13, 14, 15, 17; A, D, E, F, H, I.*

NATIONAL ACADEMY SCHOOL OF FINE ARTS, 5 E. 89th St., New York, N.Y. 10028, *7, 12, 15, 17; A, E, F, H, I.*

NAZARETH COLLEGE, 4245 E. Ave., Rochester, N.Y. 14610, *3, 4, 6, 7, 12, 13, 14, 15, 17; C, D, E, F, I, K.*

NEW SCHOOL FOR SOCIAL RESEARCH, 66 W. 12th St., New York, N.Y. 10011, *1, 3, 4, 9, 10, 12, 16; A, I.*

NEW YORK CITY COMMUNITY COLLEGE OF THE CITY UNIVERSITY OF NEW YORK, 300 Jay Street, Brooklyn, N.Y. 11201, *1, 7, 12, 13, 14; D, I.*

NEW YORK INSTITUTE OF PHOTOGRAPHY, 10 W. 33 St., New York, N.Y. 10001, *13; I.*

NEW YORK INSTITUTE OF TECHNOLOGY, 135 W. 70 St., New York, N.Y. 10023, *1, 7, 9, 11, 12, 13, 14, 15, 16; D, E.*

NEW YORK PHOENIX SCHOOL OF DESIGN, 160 Lexington Ave., New York, N.Y. 10016, *1, 3, 7, 9, 11, 12, 16, 17; A, E, F, H, I.*

NEW YORK SCHOOL OF INTERIOR DESIGN, 155 E. 56 Street, New York, N.Y. 10022, *11; I, K.*

NEW YORK STUDIO SCHOOL OF DRAWING, PAINTING & SCULPTURE, 8 W. Eighth St., New York, N.Y. 10011, *7, 12, 15; E.*

NEW YORK UNIVERSITY, Div. of Continuing Education, 1 Washington Sq. N., New York, N.Y. 10003, *1, 2, 3, 6, 7, 9, 10, 11, 12, 13, 14, 15, 17; A, F, H, I.*

NEW YORK UNIVERSITY ART DEPT., 80 Washington Sq. E., New York, N.Y. 10003, *1, 2, 3, 4, 6, 7, 9, 11, 12, 13, 14, 15, 16, 17; A, D, E, F, I, K.*

NIAGARA COUNTY COMMUNITY COLLEGE, 430 Buffalo Ave., Niagara Falls, N.Y. 14303, *3, 7, 12, 15; D, I.*

NIAGARA UNIVERSITY, Niagara Falls, N.Y. 14120, *3, 7, 12; D.*

NORTH SHORE COMMUNITY ARTS SCHOOL, 236 Middle Neck Rd., Great Neck, N.Y. 11771, *6, 12, 15; E, F, H, I.*

OLD STONE SCHOOLHOUSE GALLERY & WORKSHOPS, Middle Road, Lake George, N.Y. 12845, *12, 17; E, H.*

ORANGE COUNTY COMMUNITY COLLEGE, Middletown, N.Y. 10940, *2, 3, 7, 10, 12, 15; A, D, I.*

PACE UNIVERSITY, 41 Park Row, New York, N.Y. 10038, *1, 3, 7, 17; A, D, F, G, H, I.*

PACE UNIVERSITY, WESTCHESTER, White Plains, N.Y. 10603, *7, 12, 14, 15; D, I.*

PAN AMERICAN ART SCHOOL, 318 W. 57th St., New York, N.Y. 10019, *1, 3, 5, 7, 9, 11, 12, 17; A, F, H, I.*

PARSONS SCHOOL OF DESIGN, 410 E. 54 St., New York, N.Y. 10022, *1, 7, 8, 9, 10, 11, 12, 13, 14, 15, 16, 17; D, E, I.*

PRATT CENTER FOR CONTEMPORARY PRINTMAKING, 831 Broadway, New York, N.Y. 10003, *14; A, E, F, H, I.*

PRATT INSTITUTE SCHOOL OF ART & DESIGN, 215 Ryerson St., Brooklyn, N.Y. 11205, *1, 2, 3, 7, 8, 9, 10, 11, 12, 13, 14, 15; D, I.*

QUEENS COLLEGE, Flushing, N.Y. 11367, *1, 3, 4, 6, 7, 11, 12, 13, 14, 15, 16, 17; D, F, I.*

QUEENSBOROUGH COMMUNITY COLLEGE, 56 Ave. & Springfield Blvd., Bayside, N.Y. 11364, *1, 3, 7, 12, 15, 17; D, I.*

RENSSELAER POLYTECHNIC INSTITUTE, 110 Eighth St., Troy, N.Y. 12181, *2, 7, 12, 17; D, F.*

ROBERTS WESLEYAN COLLEGE, 2301 Westside Drive, Rochester, N.Y. 14624, *3, 6, 7, 12, 15, 17; D, G.*

ROCHESTER INSTITUTE OF TECHNOLOGY, School of Art & Design, Rochester, N.Y. 14623, *1, 3, 4, 6, 7, 9, 10, 12, 13, 14, 15, 16, 17; A, D, E, G, H, I, K.*

ROCKLAND COMMUNITY COLLEGE ART DEPT., 145 College Rd., Suffern, N.Y. 10901, *1, 3, 7, 9, 12, 13, 14, 15; A, D, E, F, H, I.*

ROSARY HILL COLLEGE, 4380 Main St., Buffalo, N.Y. 14226, *3, 4, 6, 7, 11, 12, 13, 15, 17; A, D, E, F, I, K.*

RUSSELL SAGE COLLEGE, 203 Second St., Troy, N.Y. 12180, Offers degree in fine art; *A.*

ST. JOHN'S UNIVERSITY, Grand Central & Utopia Pky., Jamaica, N.Y. 11432, *1, 3, 7, 9, 10, 12, 16; B, I.*

ST. LAWRENCE UNIVERSITY, Canton, N.Y. 13617, *3, 6, 7, 12, 14, 15, 17; A, D, E, F, K.*

ST. THOMAS AQUINAS COLLEGE, Sparkill, N.Y. 10976, *4, 6, 7, 12, 14, 15, 17; D, I.*

SARAH LAWRENCE COLLEGE, Admission Ofc., Bronxville, N.Y. 10708, *1, 3, 4, 5, 9, 10, 11, 12; B, C, F, G, I.*

SARA WHITNEY OLDS-ROBERT ZOELLER STUDIOS, Shore Rd., Mt. Sinai, N.Y. 11766, *7, 12, 17; A, F, H, I.*

SCHOOL OF BATIK PAINTING, 29 W. 84th St., New York, N.Y. 10024, *A.*

SCHOOL FOR CREATIVE MOVEMENT IN THE ARTS, 265 W. 87th St., New York, N.Y. 10024, *6, 7, 13, 14; A, H.*

SCHOOL OF VISUAL ARTS, 209-213 E. 23 St., New York, N.Y. 10010, *1, 5, 7, 9, 10, 12, 13, 14, 15, 16, 17; E, I.*

SCULPTURE CENTER, 167 E. 69th St., New York, N.Y. 10021, *A.*

SKIDMORE COLLEGE, Saratoga Springs, N.Y. 12866, *1, 3, 4, 5, 6, 7, 9, 10, 11, 12, 15, 17; B, C, I.*

SOUTHAMPTON COLLEGE OF L. I. UNIVERSITY, Southampton, N.Y. 11968, *3, 4, 7, 9, 12, 13, 14, 15, 17; A, D, E, F, H, I, K.*

STATE UNIVERSITY COLLEGE, Washington Ave., Albany, N.Y. 12203, *1, 3, 5, 7, 9, 10, 12, 16.*

STATE UNIVERSITY COLLEGE, Alfred, N.Y. 14802, *3, 11, 12, 13; G, I.*

STATE UNIVERSITY COLLEGE, Binghamton, N.Y. 13901, *3, 7, 12, 14, 15; A, D, E, F, K.*

STATE UNIVERSITY COLLEGE, Brockport, N.Y. 14420, *3, 4, 7, 12, 13, 14, 15; D, I.*

STATE UNIVERSITY COLLEGE, 1300 Elmwood Ave., Buffalo, N.Y. 14222, *1, 3, 4, 7, 10, 12, 13, 14, 15, 16, 17; A, D, F, I, K.*

STATE UNIVERSITY COLLEGE DEPT. OF ART, Foster Hall, Buffalo, N.Y. 14214, *1, 3, 4, 7, 12, 13, 14, 15; A, D, E, F, H, I, K.*

STATE UNIVERSITY COLLEGE, Agricultural & Technical College, Cobleskill, N.Y. 12043, *3, 6, 7, 12; A, D, F, H, K.*

STATE UNIVERSITY COLLEGE, Cortland, N.Y. 13045, *3, 6, 7, 12, 14, 15, 17; A, D, F, I, K.*

STATE UNIVERSITY COLLEGE, Fredonia, N.Y. 14063, *1, 3, 4, 9, 10, 11, 12; A, B, F, I.*

STATE UNIVERSITY COLLEGE, Genesco, N.Y. 14454, *3, 4, 6, 7, 8, 12, 13, 14, 15, 16, 17; D, I.*

STATE UNIVERSITY COLLEGE, New Paltz, N.Y. 12561, *1, 2, 3, 4, 6, 7, 10, 11, 12, 13, 14, 15, 17; A, D, F, I, K.*

STATE UNIVERSITY COLLEGE, Oneonta, N.Y. 13820, *3, 4, 6, 7, 12, 13, 14, 15, 16, 17; A, D, E, F, I, K.*

STATE UNIVERSITY COLLEGE, Oswego, N.Y. 13126, *3, 6, 7, 12, 13, 14, 15, 17; A, D, E, F, I, K.*

STATE UNIVERSITY COLLEGE, Pierrepont Ave., Potsdam, N.Y. 13676, *3, 6, 7, 12, 14, 15, 17; A, D, F, I, K.*

STATE UNIVERSITY COLLEGE, John P. Meyers Fine Arts Bldg., Plattsburgh, N.Y. 12901, *3, 7, 12, 13, 14, 15; D, I.*

STATE UNIVERSITY COLLEGE, Purchase, N.Y. 10577, *2, 3, 4, 6, 7, 10, 12, 13, 15; A, D, E, H.*

STATE UNIVERSITY COLLEGE, Stoney Brook, N.Y. 11790, *1, 3, 4, 9, 10, 12, 16; B, C, I.*

STATEN ISLAND COMMUNITY COLLEGE, 715 Ocean Terr., Staten Island, N.Y. 10310, *4, 6, 7, 12, 13, 15, 17; D, I.*

SULLIVAN COUNTY COMMUNITY COLLEGE, South Fallsburg, N.Y. 12779, *1, 7, 9, 10, 13; A, D, H, I.*

SYRACUSE UNIVERSITY SCHOOL OF ART, 309 University Pl., Syracuse, N.Y. 13210, *1, 3, 4, 7, 9, 10, 11, 12, 14, 15, 16, 17; A, D, E, F, H, I, K.*

TOBE-COBURN SCHOOL FOR FASHION CAREERS, 851 Madison Ave., New York, N.Y. 10021, *A.*

TRAPHAGEN SCHOOL OF FASHION, 1680 Broadway, New York, N.Y. 10019, *3, 11, 17; A, F, H, I.*

ULSTER COUNTY COMMUNITY COLLEGE, Stone Ridge, N.Y. 12484, *1, 3, 7, 8, 9, 12; D, E, I.*

UMBERTO ROMAND SCHOOL OF CREATIVE ART, 162 E. 83rd St., New York, N.Y. 10021, *7, 12, 14, 15; A.*

UNION COLLEGE, Union St., Schenectady, N.Y. 12308, *3, 7, 12, 17; B, D, E, G, H, I, K.*

UNIVERSITY OF ROCHESTER DEPT. OF ART, Rush Rhees Library, Rochester, N.Y. 14627, *1, 3, 4, 9, 10, 11, 12, 16; A, F.*

VASSAR COLLEGE DEPT. OF ART, Raymond Ave., Poughkeepsie, N.Y. 12601, *1, 3, 4, 5, 9, 10, 12; A, I.*

VILLA MARIA COLLEGE, 240 Pine Ridge Rd., Buffalo, N.Y. 14225, *1, 3, 4, 6, 7, 9, 10, 11, 12, 13, 15; D, H.*

WAGNER COLLEGE, Grymes Hill, Staten Island, N.Y. 10301, *3, 6, 7, 12, 13, 14, 15, 17; A, D, F, H, I, K.*

WELLS COLLEGE, Aurora, N.Y. 13026, *7, 12, 15, 17; D, F.*

WESTCHESTER COMMUNITY COLLEGE, 75 Grosslands Rd., Valhalla, N.Y. 10595, *3, 7; D, I.*

WOODSTOCK SCHOOL OF ART, Box 382, Woodstock, N.Y. *7, 12, 14, 15, 17; E, H, I.*

North Carolina

AGRICULTURAL & TECHNICAL COLLEGE OF NORTH CAROLINA, Greensboro, N.C. 27411, *1, 3, 4, 6, 7, 12, 14, 15, 16, 17; A, D, F, I*

ARTS & CRAFTS ASSOCIATION, INC., 610 Coliseum Dr., Winston-Salem, N.C. 27106, *3, 6, 7, 11, 12, 15, 16, 17; A, D, E, H, I, K.*

ATLANTIC CHRISTIAN COLLEGE, Wilson, N.C. 27893, *1, 4, 6, 7, 9, 12, 14, 15, 17; D, I.*

BREVARD COLLEGE, Brevard, N.C. 28712, *3, 4, 7, 15; D, E.*

CENTRAL PIEDMONT COMMUNITY COLLEGE, Elizabeth & Kings Sts., Charlotte, N.C. 28213, *1, 3, 5, 6, 7, 8, 9, 12, 14, 15, 17; D, H.*

CHOWAN COLLEGE, Murfreesboro, N.C. 27855, *1, 3, 4, 6, 7, 8, 9, 12, 14, 15, 17; D, E.*

COLLEGE OF THE ALBEMARLE, Fine Arts Center, Riverside Ave., Elizabeth City, N.C. 27909, *3, 6, 7, 11, 12, 15; A, G, H, I.*

DUKE UNIVERSITY, 6605 College Station, Durham, N.C. 27708, *4, 6, 7, 12, 13, 14, 17; D, F.*

EAST CAROLINA UNIVERSITY, Greenville, N.C. 27834, *1, 3, 4, 6, 7, 9, 10, 11, 12, 13, 14, 15, 16, 17; A, D, I, K.*

ELIZABETH CITY STATE COLLEGE, Elizabeth City, N.C. 27909, *3, 4, 6, 7, 12, 14, 15, 17; A, D, E, F, I, K.*

ELON COLLEGE, Elon, N.C. 27244, *3, 4, 6, 7, 12, 14, 15, 17; A, D, E, F, I, K.*

FAYETTEVILLE STATE UNIVERSITY, Murchison Rd., Fayetteville, N.C. 28301, *3, 4, 6, 7, 12, 13, 15, 17; I.*

GASTON COLLEGE, PO Box 1397, Gastonia, N.C. 28052, *3, 6, 7, 11, 12, 15, 17; A, E, F, H, I.*

GREENSBORO COLLEGE, W. Market Street, Greensboro, N.C. 27402, *3, 4, 6, 7, 12, 14, 15; D, E.*

GUILFORD TECHNICAL INSTITUTE, Box 309, Jamestown, N.C. 27282, *1, 3, 5, 6, 7, 9, 12, 13, 15; A, D, F, H, I.*

HIGH POINT COLLEGE, Montlieu Ave., High Point, N.C. 27262, *3, 4, 6, 7, 12, 13, 15; A, D, I, K.*

LOUISBURG COLLEGE, N. Main St., Louisburg, N.C. 27549, *3, 4, 6; D, E.*

MARS HILL COLLEGE, Mars Hill, N.C. 28754, *4, 6, 7, 12, 14, 15; C, D.*

MEREDITH COLLEGE, Raleigh, N.C. 27602, *1, 3, 4, 6, 7, 11, 12, 14, 15, 17; C, D, E, F, I, K.*

METHODIST COLLEGE, 5600 Ramsey St., Fayetteville, N.C. 28301, *3, 4, 7, 12, 17; A, D, E, F, I, K.*

NORTH CAROLINA AGRICULTURAL & TECHNICAL STATE UNIVERSITY, Greensboro, N.C. 27411, *3, 4, 6, 7, 9, 11, 12, 14; A, D, I.*

NORTH CAROLINA CENTRAL UNIVERSITY, Fayetteville St., Durham, N.C. 27707, *1, 3, 4, 6, 7, 9, 14, 15; D, E.*

NORTH CAROLINA STATE UNIVERSITY SCHOOL OF DESIGN, PO Box 5398, Raleigh, N.C. 27607, *4, 7, 12, 17; A, D, E, F, I, K.*

PEACE JR. COLLEGE, Peace St., Raleigh, N.C. 27602, *3, 7, 12, 15; C, E, F, K.*

PEMBROKE STATE UNIVERSITY, Pembroke, N.C. 28372, *1, 3, 4, 6, 7, 12, 14, 15; D, E.*

PFEIFER COLLEGE, Misenheimer, N.C. 28109, *3, 4, 6, 7, 12, 15; A, K.*

QUEENS COLLEGE, 1800 Selwyn Ave., Charlotte, N.C. 28207, *1, 3, 4, 6, 7, 12, 15, 17; C, F, K.*

SACRED HEART COLLEGE, Belmont, N.C. 28012, *3, 4, 6, 7, 8, 12, 13, 15; D, I, K.*

ST. ANDREW'S PRESBYTERIAN COLLEGE, Laurinburg, N.C. 28352, *3, 4, 6, 7, 12, 14, 15; A, D, E, I, K.*

ST. MARY'S COLLEGE, Hillsborough St., Raleigh, N.C. 27602, *3, 7, 12, 14, 17; C, E, F, K.*

SALEM COLLEGE, Winston-Salem, N.C. 27108, *3, 7, 12, 18, 21; C, D, E, F.*

UNIVERSITY OF NORTH CAROLINA, Columbia St., Chapel Hill, N.C. 27514, *1, 4, 7, 12, 14, 15; D, E, K.*

UNIVERSITY OF NORTH CAROLINA AT ASHEVILLE, King St., Asheville, N.C. 28801, *3, 4, 6, 7, 12, 14, 15; D, E, I.*

UNIVERSITY OF NORTH CAROLINA AT CHARLOTTE, Charlotte, N.C. 28213, *3, 4, 7, 12, 15; D, I.*

UNIVERSITY OF NORTH CAROLINA AT GREENSBORO, Greensboro, N.C. 27412, *1, 2, 3, 4, 6, 7, 8, 11, 12, 13, 14, 15, 16, 17; D, E, I.*

UNIVERSITY OF NORTH CAROLINA AT WILMINGTON, Wilmington, N.C. 28401, *3, 4, 6, 7, 12, 14, 15; A, D, H, I, K.*

WAKE FOREST UNIVERSITY, PO Box 7232, Winston-Salem, N.C. 27109, *3; A, F, I.*

WESTERN CAROLINA UNIVERSITY, Cullowhee, N.C. 28723, *1, 3, 4, 6, 7, 9, 10, 11, 12, 13, 14, 15, 16, 17; A, D, F, I, K.*

WINGATE COLLEGE, Wingate, N.C. 28174, *6, 7, 12, 17; D.*

North Dakota

DICKINSON STATE COLLEGE, Dickinson, N.D. 58601, *1, 3, 4, 6, 7, 12, 14, 15; A, D, H, I, K.*

JAMESTOWN COLLEGE, Jamestown, N.D. 58401, *3, 4, 7, 12, 15; A, D, E, F, H, I, K.*

LAKE REGION JR. COLLEGE, Devil's Lake, N.D. 58301, *1, 3, 6, 7, 8, 9, 12, 15, 17; D, F, I, K.*

MAYVILLE STATE COLLEGE, Mayville, N.D. 58257, *4; A, D, I.*

MINOT STATE COLLEGE, Minot, N.D. 58701, *1, 3, 4, 6, 7, 12, 14, 15, 17; A, D, E, G, I, K.*

NORTH DAKOTA SCHOOL OF SCIENCE, Sixth St., Wahpeton, N.D. 58075, *4, 6, 12, 14; A, H, I.*

UNIVERSITY OF NORTH DAKOTA, Grand Forks, N.D. 58201, *1, 3, 4, 5, 7, 9, 12, 14, 15, 17; A, D, E, F, H, I, K.*

VALLEY CITY STATE COLLEGE, Valley City, N.D. 58072, *3, 4, 6, 7, 12, 17; A, G, H, I.*

YANKTON COLLEGE, Yankton, N.D. 57078, *1, 3, 4, 6, 7, 12, 14, 15, 17; A, D, E, F, H, I, K.*

Ohio

AKA—THE SCHOOL OF FINE ARTS, 38660 Mentor Ave., Willoughby, Ohio 44094, *6, 7, 12, 13; A, H, I.*

AKRON ART INSTITUTE SCHOOL OF DESIGN, 69 E. Market Street, Akron, Ohio 44308, *3, 6, 7, 10, 12, 18, 21.*

ANTIOCH COLLEGE, Yellow Springs, Ohio 45387, *7, 8, 12, 15; D, E, H.*

ART ACADEMY OF CINCINNATI, Eden Park, Cincinnati, Ohio 45202, *1, 3, 7, 9, 12, 13, 14, 15; A, E, F, H, I.*

ART SCHOOL OF WILLIAM E. GEBHARDT ASSOCIATES, 228 E. 5th St., Cincinnati, Ohio 45202, *1, 3, 5, 7, 9, 11, 12, 16, 17; A, E, F, H, I.*

ASHLAND COLLEGE, College Ave., Ashland, Ohio 44805, *3, 4, 7, 12, 14, 15, 17; D, E, I.*

BALDWIN WALLACE COLLEGE, Front Street, Berea, Ohio 44017, *3, 5, 6, 7, 12, 14, 15; D, E, H, I.*

BLUFFTON COLLEGE, Bluffton, Ohio 45817, *4, 6, 7, 12, 13, 14, 15, 17; D, I.*

BOWLING GREEN STATE UNIVERSITY, Bowling Green, Ohio 43402, *3, 7, 10, 12, 15, 18, 21; D, H.*

BUTLER INSTITUTE OF AMERICAN ART, 524 Wick Ave., Youngstown, Ohio 44502, *7, 12, 17; F, H, I.*

CAPITAL UNIVERSITY, E. Main St., Columbus, Ohio, 43209, *3, 4, 6, 7, 12, 14, 15, 16, 17; A, D, E, F, H, I, K.*

CASE WESTERN RESERVE UNIVERSITY, Cleveland, Ohio 44106, *3, 4; A, D, H, I.*

CENTRAL ACADEMY OF COMMERCIAL ART, 2326 Upland Place, Cincinnati, Ohio 45206, *1, 7, 9.*

CENTRAL STATE UNIVERSITY, Wilberforce, Ohio 45384, *2, 3, 6, 7, 12, 15, 18, 19, 21.*

CLEVELAND INSTITUTE OF ART, 11141 E. Blvd., Cleveland, Ohio 44106, *3, 4, 6, 7, 10, 12, 13, 14, 15, 17; A, D, E, F, H, I.*

CLEVELAND STATE UNIVERSITY, Euclid at 24th, Cleveland, Ohio 44115.

COLLEGE OF MOUNT ST. JOSEPH ON THE OHIO, Mount St. Joseph, Ohio 45051, *1, 3, 4, 6, 7, 11, 12, 13, 14, 15, 17; D, E.*

COLLEGE OF STEUBENVILLE, Franciscan Way, Steubenville, Ohio 43952, *3, 4; A, D, F, I, K.*

COLLEGE OF THE DAYTON ART INSTITUTE, 456 Belmonte Park N., Dayton, Ohio 45495, *1, 3, 6, 7, 9, 12, 13, 14, 15; A, D, H, I.*

COLLEGE OF WOOSTER, Wooster, Ohio 44691, *2, 3, 4, 7, 12, 14, 15, 17; A, D, F, I, K.*

COLUMBUS COLLEGE OF ART & DESIGN, 486 Hutton Place, Columbus, Ohio 43215, *1, 3, 5, 7, 9, 10, 11, 12, 13, 14, 15, 17; A, D, E, F, H, K.*

COOPER SCHOOL OF ART, 2341 Carnegie Ave., Cleveland, Ohio 44715, *3, 7, 8, 10, 12; D, H, I.*

CUYAHOGA COMMUNITY COLLEGE, 700 Carnegie Ave., Cleveland, Ohio 44115, *3, 4, 7, 12, 14, 17; D, E, F, H, I.*

CUYAHOGA VALLEY ART CENTER, 1886 Front St., Cuyahoga Falls, Ohio 44221, *6, 7, 12, 17; F, H, I.*

DEFIANCE COLLEGE, N. Clinton St., Defiance, Ohio 43512, *3, 4, 6, 7, 12, 13, 14, 15, 17; A, D, F, I, K.*

DENISON UNIVERSITY, Granville, Ohio 43023, *3, 4, 7, 12, 13, 14, 15, 16, 17; D, E, F.*

EDGECLIFF COLLEGE, 2220 Victory Parkway, Cincinnati, Ohio 45206, *3, 4, 6, 7, 11, 12, 14, 15, 16, 17; D, E, I.*

FINDLAY COLLEGE, Findlay, Ohio 45840, *1, 3, 4, 6, 7, 12, 14, 15, 17; A, D, E, F, H, I, K.*

GEBHART ART SCHOOL, 124 E. Seventh St., Cincinnati, Ohio 45202, *6, 7, 8, 9, 10, 11, 12, 13, 14; A, H.*

HEIDELBERG COLLEGE, Tiffin, Ohio 44883, *1, 3, 4, 6, 7, 9, 10, 11, 12, 15; A, D, E, I, K.*

HIRAM COLLEGE, Hiram, Ohio 44234, *3, 4, 6, 7, 12, 14, 15; A, D, E, I, K.*

226

KENT STATE UNIVERSITY, Kent, Ohio 44242, *2, 4, 7, 10, 12, 18; D, H, I.*

KENYON COLLEGE, Gambier, Ohio 43022, *3, 7, 12, 15; B, D, E, F, K.*

LAKE ERIE COLLEGE, Painesville, Ohio 44077, *1, 3, 4, 6, 7, 12, 13, 15, 17; C, D, E, G, H, I.*

LAKELAND COMMUNITY COLLEGE, Mentor, Ohio 44060, *1, 3, 7, 12, 14, 15, 17; D, H, I.*

LORAINE COUNTY COMMUNITY COLLEGE, 1005 N. Abbe Rd., Elyria, Ohio 44035, *3, 4, 7; A, F, H, I.*

MALONE COLLEGE, 515 25th St. N.W., Canton, Ohio 44709, *3, 4, 7, 12, 17; A, D, E, F, H, I, K.*

MARIETTA COLLEGE, Marietta, Ohio 45750, *3, 4, 7, 12, 14, 15, 17; A, D, E, F, H, I, K.*

MIAMI UNIVERSITY SCHOOL OF FINE ARTS, Oxford, Ohio 45056, *1, 3, 6, 7, 9, 12, 14, 15, 16, 17; A, D, F, G, K.*

MOUNT UNION COLLEGE, Art Dept., Alliance, Ohio 44601, *3, 4, 6, 7, 12, 14, 15, 17; A, D, G.*

MUSKINGUM COLLEGE, New Concord, Ohio 43762, *1, 3, 4, 6, 7, 12, 14, 15, 17; A, D, E, F, H, I, K.*

NOTRE DAME COLLEGE, 4545 College Road, Cleveland, Ohio 44121, *3, 4, 6, 7, 11, 12, 14, 15, 16, 17; C, D, E, F, K.*

OBERLIN COLLEGE, Oberlin, Ohio 44074, *3, 7, 12, 15, 18; D, E, F.*

OHIO DOMINICAN COLLEGE, 1216 Sunbury Rd., Columbus, Ohio 43219, *3, 4, 6, 7, 12, 15, 17; D, E, I.*

OHIO NORTHERN UNIVERSITY, 501 S. Main St., Ada, Ohio 45810, *3, 4, 6, 7, 12, 14, 15, 17; A, D, G, K.*

OHIO STATE UNIVERSITY SCHOOL OF ART, 127 N. Oval Dr., Columbus, Ohio 43210, *1, 3, 4, 6, 9, 10, 11, 12, 13, 16, 17; A, B, C, I.*

OHIO UNIVERSITY, School of Art, Athens, Ohio 45701, *1, 3, 4, 6, 7, 9, 10, 11, 12, 13, 14, 15, 16, 17; A, D, E, F, I, K.*

OHIO UNIVERSITY AT BELMONT COUNTY, National Rd. W. St., Clairsville, Ohio 43950, *3, 4, 6, 12, 13, 14, 15, 16; H, I.*

OHIO UNIVERSITY AT CHILLICOTHE, Chillicothe, Ohio 45601, *7, 12, 13, 14, 15, 17; H, I.*

OHIO UNIVERSITY, Lancaster Campus, 1000 Lancaster-Newark Rd. N.E., Lancaster, Ohio 43130, *4, 7, 12, 15; H, I.*

OHIO WESLEYAN UNIVERSITY, Dept. of Fine Arts, Delaware, Ohio 43015, *1, 3, 4, 6, 7, 11, 12, 14, 15, 17; A, D, E, G, I, K.*

OTTERBEIN COLLEGE, Westerville, Ohio 43081, *2, 3, 4, 6, 7, 12, 13, 14, 15; A, D.*

OUR LADY OF CINCINNATI COLLEGE, Edgecliff Walnut Hills, Cincinnati, Ohio 45206, *3, 4, 6, 7, 11, 12, 14, 15, 17; C, D, E, F, I, K.*

SCHOOL OF THE DAYTON ART INSTITUTE, Forest & Riverview Ave., Dayton, Ohio 45405, *1, 3, 7, 9, 10, 12, 13, 14, 15, 17; A, E, F, H, I.*

SINCLAIR COMMUNITY COLLEGE, 444 W. Third St., Dayton, Ohio 45402, *1, 6, 7, 9, 10, 11, 12, 15; A, D, H.*

SPRINGFIELD ART CENTER, 107 Cliff Park Rd., Springfield, Ohio 45501, *6, 7, 9, 10, 11, 12, 13, 15; A, H.*

TOLEDO MUSEUM OF ART SCHOOL, Monroe St. at Scottwood Ave., Toledo, Ohio 43609, *3, 6, 7, 10, 11, 12, 15, 18, 21.*

UNIVERSITY OF AKRON, Akron, Ohio 44325, *3, 4, 6, 7, 9, 10, 11, 12, 13, 14, 15; A, D, E, H, I.*

UNIVERSITY OF CINCINNATI, College of Design, Architecture & Art, Cincinnati, Ohio 45221, *1, 2, 3, 4, 6, 7, 9, 10, 11, 12, 13, 14, 15, 17; A, D, E, F, H, I, K.*

UNIVERSITY OF DAYTON, 300 College Park, Dayton, Ohio 45409, *1, 4, 7, 12, 14, 15, 17; D.*

URSULINE COLLEGE FOR WOMEN, 2600 Lander Rd., Pepper Pike, Cleveland, Ohio 44124, *3, 4, 6, 7, 11, 12, 15, 16, 17; C, D, E, F, K.*

WESTERN COLLEGE FOR WOMEN, Oxford, Ohio 45056, *3, 7, 11, 12, 14, 15, 17; C, D, E, F, K.*

WESTERN RESERVE UNIVERSITY, Div. of Art & Architecture, Cleveland, Ohio 44106, *2, 3, 4; D, E, F, I, K.*

WILMINGTON COLLEGE, Wilmington, Ohio 45177, *3, 4, 6, 7, 12, 15; A, D, F, G, I, K.*

WITTENBERG UNIVERSITY, 818 N. Fountain, Springfield, Ohio 45501, *1, 3, 4, 6, 7, 8, 9, 10, 12, 14, 15, 17; D, E, G, I, J.*

XAVIER UNIVERSITY, Dava & Victory Parkway, Cincinnati, Ohio 45207, *D, E, I.*

YOUNGSTOWN STATE UNIVERSITY, 410 Wick Ave., Youngstown, Ohio 44503, *4, 6, 7, 9, 12, 14, 15, 16; D, H, I.*

ZANESVILLE ART CENTER, 1145 Maple Ave., Zanesville, Ohio 43701, *6, 7, 12, 15; A, H.*

Oklahoma

BACONE COLLEGE, Bacone, Okla. 74420, *3, 6, 7, 10, 12, 15, 17; D, E.*

BETHANY NAZARENE COLLEGE, Bethany, Okla. 73008, *2, 3, 6, 7, 12, 17; D.*

CAMERON UNIVERSITY, 2800 Gore Blvd., Lawton, Okla. 73501, *3, 4, 6, 7, 12, 14, 15; A, D, H, I, K.*

CENTRAL PILGRIM COLLEGE, Old Tulsa Road, Bartlesville, Okla. 74003; *3, 4, 7, 12, 17; A, E, F, H, K.*

CENTRAL STATE UNIVERSITY, North College, Edmond, Okla. 73034, *1, 3, 4, 6, 7, 12, 14, 15, 17; A, D, E, F, H, I, K.*

CLAREMORE JR. COLLEGE, College Hill, Claremore, Okla. 74017, *3, 4, 6, 7, 9, 10, 11, 12, 14, 15; A, D, H, I, K.*

CONNORS STATE COLLEGE, Warner, Okla. 74469, *1, 3, 7, 12, 14; A, D, K.*

EAST CENTRAL STATE UNIVERSITY, Art Dept., Ada, Okla. 74820, *1, 3, 4, 6, 7, 12, 13, 14, 15, 17; A, D, F, I, K.*

GOETZ ART SCHOOL, 800 N.E. 21st St., Oklahoma City, Okla. 73105, *7, 12; I.*

GREENWICH VILLAGE ART INSTITUTE, 13161 E. Sixth St., Tulsa, Okla. 74120, *1, 3, 4, 6, 7, 8, 9, 10, 11, 12, 15; A, D, H, I, K.*

LANGSTON UNIVERSITY, Langston, Okla. 73050, *3, 4, 6, 7, 9, 10, 11, 12, 14, 15; A, D, H, I, K.*

MONTE CASSINO SCHOOL, 2200 S. Lewis, Tulsa, Okla. 74114, *6, 12, 14, 17; A, E, I.*

MURRAY STATE AGRICULTURAL COLLEGE, Tishomingo, Okla. 73460, *3, 7, 12, 13, 17; A, F, H, K.*

NORTHEASTERN OKLAHOMA A&M COLLEGE, 1 St. N.E., Miami, Okla. 74354, *3, 7, 12, 13, 17; A, D, E, F, H.*

NORTHEASTERN OKLAHOMA STATE UNIVERSITY, Tahlequah, Okla. 74464, *3, 6, 7, 8, 10, 12, 15; D, E, I, K.*

NORTHERN OKLAHOMA COLLEGE, 1220 E. Grand, Tonkawa, Okla. 74653, *1, 3, 7, 12, 17; A, D, F, I, K.*

NORTHWESTERN OKLAHOMA STATE UNIVERSITY, Oklahoma Blvd., Alva, Okla. 73717, *1, 3, 4, 6, 7, 9, 12, 15, 17; D, E, I, K.*

OKLAHOMA BAPTIST UNIVERSITY, Shawnee, Okla. 74801, *3, 4, 7, 13; A, F, K.*

OKLAHOMA CHRISTIAN COLLEGE, S. Eastern & Memorial Rd., Oklahoma City, Okla. 73111, *1, 3, 4, 5, 6, 7, 9, 10, 11, 12, 17; A, F, I, K.*

OKLAHOMA CITY UNIVERSITY, 2501 N. Blackwelder, Oklahoma City, Okla. 73106, *1, 3, 4, 7, 12, 14, 15; D, I.*

OKLAHOMA COLLEGE OF LIBERAL ARTS, Box 3228 Ocla, Chickasha, Okla. 73018, *1, 3, 4, 6, 7, 9, 12, 14, 15, 17; A, D, E, K.*

OKLAHOMA MILITARY ACADEMY, Military Hill, Claremore, Okla. 74017, *1, 3, 7, 12, 15; D, E, I.*

OKLAHOMA STATE UNIVERSITY, Stillwater, Okla. 74074, *2, 7, 12, 14, 18.*

PANHANDLE A&M COLLEGE, Goodwell, Okla. 73939, *7, 12, 17; A, D, F, I, K.*

PHILLIPS UNIVERSITY, Enid, Okla. 73701, *6; A, D, H, I.*

SOUTHEASTERN STATE COLLEGE, Durant, Okla. 74701, *3, 6, 7, 12, 17; A, D, H.*

SOUTHWESTERN STATE COLLEGE, Weatherford, Okla. 73096, *1, 3, 4, 5, 6, 7, 9, 12, 14, 15, 17; A, D, F, I, K.*

UNIVERSITY OF OKLAHOMA, Norman, Okla. 73069, *2, 4, 7, 10, 12, 15, 18; D, E.*

UNIVERSITY OF TULSA, Tulsa, Okla. 74104, *4, 7, 10, 12, 14, 15, 18; D, E, I.*

Oregon

BLUE MOUNTAIN COMMUNITY COLLEGE, 2410 N. W. Cardu Ave., Pendelton, Ore. 97801, *3, 7, 12; A, G, H.*

CENTRAL OREGON COMMUNITY COLLEGE, Bend, Ore. 97701, *3, 6, 7, 12, 17; A, D, H, I.*

CLATSOP COMMUNITY COLLEGE, 16 & Jerome, Astoria, Ore. 97103, *3, 7, 12, 15, 17; D, H, I.*

COLUMBIA CHRISTIAN COLLEGE, 200 N.E. 91 St., Portland, Ore. 97220, *1, 3, 6, 7, 17; A, D, E, F, H, K.*

EASTERN OREGON STATE COLLEGE, LeGrande, Ore. 97850, *1, 6, 7, 8, 9, 10, 11, 12, 13, 14, 15, 16; A, D, H, I, K.*

JUDSON BAPTIST COLLEGE, 9201 N. E. Fremont St., Portland, Ore. 97220, *1, 3, 7, 12; H.*

LANE COMMUNITY COLLEGE, 4000 E. 30th Ave., Eugene, Ore. 97405, *3, 6, 7, 12, 13, 14, 15; A, D, H, I.*

LEWIS AND CLARK COLLEGE, Portland, Ore. 97219, *1, 3, 6, 7, 12, 14, 15; A, D, I, K.*

LINFIELD COLLEGE, McMinnville, Ore. 97128, *1, 3, 4, 6, 7, 9, 11, 12, 15; A, D, E, F, I, K.*

LINN BENTON COMMUNITY COLLEGE, 6500 S.W. Pacific Blvd., Albany, Ore. 97321, *1, 2, 3, 4, 6, 7, 8, 9, 10, 11, 12, 13, 14, 15, 16, 17; A, D, H.*

MARYLHURST COLLEGE, Marylhurst, Ore. 97036, *1, 3, 4, 6, 7, 9, 12, 14; C, D, E, F, I, K.*

MAUDE KERNS ART CENTER, 1910 E. 15th Ave., Eugene, Ore. 97403, *6, 7, 12, 13; A, H, I.*

MOUNT ANGEL COLLEGE, Mount Angel, Ore. 97362, *3, 4, 6, 7, 12, 14, 15; A, D, E, F, I, K.*

MUSEUM ART SCHOOL, S.W. Park & Madison, Portland, Ore. 97205, *1, 3, 7, 9, 12, 14, 15, 17; A, D, E, F, H, I.*

OREGON COLLEGE OF ART, 30 S. First St., Ashland, Ore. 97520, *1, 3, 4, 6, 7, 8, 9, 10, 11, 12, 14, 15, 16; A, K.*

OREGON COLLEGE OF EDUCATION, Monmouth, Ore. 97361, *1, 3, 4, 6, 7, 12, 13, 14, 15, 16, 17; D, E, H, I.*

OREGON STATE UNIVERSITY, Corvallis, Ore. 97330, *2, 4, 7, 11, 12, 14, 15.*

PORTLAND STATE UNIVERSITY, P.O. Box 751, Portland, Ore. 97207 *1, 2, 4, 6, 7, 9, 10, 11, 12, 13, 14, 15, 16, 17; D, H, I.*

REED COLLEGE, Portland, Ore. 97202, *3, 7, 12, 14, 15; A, D, E, F, K.*

SCHOOL OF THE ARTS AND CRAFTS SOCIETY, 616 N.W. 18th Ave., Portland, Ore. 97209, *6, 7, 8, 9, 12, 13, 14, 15, 16; A, H, I.*

SOUTHERN OREGON COLLEGE, Ashland, Ore. 97520, *4, 6, 7, 12, 14, 15, 16, 17; D, H, I.*

SOUTHWESTERN OREGON COMMUNITY COLLEGE, Coos Bay, Ore. 97420, *1, 7, 12, 15, 17; D, H, I.*

TREASURE VALLEY COMMUNITY COLLEGE, 650 College Blvd., Ontario, Ore. 97914, *1, 3, 7, 12, 13, 17; A, H, I, K.*

UMPQUA COMMUNITY COLLEGE, P.O. Box 699, Roseburg, Ore. 97470, *7, 12.*

UNIVERSITY OF OREGON, Eugene, Ore. 97403, *2, 4, 7, 8, 10, 11, 12, 15.*

Pennsylvania

ACADEMY OF THE ARTS, 107 Sixth St. (Fulton Bldg.), Pittsburgh, Pa. 15222, *1, 3, 5, 7, 9, 10, 11, 12, 14, 15, 17; A, G, H, I, K.*

ALLEGHENY COLLEGE, Meadville, Pa. 16335, *3, 6, 7, 12, 13, 14, 15, 17; A, D, E, G, I, K.*

ANTONELLI SCHOOL OF PHOTOGRAPHY, 209 N. Broad St., Philadelphia, Pa. 19107, *3; A, G, H.*

ART INSTITUTE OF PHILADELPHIA, 125 S. Ninth St., Philadelphia, Pa. 19107, *1, 5, 7, 9, 12, 13, 14, 15, 17; E, H, I.*

ART INSTITUTE OF PITTSBURGH, 635 Smithfield St., Pittsburgh, Pa. 15222, *1, 3, 5, 7, 9, 10, 11, 12, 13, 14, 17; A, E, F, G, H, I, K.*

THE ART SCHOOL, 18 N. Park Row, Erie, Pa. 16501, *7, 12, 17; A, E, F, H, I.*

BEAVER COLLEGE, Glenside, Pa. 19038, *1, 3, 9, 11, 12, 14, 17; C, D, E, F.*

BLOOMSBURG STATE COLLEGE, Bloomsburg, Pa. 17815, *3, 6, 7, 12, 15; A, D, F, I, K.*

BRYN MAWR COLLEGE, Bryn Mawr, Pa. 19010, *7, 12, 14; D, E, F.*

BUCKNELL UNIVERSITY, Lewisburg, Pa. 17837, *3, 7, 12, 14, 15, 17; D, E.*

BUCKS COUNTY COMMUNITY COLLEGE, Swamp Rd., Newtown, Pa. 18940, *1, 3, 6, 7, 9, 12, 13, 14, 15; A, D, H.*

CABRINI COLLEGE, Radnor, Pa. 19087, *3, 4, 7, 12, 17; C, D, E, F.*

CAMP HILL GALLERY & ACADEMY OF ART, 2208 Market St., Camp Hill, Pa. 17011, *3, 6, 7, 11, 12, 17; H, I.*

CARLOW COLLEGE, Pittsburgh, Pa. *4, 6, 7, 12, 14, 15, 17; D, F.*

CARNEGIE-MELLON UNIVERSITY, Schenley Park, Pittsburg, Pa. 15213, *1, 2, 4, 6, 7, 9, 10, 12, 13, 14, 15, 17; D, E, I.*

CEDAR CREST COLLEGE, Allentown, Pa. 18104, *3, 4, 6, 7, 12, 15; A, D, H, I, K.*

CHATHAM COLLEGE, Pittsburgh, Pa. 15232, *3, 7, 12, 15; D, F.*

CHEYNEY STATE COLLEGE, Cheyney, Pa. 19319, *3, 4, 6, 7, 12, 14, 15; A, D, H, K.*

CLARION STATE COLLEGE, Clarion, Pa. 16214, *4, 6, 7, 12, 14, 15, 17; D.*

COLLEGE MISERICORDIA, Dallas, Pa. 18612, *4, 7, 9, 12, 14, 15, 17; D, E, I.*

COMMUNITY COLLEGE OF PHILADELPHIA, 34 S. 11th St., Philadelphia, Pa. 19107, *1, 12, 13; I.*

DICKINSON COLLEGE, Carlisle, Pa. 17013, *3, 7, 12, 14, 15, 17; D, E, F.*

DREXEL UNIVERSITY, 33rd & Market Sts., Philadelphia, Pa. 19104, *8, 10; A, D, H, I, K.*

EAST STROUDSBURG STATE COLLEGE, East Stroudsburg, Pa. 18301, *3, 4, 6, 7, 12, 14, 15, 17; D, F, I.*

EDINBORO STATE COLLEGE, Edinboro, Pa. 16412, *1, 3, 4, 6, 7, 12, 14, 15, 17; A, D, E, F, I.*

FRANKLIN & MARSHALL COLLEGE, Lancaster, Pa. 17604, *7, 12, 15, 17; D, E, I.*

GANNON COLLEGE, Perry Sq., Erie, Pa. 16501, *3; D, E, I.*

GETTYSBURG COLLEGE, Gettysburg, Pa. 17325, *3, 7, 12, 14, 15, 17; A, D, E, F, K.*

GROVE CITY COLLEGE, Grove City, Pa. 16127, *3, 6, 7, 11, 12, 17; A, F, K.*

HARRISBURG AREA COMMUNITY COLLEGE, 3300 Cameron St. Rd., Harrisburg, Pa. 17110, *2, 3, 4, 7, 12, 13, 14, 15, 17; D, E.*

HAVERFORD COLLEGE, Haverford, Pa. 19041, *3, 4, 6, 7, 12, 13, 14, 15; A, D, K.*

HOLY FAMILY COLLEGE, Philadelphia, Pa. 19114, *3, 7, 9, 10, 12, 15; C.*

HUSSIAN SCHOOL OF ART, 34 S. 17th St., Philadelphia, Pa. 19103, *1, 3, 7, 9, 12, 17; A, F.*

INDIANA UNIVERSITY OF PENNSYLVANIA, Indiana, Pa. 15701, *3, 4, 6, 7, 12, 14, 15, 17; A, D, F, I, K.*

IVY SCHOOL OF PROFESSIONAL ART, 207 Market St., Pittsburgh, Pa. 15222, *1, 7, 8, 9, 11, 12, 13, 14, 17; H.*

JUNIATA COLLEGE, Moore St., Huntingdon, Pa. 16652, *7, 12, 14; D.*

KUTZTOWN STATE COLLEGE, Kutztown, Pa. 19530, *1, 3, 4, 6, 7, 9, 10, 11, 12, 13, 14, 15, 17; A, D, F, I, K.*

LAFAYETTE COLLEGE, College Hill, Easton, Pa. 18042, *1, 3, 7; B, F.*

LA SALLE COLLEGE, 20th & Olney Ave., Philadelphia, Pa. 19141, *3, 12, 13, 14; A, D, H, I, J.*

LEBANON VALLEY COLLEGE, Annville, Pa. 17003, *3, 4, 7, 12, 17; A, F, H.*

LEHIGH UNIVERSITY, Bethlehem, Pa. 18015, *2, 3, 7, 12, 14, 15, 17; B, D, E, F, I, K.*

LOCK HAVEN STATE COLLEGE, Lock Haven, Pa. 17745, *3, 6, 7, 12, 14, 15; A, D, F, I, K.*

LYCOMING COLLEGE, Williamsport, Pa. 17704, *3, 7, 12, 17; A, D, E, F, H, I.*

MANOR JR. COLLEGE, Fox Chase Manor, Jenkintown, Pa. 19046, *3, 4, 6; C, D.*

MANSFIELD STATE COLLEGE, Mansfield, Pa. 16933, *3, 4, 6, 7, 12, 15, 17; A, D, F, I, K.*

MARYWOOD COLLEGE, 2300 Adams Ave., Scranton, Pa. 18509, *1, 3, 4, 6, 7, 9, 11, 12, 14, 15, 17; C, D, F, I, K.*

MERCERSBURG ACADEMY, Mercersburg, Pa. 17236, *3, 6, 7, 8, 12, 14, 15, 16; A.*

MERCYHURST COLLEGE, 508 E. 38th St. Blvd., Erie, Pa. 16501, *1, 3, 4, 6, 7, 11, 12, 14, 15, 17; A, D, E, F, H, I, K.*

MESSIAH COLLEGE, Grantham, Pa. 17028, *3, 12; A, D, E, F, K.*

MILLERSVILLE STATE COLLEGE, Millersville, Pa. 17551, *1, 3, 4, 6, 7, 9, 12, 13, 14, 15, 17; A, D, E, F, H, I, K.*

MOORE COLLEGE OF ART, 20th & Race, Philadelphia, Pa. 19103, *1, 3, 4, 6, 7, 9, 12, 13, 14, 15, 17; C, D, E.*

MT. ALOYSIUS JR. COLLEGE, Cresson, Pa. 16630, *3, 6, 7, 12, 14, 15, 17; C, D, E, F, H, I, K.*

PENN STATE UNIVERSITY, 3550 Seventh St. Rd., New Kensington, Pa. 15068, *3, 4, 7, 12, 17; D, G, I.*

PENNSYLVANIA ACADEMY OF THE FINE ARTS, Broad & Cherry Sts., Philadelphia, Pa. 19102, *3, 7, 12, 14, 15, 17; A, D, E, F, H, I, K.*

PENNSYLVANIA STATE UNIVERSITY, 1600 Woodland Road, Abington, Pa. 19001, *1, 3, 4, 7, 9, 12, 14, 15, 17; A, G, I.*

PENNSYLVANIA STATE UNIVERSITY, University Pk., Pa. 16802, *2, 3, 4, 6, 7, 12, 13, 14, 15, 16, 17; A, E, G, I, K.*

PENNSYLVANIA STATE UNIVERSITY, FAYETTE CAMPUS, Hwy. 119 S., Uniontown, Pa. 15401, *2, 3, 4, 6, 7; A, D, H.*

PENNSYLVANIA STATE UNIVERSITY, NEW KENSINGTON, New Kensington, Pa. 15068, *3, 4, 7, 12, 17; A, D.*

PHILADELPHIA COLLEGE OF ART, Broad & Pine Sts., Philadelphia, Pa. 19102, *1, 3, 4, 7, 9, 10, 11, 12, 13, 14, 15, 16, 17; A, D, E, F, H, I, K.*

PHILADELPHIA COLLEGE OF TEXTILES & SCIENCE, School House Dr., Philadelphia, Pa. 19144, *7, 8, 11, 14, 16; D, E, I.*

POINT PARK COLLEGE, Pittsburgh, Pa. 15222, *1, 4, 7, 9, 10, 12, 13, 14; D, E, I.*

ROSEMONT COLLEGE, Rosemont, Pa. 19010, *1, 3, 4, 7, 12, 14, 15, 17; C, D, E, F, K.*

SACRED HEART JR. COLLEGE, Quarry Road, Yardley, Pa. 19067, *3, 4, 7; C, G.*

ST. FRANCIS COLLEGE, Loretto, Pa. 15940, *3, 4, 6, 7, 12; D.*

SCHOOL OF ART & DESIGN, 1230 Arch St., Philadelphia, Pa. 19107, *7, 12, 14, 15.*

SAMUEL S. FLEISHER ART MEMORIAL, 719 Catharine St., Philadelphia, Pa. 19147, *3, 7, 12, 13, 14, 15, 17; I.*

SENTON HILL COLLEGE, Greensburg, Pa. 15601, *3, 4, 7, 12, 14, 15, 17; D, F, I, K.*

SLIPPERY ROCK STATE COLLEGE, Slippery Rock, Pa. 16057, *3, 6, 7, 12, 13, 15, 16; A, D, H, I, K.*

STATE COLLEGE, Shippersburg, Pa. 17257, *3, 6, 7, 12; A, G.*

SUSQUEHANNA UNIVERSITY, Selingsgrove, Pa. 17870, *7, 12, 17; D.*

SWARTHMORE COLLEGE, Swarthmore, Pa. 19081, *6, 12, 14, 15; A, D.*

TEMPLE UNIVERSITY, Beech and Penrose Ave., Philadelphia, Pa. 19126, *1, 3, 4, 6, 7, 9, 12, 13, 14, 15, 16, 17; A, D, E, F, H, I, K.*

THIEL COLLEGE, Greenville, Pa. 16125, *3, 4, 7, 12, 14; A, D, F, I, K.*

TRACEY-WARNER SCHOOL OF FASHION DESIGN, 663-65 N. Broad St., Philadelphia, Pa. 19123, *3; A, H, I.*

UNIVERSAL ART ACADEMY, 313 Sixth Ave., Pittsburgh, Pa. 15222, *1, 7, 8; E, I.*

UNIVERSITY OF PENNSYLVANIA, Philadelphia, Pa. 19104, *7, 11, 12, 15, 18; D, E, I.*

UNIVERSITY OF PITTSBURG, 728 Cathedral of Learning, Pittsburgh, Pa. 15213, *3, 7, 12, 14, 15; A, D, E, G, H.*

URSINUS COLLEGE, Collegeville, Pa. 19426, *12; D, F, I.*

VILLANOVA UNIVERSITY, Villanova, Pa. 19085, *2, 3, 4, 12, 14, 15, 17; D, H, I.*

WASHINGTON & JEFFERSON COLLEGE, Washington, Pa. 15301, *3, 7, 12, 14; B, F, I, K.*

WEST CHESTER STATE COLLEGE, S. High St., West Chester, Pa. 19380, *1, 3, 6, 7, 12, 14, 15, 16, 17; D, E, I.*

WESTMINSTER COLLEGE, New Wilmington, Pa. 16142, *3, 4, 7, 12, 14, 15, 17; D.*

WILKES COLLEGE, Wilkes-Barre, Pa. 18703, *4, 7, 12, 14, 15, 17; D, I.*

WILLIAMSPORT AREA COMMUNITY COLLEGE, 1005 W. Third St., Williamsport, Pa. 17701, *10; I.*

WILSON COLLEGE, Chambersburg, Pa. 17201, *3, 7, 12, 14, 15, 17; C, D, E, F, K.*

YORK ACADEMY OF ARTS, P.O. Box 1441, 205 S. George St., York, Pa. 17405, *1, 3, 7, 9, 11, 12, 13, 14, 17; A.*

Rhode Island

BROWN UNIVERSITY, Providence, R.I. 02912, *7, 12, 14, 15; D, F.*

PEMBROKE COLLEGE, Benefit St., Providence, R.I. 02912, *4, 7, 12, 14, 15; E.*

PROVIDENCE COLLEGE, River Ave., Providence, R.I. 02918, *3, 4, 6, 7, 12, 13, 14, 15; A, D, H, I, K.*

RHODE ISLAND COLLEGE, 600 Mount Pleasant Ave., Providence, R.I. 02908, *4, 6, 7, 12, 14, 15; D, E, I.*

RHODE ISLAND JUNIOR COLLEGE, 400 East Ave., Warwick, R.I. 02886, *3, 6, 7, 9, 10, 11, 12, 13, 14, 15; A, D, H,* Continuing Education Program.

RHODE ISLAND SCHOOL OF DESIGN, 2 College Hill, Providence, R.I. 02903, *1, 2, 3, 4, 6, 7, 9, 10, 11, 12, 13, 14, 15, 16, 17; A, D, E, F, H, I, K.*

ROGER WILLIAMS COLLEGE, Old Ferry Road, Bristol, R.I. 02809, *4, 7, 12, 14, 15; D.*

SCHOOL OF THE ART ASSOCIATION, 76 Bellevue Avenue, Newport, R.I. 02840, *12; G, H, I.*

UNIVERSITY OF RHODE ISLAND, Kingston, R.I. 02881, *3, 7, 12, 14, 15; D, E, I.*

VERNON COURT JR. COLLEGE, Baker School of Fine Arts, Newport, R.I. 02840, *1, 2, 3, 7, 9, 11, 12, 14, 15; C, D, E, F, I, K.*

South Carolina

ALLEN UNIVERSITY, Harden & Taylor, Columbia, S.C. 29204, *3, 4, 7, 12, 15, 17; A, D, I, K.*

ANDERSON JR. COLLEGE, 410 Blvd., Anderson, S.C. 29621, *1, 3, 7, 12, 17; A, D, E, F, I, K.*

BAPTIST COLLEGE AT CHARLESTON, Hwy. 78 at I-26, Charleston, S.C. 29411, *3, 4, 6, 7, 12, 15; A, D, H, I, K.*

BENEDICT COLLEGE, Taylor & Harden Sts., Columbia, S.C. 29204, *3, 4, 6, 7, 12, 13, 14, 15; A, D, H, I, K.*

BOB JONES UNIVERSITY, Wade Hampton Blvd., Greenville, S.C. 29614, *1, 3, 4, 6, 7, 12, 14, 15, 17; A, D, F, K.*

THE CITADEL, Charleston, S.C. 29409, *B, D, F.*

CLAFLIN COLLEGE, Orangeburg, S.C. 29115, *3, 4, 6, 7, 12, 15, 16, 17.*

CLEMSON UNIVERSITY, Clemson, S.C. 29631, *2, 3, 7, 11, 12, 13, 14, 15, 17; D, E, I.*

COKER COLLEGE, Hartsville, S.C. 29550, *3, 7, 9, 10, 11, 12, 14, 15; B, C, F.*

COLLEGE OF CHARLESTON, 66 George St., Charleston, S.C. 29401, *7, 12, 17; D, F.*

COLUMBIA COLLEGE, Columbia, S.C. 29203, *3, 7, 9, 12, 14, 15, 17; C, D, G, H, I.*

CONVERSE COLLEGE, Spartanburg, S.C. 29301, *3, 6, 7, 10, 12, 13, 15; A, D, H.*

ERSKINE COLLEGE, Due West, S.C. 29639, *4; A, D, I.*

FURMAN UNIVERSITY, Greenville, S.C. 29613, *1, 4, 6, 7, 9, 12, 14, 15; D, E, I.*

LIMESTONE COLLEGE, Gaffney, S.C. 29340, *3, 4, 6, 7, 12, 15; A, D, H, I, K.*

NEWBURY COLLEGE, Box 70, Newbury, S.C. 29108, *3, 7, 12; D.*

PRESBYTERIAN COLLEGE, Broad St., Clinton, S.C. 29325, *3, 7, 12, 15; A, D, E, F, H, I, K.*

RICHLAND ART SCHOOL OF THE COLUMBIA MUSEUM OF ART, 1112 Bull St., Columbia, S.C. 29201, *1, 3, 6, 7, 12, 15, 17; A, F, H, I.*

SOUTH CAROLINA COLLEGE, Orangeburg, S.C. 29115, *4, 6, 7, 12, 15, 16; A, D.*

UNIVERSITY OF SOUTH CAROLINA, Columbia, S.C. 29208, *1, 3, 4, 6, 7, 11, 12, 14, 15, 17; A, D, E, F, H, I, K.*

WINTHROP COLLEGE, Rock Hill, S.C. 29733, *4, 6, 12, 13, 14, 15; A, D, I.*

WOFFORD COLLEGE, Spartanburg, S.C. 29301, *3, 4; B, F, K.*

South Dakota

AUGUSTANA COLLEGE, Sioux Falls, S.D. 57102, *3, 4, 7, 10, 12, 14, 15, 17; A, D, E, F, H, I, K.*

BLACK HILLS STATE COLLEGE, Spearfish, S.D. 57783, *4, 6, 7, 9, 10, 11, 12, 13, 15; A, D, I, K.*

COLLEGE OF ST. MARTIN, Box 3087, Rapid City, S.D. 57701, *3, 4, 6, 7, 12, 14, 17; C.*

DAKOTA STATE COLLEGE, Madison, S.D. 57042, *3, 4, 6, 7, 12, 17; D, E.*

DAKOTA WESLEYAN UNIVERSITY, University Blvd., Mitchell, S.D. 57301, General Art, *A, D, I.*

HURON COLLEGE, Huron, S.D. 57350, *1, 4, 7, 12, 14, 15, 17; D, E.*

MOUNT MARTY COLLEGE, Yankton, S.D. 57078, *3, 4, 6, 7, 12, 14, 15; C, D, F, H, I, K.*

NORTHERN STATE COLLEGE, 12 St., Aberdeen, S.D. 57401, *1, 3, 4, 6, 7, 9, 10, 11, 12, 14, 15, 16, 17; A, D, E, F, I, K.*

RUSHMORE COLLEGE, Box 1130, Rapid City, S.D. 57701, *3, 4, 6, 7, 12, 13; A, F, K.*

SIOUX FALLS COLLEGE, Sioux Falls, S.D. 57101, *3, 6, 7, 12, 15, 21.*

SOUTH DAKOTA STATE UNIVERSITY, Brookings, S.D. 57006, *1, 3, 4, 6, 7, 9, 12, 13, 14, 15, 16, 17; D, E, I.*

SOUTHERN STATE COLLEGE, Springfield, S.D. 57062, *4, 6, 12, 14, 15, 17; D.*

UNIVERSITY OF SOUTH DAKOTA, SPRINGFIELD, Springfield, S.D. 57062, *7, 10, 12, 14, 15; A, D, I, K.*

UNIVERSITY OF SOUTH DAKOTA, Vermillion, S.D. 57069, *1, 3, 4, 5, 7, 9, 12, 17; A, D, F, I, K.*

YANKTON COLLEGE, Yankton, S.D. 57078, *1, 4, 6, 7, 12, 13, 14, 15, 17; D, E, I.*

Tennessee

AUSTIN PEAY STATE UNIVERSITY, Clarksville, Tenn. 37040, *1, 3, 4, 6, 7, 9, 12, 14, 15, 17; A, D, E, F, H, I, K.*

BRYAN COLLEGE, Dayton, Tenn. 37321, *4, 7, 12, 17; D, F.*

CARSON-NEWMAN COLLEGE, Jefferson City, Tenn. 37760, *3, 4, 6, 7, 12, 14, 15, 17; D, E.*

CUMBERLAND COLLEGE, Lebanon, Tenn. 37087, *7, 9, 12, 17; A, F, G, H, I.*

EAST TENNESSEE STATE UNIVERSITY, Johnson City, Tenn. 37601, *3, 4, 6, 7, 12, 13, 14, 15, 17; A, D, E, H, I, K.*

FISK UNIVERSITY DEPT. OF ART, Nashville, Tenn. 37203, *3, 4, 6, 7, 12, 14, 15; D, E, H.*

GEORGE PEABODY COLLEGE FOR TEACHERS, 21 Ave. South, Nashville, Tenn. 37203, *3, 6, 7, 10, 12, 15, 18, 21; D, E, G.*

HARRIS SCHOOL OF ADVERTISING ART INC., 2000 Warfield, Nashville, Tenn. 37215, *1, 3, 7, 9, 12, 13, 17; A, F, K.*

LAMBUTH COLLEGE, Jackson, Tenn. 38302, *3, 4, 7, 12, 14, 15; A, D, E, F, K.*

LANE COLLEGE, Jackson, Tenn. 38301, *4, 6, 7, 12, 17; D, E.*

LE MOYNE COLLEGE, 807 Walker Ave., Memphis, Tenn. 38106, *6, 12, 15; A, F.*

MARTIN COLLEGE, Pulaski, Tenn. 37478, *3, 4, 7, 14, 15; D, G.*

MARYVILLE COLLEGE, Maryville, Tenn. 37801, *3, 4, 6, 7, 12, 14; A, D.*

MEMPHIS ACADEMY OF ARTS, Overton Park, Memphis, Tenn. 38112, *1, 3, 6, 7, 9, 12, 14, 15, 16, 17; A, D, E, F, H, I.*

MEMPHIS STATE UNIVERSITY ART DEPT., Memphis, Tenn. 38111, *1, 2, 3, 4, 7, 9, 11, 12, 14, 15, 17; D, F, H, I, K.*

MIDDLE TENNESSEE STATE UNIVERSITY, Murfreesboro, Tenn. 37130, *3, 4, 6, 7, 12, 13, 14, 15, 17; D, F, H, I, K.*

SOUTHERN MISSIONARY COLLEGE, Collegedale, Tenn. 37315, *4, 6, 7, 10, 12, 13, 14, 15, 17; D.*

SOUTHWESTERN AT MEMPHIS, 2000 N. Parkway, Memphis, Tenn. 38112, *3, 4, 6, 7, 12, 13, 15; A, D, E, K.*

TENNESSEE TECHNOLOGICAL UNIVERSITY, Cookeville, Tenn. 38501, *3, 4; A, F, K.*

TENNESSEE WESLEYAN COLLEGE, P.O. Box 40, Athens, Tenn. 37303, *3, 7, 12, 15; A, D, H, I, K.*

TUSCULUM COLLEGE, Greeneville, Tenn. 37743, *3, 7, 12, 15; A, F, K.*

UNION UNIVERSITY, Jackson, Tenn. 38301, *1, 3, 6, 7, 12, 13, 17; A, D, E, F, H, I, K.*

UNIVERSITY OF TENNESSEE AT CHATTANOOGA, Chattanooga, Tenn. 37403, *1, 4, 7, 12, 14, 15, 17; D, E, I.*

UNIVERSITY OF TENNESSEE, Knoxville, Tenn. 37916, *3, 6, 8, 11, 21; D, E, I.*

UNIVERSITY OF THE SOUTH, Sewanee, Tenn. 37375, *3, 7, 12, 13, 14, 15; A, D, I.*

VANDERBILT UNIVERSITY DEPT. OF FINE ARTS, Box 1801, Station B, Nashville, Tenn. 37203, *3, 7, 12, 15; A, D, F, I.*

Texas

ABILENE CHRISTIAN COLLEGE, Abilene, Tex. 79601, *3, 4, 7, 12, 15; A, D, F, K.*

AMARILLO COLLEGE, Box 447, Amarillo, Tex. 79105, *3, 7, 12, 13, 15; A, F, I.*

ARLINGTON STATE COLLEGE OF THE UNIVERSITY OF TEXAS, ART DEPT., Box 308, Arlington, Tex. 76010, *1, 2, 3, 4, 7, 11, 12; A, D, E, F, I, K.*

AUSTIN COLLEGE, Sherman, Tex. 75090, *3, 4, 7, 12, 13, 14, 15; D, E.*

BAYLOR UNIVERSITY DEPT. OF ART, Waco, Tex. 76703, *1, 3, 4, 6, 7, 12, 14, 17; A, D, E, F, H, I, K.*

CHRISTIAN COLLEGE OF THE SOUTHWEST, PO Box 28295, Dallas, Tex. 75228, *7, 12; D, I.*

CISCO JR. COLLEGE, Cisco, Tex. 96437, *7, 12, 15; D, E, I.*

CONCORDIA LUTHERAN COLLEGE, Austin, Tex. 78705, *4, 7, 12; A, D, K.*

DALLAS ART INSTITUTE, 2523 McKinney Ave., Dallas, Tex. 75201, *1, 5, 7, 8, 9, 10, 11, 12, 14, 15, 16, 17; E, I.*

DALLAS BAPTIST COLLEGE, P. O. Box 21206, Dallas, Tex. 75211, *4, 6, 7, 12, 14, 15; D.*

DEL MAR COLLEGE, Corpus Christi, Texas 78404, *1, 3, 7, 12, 17; F, H, I, K.*

DOMINICAN COLLEGE, 2401 E. Holcombe, Houston, Tex. 77021, *2, 4, 6, 7, 12, 14, 15, 16, 17; D, E, I.*

EAST TEXAS STATE UNIVERSITY, Commerce, Tex. 75428, *1, 3, 4, 6, 7, 8, 9, 12, 14, 15, 16, 17; D, E.*

FORT WORTH ART CENTER MUSEUM & SCHOOL, 1309 Montgomery, Fort Worth, Tex. 76107, *1, 3, 5, 7, 9, 12, 14, 15, 16, 17; A, E, G, H, I.*

FORT WORTH CHRISTIAN COLLEGE, 7517 Bogart Dr., Fort Worth, Tex. 76118, *12, 17; D, E, F.*

FRANK PHILLIPS COLLEGE, 50 Acres on Roosevelt, Borger, Tex. 79007, *3, 7, 12, 14, 15, 17; A, D, F, H, K.*

GARLAND COLLEGE, 2004 16th St., Garland, Tex. 75040, *5, 13; A, D, F, H, I, K.*

HARDIN-SIMMONS UNIVERSITY, Abilene, Tex. 79601, *3, 4, 6, 7, 12, 14, 15; A, D, E, H, I, K.*

HILL COUNTRY ARTS FOUNDATION, Box 176, Ingram, Tex. 78025, *6, 12, 17; A, E, I.*

HOUSTON BAPTIST COLLEGE, 7502 Fondren Rd., Houston, Tex. 77036, *3, 4, 6, 7, 12, 14, 15, 17; A, D, F, I, K.*

HOWARD COLLEGE, Birdwell Lane, Big Spring, Tex. 79720, *1, 3, 4, 6, 7, 12, 14; A, D, H, I, K.*

HOWARD PAYNE UNIVERSITY, Howard Payne Station, Brownwood, Tex. 76801, *1, 3, 4, 6, 7, 9, 10, 11, 12, 13, 15; A, D, E, H, I, K.*

INCARNATE WORD COLLEGE, 4301 Broadway, San Antonio, Tex. 78209, *3, 4, 7, 12, 14; D, E, I.*

KILGORE COLLEGE, 1100 Broadway, Kilgore, Tex. 75662, *1, 7, 9, 10, 12, 14; D, E, H, I.*

LAMAR UNIVERSITY, Box 10027, Beaumont, Tex. 77705, *1, 3, 4, 7, 9, 12, 13, 14, 15, 17; D, I.*

LUBBOCK CHRISTIAN COLLEGE, 5601 19th St., Lubbock, Tex. 79407, *1, 3, 7, 12; A, E, F, I, K.*

MARY HARDIN-BAYLOR COLLEGE, Belton, Tex. 76513, *3, 4, 6, 7, 12, 14, 15, 17; D, F, I, K.*

MC MURRAY COLLEGE, Sayles at 14th Streets, Abilene, Tex. 79605, *3, 4, 7, 12, 17; A, D, F, H, I, K.*

MIDWESTERN UNIVERSITY DEPT. OF ART, 3400 Taft, Wichita Falls, Tex. 76308, *1, 3, 4, 7, 12, 14, 15, 17; A, F, H, I, K.*

NAVARRO COLLEGE, Corsicana, Tex. 75110, *1, 6, 7, 9, 12, 15, 17; A, D, F, K.*

NAZARETH ACADEMY, 205 W. Church St., Victoria, Tex. 77901, *6, 7, 12, 17.*

NORTH TEXAS STATE COLLEGE, Houston, Tex. *2, 4, 7, 8, 10, 11, 12, 14.*

NORTH TEXAS STATE UNIVERSITY, Denton, Tex. 76203, *3, 6, 7, 8, 10, 11, 12, 15, 18, 21; D.*

ODESSA COLLEGE, PO Box 3752, Odessa, Tex. 79760, *1, 3, 4, 6, 7, 9, 10, 12, 15, 17; A, D, E, F, H, I, K.*

OUR LADY OF THE LAKE COLLEGE, 411 S. W. 24th St., San Antonio, Tex. 78707, *3, 4, 6, 7, 12, 14, 15, 17; A, D, E, F, H, I, K.*

PAN AMERICAN UNIVERSITY, Edinburg, Tex. 78539, *1, 3, 4, 7, 12, 14, 15; A, D, E, F, H, I, K.*

RICE UNIVERSITY DEPT. OF FINE ARTS, Houston, Tex. 77001, *3, 7, 12, 14, 15, 17; A, F, K.*

ROCKPORT SCHOOL OF FINE ARTS, PO Box 1283, King St., Rockport, Tex. 78382, *7, 12, 17; A, H, I.*

ST. EDWARD'S UNIVERSITY, 3001 S. Congress, Austin, Tex. 78704, *3, 4, 7, 13, 14, 17.*

ST. MARY'S UNIVERSITY OF SAN ANTONIO, 2700 Cincinnati Ave., San Antonio, Tex. 78284, *3, 4, 6, 7, 12, 13, 14, 15; A, D, H, I, K.*

SAM HOUSTON STATE UNIVERSITY, Huntsville, Tex. 77340, *3, 4, 6, 7, 9, 12, 14, 15, 17; A, D, F, I, K.*

SAN ANTONIO ART INSTITUTE, 6000 N. New Braunfels Ave., San Antonio, Tex. 78209, *3, 7, 10, 12, 15, 18, 21.*

SAN ANTONIO COLLEGE ART DEPT., 1300 San Pedro, San Antonio, Tex. 78212, *2, 3, 6, 7, 14, 17; A, D, F, H, I.*

SAN JACINTO COLLEGE, 8060 Spencer Hwy., Pasadena, Tex. 77505, *1, 7, 15, 17; A, F, H, I.*

SCHOOL OF ART, MUSEUM OF FINE ARTS, PO Box 6826, 1001 Bissonnet, Houston, Tex. 77005, *7, 12, 14, 17; E.*

SIMON MICHAEL SCHOOL OF FINE ART, PO Box 1283, 510 E. King St., Rockport, Tex. 78382, *2, 7, 12, 15; A, H.*

SOUTH PLAINS COLLEGE, Levelland, Tex. 79336, *1, 6, 7, 11, 12, 13, 17; A, F, H, I, K.*

SOUTHERN METHODIST UNIVERSITY, Dallas, Tex. 75222, *1, 3, 4, 6, 7, 12, 14, 15; A, D, E, F, I, K.*

SOUTHWEST TEXAS STATE UNIVERSITY, San Marcos, Tex. 78666, *1, 3, 4, 6, 7, 9, 12, 15, 16, 17; A, D, H, I, K.*

SOUTHWESTERN UNIVERSITY, Box 272 SU Sta., Georgetown, Tex. 78626, *3, 4, 7, 12, 14, 15, 17; A, D, E, F, K.*

STEPHEN F. AUSTIN STATE UNIVERSITY, SFA Sta., Nacogdoches, Tex. 75961 *1, 3, 4, 6, 7, 9, 11, 12, 13, 14, 15, 17; D, E.*

SUL ROSS STATE UNIVERSITY, Alpine, Tex. 79830, *1, 3, 4, 6, 7, 12, 14, 15, 16, 17; D.*

TARLETON STATE COLLEGE, Tarleton Station, Stephenville, Tex. 76401, *3, 4, 6, 7, 9, 12, 17; A, F, I.*

TEMPLE JR. COLLEGE, 2600 S. First St., Temple, Tex. 76501, *1, 6, 12, 14, 15, 17; D, E, I.*

TEXARKANA COLLEGE, Texarkana, Tex. 75501, *3, 4, 6, 7, 12, 13, 15; D, E, I.*

TEXAS A&I UNIVERSITY, Kingsville, Tex. 78363, *3, 4, 6, 7, 12, 14, 15, 17; D, E.*

TEXAS A&M UNIVERSITY, College Station, Tex. 77843, *2; D, E.*

TEXAS CHRISTIAN UNIVERSITY, Fort Worth, Tex. 76129, *1, 3, 4, 6, 7, 9, 12, 14, 15; A, D, E, F, H, I, K.*

TEXAS COLLEGE, Tyler, Tex. 75703, *1, 3, 4, 6, 7, 12; A, D, F, I, K.*

TEXAS COLLEGE OF ARTS & INDUSTRIES, Kingsville, Tex. 78363, *3, 4, 6, 7, 12, 13, 14, 15, 17; A, E, F, H, I, K.*

TEXAS LUTHERAN COLLEGE, Sequin, Tex. 78155, *1, 4, 6, 7, 12, 14, 15; A, D, F, I, K.*

TEXAS SOUTHERN UNIVERSITY, 3201 Wheeler, Houston, Tex. 77004, *4, 6, 7, 12, 14, 15; D.*

TEXAS SOUTHMOST COLLEGE, 83 Fort Brown, Brownsville, Tex. 78520, *3, 7, 12, 14, 17; D, E, I.*

TEXAS TECHNOLOGICAL COLLEGE, Lubbock, Tex. 79406, *2, 4, 7, 10, 11, 12, 14, 18; D.*

TEXAS WESLEYAN COLLEGE, PO Box 3277, Fort Worth, Tex. 76105, *3, 4, 6, 7, 12, 14; A, D, E, H, I, K.*

TEXAS WOMEN'S UNIVERSITY, Denton, Tex. 76201, *2, 7, 10, 12, 15, 18; C, D, E.*

TRINITY UNIVERSITY, 715 Stadium Drive, San Antonio, Tex. 78212, *1, 3, 4, 7, 9, 12, 14, 15, 17; A, D, E, F, H, I, K.*

TYLER JR. COLLEGE, 5th St., Tyler, Tex. 75701, *3, 7, 12; A, F, H, K.*

UNIVERSITY OF CORPUS CHRISTI, Corpus Christi, Tex. 78411, *3, 4, 7, 12, 14, 15; A, D, E, F, H, I, K.*

UNIVERSITY OF DALLAS, Dallas, Tex. 75061, *3, 7, 10, 12, 15, 18.*

UNIVERSITY OF HOUSTON ART DEPT., Cullen Blvd., Houston, Tex. 77004, *1, 2, 3, 4, 6, 7, 9, 10, 11, 12, 13, 14, 15, 17; A, D, E, F, H, I, K.*

UNIVERSITY OF ST. THOMAS, 3812 Montrose, Houston, Tex. 77006, *7, 12, 15; D, F.*

UNIVERSITY OF TEXAS AT AUSTIN, Austin, Tex. 78712, *1, 3, 4, 6, 7, 9, 11, 12, 13, 14; A, D, E, F, I, K.*

UNIVERSITY OF TEXAS AT EL PASO, Texas Western College, El Paso, Tex. 79999, *3, 4, 7, 12, 15; A, D, F, H, I, K.*

UNIVERSITY OF TEXAS OF THE PERMIAN BASIN, Odessa, Tex. 79762, *3, 4, 6, 7, 12, 13, 14, 15; A, D, H, I.*

VICTORIA COLLEGE, Victoria, Tex. 77901, *4, 6, 12; D.*

WAYLAND BAPTIST COLLEGE, 1900 W. Seventh, Plainview, Tex. 79072, *3, 4, 7, 12, 14, 15, 17; D, E, I.*

WEATHERFORD COLLEGE, 407 S. Main, Weatherford, Tex. 76086, *4, 7, 12, 17; A, D, E, F, H, I.*

WEST TEXAS STATE UNIVERSITY, Canyon, Tex. 79015, *1, 3, 4, 6, 7, 12, 14, 15, 16, 17; A, D, E, F, H, I, K.*

WHARTON COUNTY COLLEGE, 911 Boling Highway, Wharton, Tex. 77488, *3, 4, 6, 7, 12, 15; A, D, H, I.*

WILEY COLLEGE, Marshall, Tex. 75670, *4, 6, 7, 10, 12, 14, 15, 17; F.*

Utah

BRIGHAM YOUNG UNIVERSITY, Provo, Utah 84601, *3, 6, 7, 8, 10, 12, 15, 18, 21; D, E, I, K.*

COLLEGE OF EASTERN UTAH, Price, Utah 84501, *1, 3, 7, 12, 14, 15, 17; A, D, E, G, H, K.*

COLLEGE OF SOUTHERN UTAH, Cedar City, Utah 84720, *1, 3, 4, 6, 7, 9, 11, 12, 13, 14, 15, 17; A, D, E, G, H, I, K.*

DIXIE COLLEGE, St. George, Utah 84770, *1, 3, 6, 7, 12, 13, 14, 15, 16, 17; A, E, G, H.*

SNOW COLLEGE, Ephraim, Utah 84627, *1, 3, 4, 7, 11, 12, 13, 17; H.*

SOUTHERN UTAH STATE COLLEGE, Cedar City, Utah 84720, *1, 3, 4, 7, 11, 12, 13, 14, 15, 17; D, E, H, I.*

UNIVERSITY OF UTAH, Fine Arts Building, Salt Lake City, Utah 84112, *1, 2, 3, 4, 6, 7, 9, 10, 12, 14, 15, 17; D, E, G, H, I, K.*

UTAH STATE AGRICULTURAL COLLEGE, Logan, Utah 84321, *4.*

UTAH STATE UNIVERSITY, Logan, Utah 84321, *1, 3, 4, 6, 7, 9, 11, 12, 14, 15, 16, 17; E, H, I, K.*

WEBER STATE COLLEGE, 3750 Harrison Blvd., Ogden, Utah 84403, *1, 3, 4, 6, 7, 12, 13, 14, 15, 17; D, E, H.*

WESTMINSTER COLLEGE OF UTAH, 1840 S. 13th St. E., Salt Lake City, Utah 84105, *3, 4, 7, 12; A, D, F, I, K.*

Vermont

BENNINGTON COLLEGE, Bennington, Vt. 05201, *2, 4, 7, 12, 14, 15; D, E, F.*

CASTLETON STATE COLLEGE, Castleton, Vt. 05735, *1, 3, 4, 7, 12, 15, 17; D.*

GODDARD COLLEGE, Plainfield, Vt. 05667, *2, 3, 6, 7, 12, 13, 14, 15, 17; D, G.*

GREEN MOUNTAIN COLLEGE, Poultney, Vt. 05764, *1, 3, 7, 12; C, G.*

JOHNSON STATE COLLEGE, Johnson, Vt. 05656, *3, 7, 12.*

MIDDLEBURY COLLEGE, Middlebury, Vt. 05753, *3, 6, 7, 9, 10, 12, 15; D, F.*

NORWICH UNIVERSITY, Northfield, Vt. 05663, *3, 13; B, F.*

SOUTHERN VERMONT ART CENTER, Manchester, Vt. 05254, *7, 12, 14, 15, 17; A, E, I.*

THE UNIVERSITY OF VERMONT, Dept. of Art, Burlington, Vt. 05401, *2, 3, 6, 7, 12, 15; A, D, F, H, I, K.*

WINDHAM COLLEGE, Putney, Vt. 05346, *7, 12, 13, 14, 15, 17; D, E, F.*

WRIGHT SCHOOL OF ART, Stowe, Vt. 05672, *7, 12, 17; A, F, H, I.*

Virginia

AVERETT COLLEGE, Danville, Va. 24541, *1, 3, 4, 7, 12, 14, 15, 17; D, E, I.*

BRIDGEWATER COLLEGE, Bridgewater, Va. 22812, *3, 7, 12, 15; A, F, I, K.*

COLLEGE OF WILLIAM AND MARY, Williamsburg, Va. 23185, *2, 3, 4, 6, 7, 12, 14, 15, 17; A, D, F, I, K.*

COLUMBIA TECHNICAL INSTITUTE-SCHOOL OF TECHNOLOGY, 112 S. Wayne Street, Arlington, Va. 22180, *1, 2, 5, 7, 8, 9, 10, 11, 14, 17; I.*

FREDERICK COLLEGE, Portsmouth, Va. 23703, *3, 4, 7, 17; A, D, F, K.*

HAMPTON INSTITUTE, Hampton, Va. 23368, *1, 3, 4, 6, 7, 9, 10, 12, 13, 14, 15, 16, 17; A, D, E, F, I, K.*

HOLDEN SCHOOL OF ART & DESIGN, 215 E. High, Charlottesville, Va. 22902, *7, 9, 11, 12, 14, 17.*

HOLLINS COLLEGE, Hollins College, Va. 24020, *7, 12, 14, 15; C, D, G.*

LONGWOOD COLLEGE, Farmville, Va. 23901, *1, 4, 6, 7, 12, 13, 14, 15, 16, 17; C, D.*

LYNCHBURG COLLEGE, Lynchburg, Va. 24501, *3, 4, 6, 7, 12, 13, 14, 15; A, D.*

MADISON COLLEGE, Harrisonburg, Va. 22801, *1, 3, 4, 6, 7, 11, 12, 13, 14, 15, 16, 17; D, E, I.*

MARION COLLEGE, Main St., Marion, Va. 24354, *3, 6; C, F, K.*

MARY BALDWIN COLLEGE, Frederick Street, Staunton, Va. 24401, *3, 4, 6, 7, 12, 14, 15, 17; C, D, E, F.*

MARY WASHINGTON COLLEGE, Fredericksburg, Va. 22401, *3, 4, 6, 7, 9, 12, 14, 15; A, D, E, H.*

NORFOLK STATE COLLEGE, 2401 Corprew Ave., Norfolk, Va. 23504, *1, 4, 6, 7, 9, 12, 13, 14, 15, 17; D.*

OLD DOMINION COLLEGE, 5215 Hampton Blvd., Norfolk, Va. 23508, *3, 4, 6, 7, 12, 13, 14, 15, 17; A, D, E, F, H, I, K.*

RADFORD COLLEGE, Radford, Va. 24142, *2, 3, 4, 6, 7, 12, 14, 15, 17; D, E.*

RANDOLPH-MACON WOMAN'S COLLEGE, Lynchburg, Va. 24503, *6, 14, 15; C, D, K.*

RICHARD BLAND COLLEGE OF THE COLLEGE OF WILLIAM & MARY, Petersburg, Va. 23803, *7, 12, 14, 15; D, I.*

RICHMOND PROFESSIONAL INSTITUTE, School of Art, Richmond, Va. 23220, *1, 3, 4, 6, 7, 9, 10, 11, 12, 13, 14, 15, 16, 17; A, D, E, F, H, I, K.*

ROANOKE COLLEGE, Salem, Va. 24153, *7, 12, 13, 17; D, I.*

ST. PAUL'S COLLEGE, Lawrenceville, Va. 23868, *3, 4, 6, 7, 12, 15, 17; E, G.*

SOUTHERN SEMINARY JUNIOR COLLEGE, Buena Vista, Va. 24416, *4, 6, 7, 8, 9, 11, 12, 15; C, D, K.*

SULLINS COLLEGE, Bristol, Va. 24201, *3, 6, 7, 11, 12, 13, 15; C, D, K.*

SWEET BRIAR COLLEGE, Sweet Briar, Va. 24595, *3,* Art studio; *C, D, K.*

UNIVERSITY OF RICHMOND, Richmond, Va. 23220, *3, 12; A, D, F, K.*

UNIVERSITY OF VIRGINIA, Charlottesville, Va. 22903, *3, 7, 12, 14, 15; A, D, I, K.*

VIRGINIA ART INSTITUTE, 2007 Earhart, Charlottesville, Va. 22903, *1, 7, 9, 12, 13, 14, 15, 17; E, I.*

VIRGINIA COMMONWEALTH UNIVERSITY SCHOOL OF THE ARTS, 901 W. Franklin, Richmond, Va. 23220, *1, 3, 4, 6, 7, 8, 9, 11, 12, 13, 14, 15, 16; D, E, I.*

VIRGINIA INTERMONT COLLEGE, Moore Street, Bristol, Va. 24210, *4, 6, 7, 11, 12, 13, 14, 15, 17; C, D, F.*

VIRGINIA POLYTECHNIC INSTITUTE & STATE UNIVERSITY, College of Architecture, Blacksburg, Va. 24061, *2, 3, 7, 12, 13, 14, 15, 17; D, I, K.*

VIRGINIA STATE COLLEGE, Norfolk Div., 2401 Corprew Ave., Norfolk, Va. 23504, *3, 4, 6, 7, 13, 14, 15; A, D, F, H, I.*

VIRGINIA STATE COLLEGE, Box 26, Petersburg, Va. 23802, *3, 4, 6, 7, 12, 14, 15, 17; D, E.*

VIRGINIA WESLEYAN COLLEGE, Wesleyan Dr., Norfolk, Va. 23502, *3, 4, 7, 12, 15, 17; D, E, F, I.*

WASHINGTON & LEE UNIVERSITY, Lexington, Va. 24450, *7, 12, 14, 15, 17; B, D, F.*

Washington

BELLEVUE COMMUNITY COLLEGE, Bellevue, Wash. 98007, *3, 6, 7, 12, 13, 15, 16; A, D, H.*

BIG BEND COMMUNITY COLLEGE, Moses Lake, Wash. 98837, *1, 3, 6, 7, 12, 14, 15, 17; A, D, H, I, K.*

BURNLEY SCHOOL OF PROFESSIONAL ART, 905 E. Pine St., Seattle, Wash. 98122, *1, 3, 5, 7, 9, 10, 11, 13, 17; A, E, F.*

CENTRAL WASHINGTON STATE COLLEGE, Ellensburg, Wash. 98926, *1, 4, 6, 7, 11, 12, 13, 14, 15, 17; D, H.*

CENTRALIA COLLEGE, Locust at Oak, Centralia, Wash. 98531, *3, 7, 12, 17; A, E, G, K.*

CLARK COLLEGE, 1800 E. McLoughlin Blvd., Vancouver, Wash. 98663, *3, 7, 9, 12, 13, 14, 15, 16, 17; D, H.*

COLUMBIA BASIN COLLEGE, 2600 N. Chase, Pasco, Wash. 99301, *1, 3, 6, 7, 12, 14, 15, 17; A, D, E, H, I.*

CORNISH SCHOOL OF ALLIED ARTS, 710 E. Roy St., Seattle, Wash. 98102, *6, 7, 9, 11, 14, 15, 17; E, I.*

EASTERN WASHINGTON STATE COLLEGE, Cheney, Wash. 99004, *1, 3, 4, 6, 7, 11, 12, 14, 15, 17; A, D, F, H, I, K.*

EVERETT COMMUNITY COLLEGE, 801 Wetmore, Everett, Wash. 98201, *1, 3, 6, 7, 11, 12, 13, 15, 16, 17; A, D, F, H, I, K.*

FORT WRIGHT COLLEGE, Spokane, Wash. 99204, *1, 3, 4, 7, 12, 14, 15; A, D, E, G, H, I, K.*

GONZAGA UNIVERSITY, Spokane, Wash. 99202, *1, 3, 4, 7, 9, 12, 14, 15; A, D, F, H, I.*

GRAYS HARBOR JR. COLLEGE, Aberdeen, Wash. 98520, *3, 7, 12.*

GREEN RIVER COMMUNITY COLLEGE, Auburn, Wash. 98002, *1, 6, 7, 9, 12, 13, 14, 15, 16, 17; D, E, H, I.*

LOWER COLUMBIA COLLEGE, Longview, Wash. 98632, *3, 6, 7, 12, 15, 17; D, E, H, I.*

OLYMPIC COMMUNITY COLLEGE, 16 & Chester, Bremerton, Wash. 98310, *3, 7, 11, 12, 14, 17; A, D, E, F, H, I.*

PACIFIC LUTHERAN UNIVERSITY, Tacoma, Wash. 98447, *3, 4, 7, 9, 12, 13, 14, 15; A, D, I, K.*

PENINSULA COLLEGE, Port Angeles, Wash. 98362, *7, 9, 12, 14, 17; D, G, I.*

SEATTLE CENTRAL COMMUNITY COLLEGE, 1718 Broadway, Seattle, Wash. 98122, *1, 3, 12, 13, 15; A, D, H.*

SEATTLE UNIVERSITY DEPT. OF FINE ARTS, Broadway & Madison, Seattle, Wash. 98122, *3, 7, 12, 14, 15; A, D, K.*

SHORELINE COMMUNITY COLLEGE, N. 160 St., Greenwood Ave., Seattle, Wash. 98132, *1, 3, 7, 12, 14, 15, 17; A, F, H, I.*

SKAGIT VALLEY COLLEGE, Mount Vernon, Wash. 98273, *3, 6, 7, 12, 14, 15, 16, 17; D, E, H, I.*

SPOKANE FALLS COMMUNITY COLLEGE, 3410 Fort Wright Dr., Spokane, Wash. 99204, *1, 3, 5, 7, 9, 12, 13, 14, 15, 17; D, E, H, I.*

TACOMA COMMUNITY COLLEGE, 5900 S. 12 St., Tacoma, Wash. 98465, *3, 7, 12, 15, 17; A, G, H.*

UNIVERSITY OF PUGET SOUND, 1500 N. Warner, Tacoma, Wash. 98416, *1, 3, 4, 6, 7, 11, 12, 14, 15, 17; A, D, F, I, K.*

UNIVERSITY OF WASHINGTON, Seattle, Wash. 98105, *1, 2, 3, 4, 5, 6, 7, 9, 10, 11, 12, 13, 14, 15, 16, 17; A, D, E, G, H, I, K.*

WALLA WALLA COMMUNITY COLLEGE, College Place, Wash. 99324, *1, 3, 7, 12, 14, 15; A, G, I, K.*

WASHINGTON STATE UNIVERSITY, Pullman, Wash. 99163, *1, 2, 3, 4, 6, 7, 9, 11, 12, 14, 15, 17; A, D, E, F, I, K.*

WENATCHEE VALLEY COLLEGE, 5th Street, Wenatchee, Wash. 98801, *3, 6, 7, 11, 12, 13, 14, 15, 17; A, D, E, G, H, I, K.*

WESTERN WASHINGTON STATE COLLEGE, Bellingham, Wash. 98225, *3, 4, 7, 12, 14, 15, 17; A, D, E, F, H, I, K.*

WHITMAN COLLEGE, Boyer Ave., Walla Walla, Wash. 99362, *3, 6, 7, 12, 14, 15, 17; A, D, E, F, K.*

WHITWORTH COLLEGE, Spokane, Wash. 99218, *3, 4, 6, 7, 12, 13, 14, 15, 17; A, D, E, F, H, I, K.*

West Virginia

BETHANY COLLEGE, Bethany, W. Va. 26032, *3, 4, 6, 7, 12, 15, 17; A, D, E, F, K.*

CONCORD COLLEGE, Athens, W. Va. 24712, *4, 6, 7, 9, 12, 14, 15, 17; D.*

DAVIS & ELKINS COLLEGE, Elkins, W. Va. 26241, *1, 3, 4, 7, 12, 14, 15, 17; A, D, E, F, K.*

FAIRMONT STATE COLLEGE, Fairmont, W. Va. 26555, *3, 4, 7, 11, 12, 14, 15, 17; A, D, E, F, I, K.*

GLENVILLE STATE COLLEGE, Glenville, W. Va. 26351, *3, 4, 6, 7, 12, 14, 15, 16, 17; A, D, E, F, H, I, K.*

MARSHALL UNIVERSITY, Huntington, W. Va. 25705, *3, 4, 6, 7, 12, 14, 15, 17; A, F, H, I, K.*

MORRIS HARVEY COLLEGE, 2300 Maccorkle Avenue, Charleston, W. Va. 25304, *3, 4, 7, 11, 12, 15, 17; A, D, E, F, H, I, K.*

SHEPHERD COLLEGE, Shepherdstown, W. Va. 25443, *3, 4, 6, 7, 12, 14, 15, 17; D.*

WEST LIBERTY STATE COLLEGE INSTITUTE, West Liberty, W. Va. 25112, *3, 4, 7, 12, 14, 15, 17; D, E, I.*

WEST VIRGINIA INSTITUTE OF TECHNOLOGY, Montgomery, W. Va. 25136, *3, 6; A, F, K.*

WEST VIRGINIA STATE COLLEGE INSTITUTE, W. Va. 25112, *3, 4, 7, 12, 14, 15, 17; D, E, I.*

WEST VIRGINIA UNIVERSITY, Morgantown, W. Va. 26506, *3, 4, 7, 12, 15, 17; A, D, E, F, H, I, K.*

WEST VIRGINIA WESLEYAN COLLEGE, Buckhannon, W. Va. 26201, *3, 4, 6, 7, 12, 14, 15, 17; A, D.*

Wisconsin

ALVERNO COLLEGE, 3401 S. 39th Street, Milwaukee, Wisc. 53215, *3, 4, 6, 7, 12, 14, 15, 16, 17; D, E, F, G, H, I, K.*

BELOIT COLLEGE, Beloit, Wisc. 53511, *3, 7, 12, 15.*

CARDINAL STRITCH COLLEGE, 6801 N. Yates Rd., Milwaukee, Wisc. 53217, *3, 7, 12.*

CARTHAGE COLLEGE, Kenosha, Wisc. 53140, *4, 6, 7, 12, 14, 15; A, D, E, F, H, I, K.*

CONCORDIA COLLEGE, 3201 W. Highland, Milwaukee, Wisc. 53209, *3, 6, 7, 12, 15; A, D.*

DODGE COUNTY TEACHERS COLLEGE, Oak St., Mayville, Wisc. 53050, *4; A, F.*

DOMINICAN COLLEGE, 5915 Erie Street, Racine, Wisc. 53402, *3, 4, 6, 7, 12, 14, 15, 16, 17; A, D, F, H, K.*

EDGEWOOD COLLEGE, 855 Woodrow Street, Madison, Wisc. 53711, *3, 4, 6, 7, 12, 14, 15, 16; C, D, F, I, K.*

LAWRENCE UNIVERSITY ART DEPT., Appleton, Wisc. 54911, *2, 3, 4, 6, 7, 14, 15, 17; G.*

LAYTON SCHOOL OF ART, 4650 N. Port Washington Rd., Milwaukee, Wisc. 53212, *1, 3, 7, 9, 10, 11, 12, 13, 14, 15, 17; A, D, E, F, H, K.*

MADISON AREA TECHNICAL COLLEGE, 211 N. Carroll St., Madison, Wisc. 53703, *1, 6, 7, 9, 12, 14, 17; D, F, I.*

MARIAN COLLEGE OF FOND DU LAC, 45 National Avenue, Fond du Lac, Wisc. 54935, *3, 4, 6, 7, 9, 10, 12, 17; C, D, E, F, H, I, K.*

MILTON COLLEGE, Milton, Wisc. 53563, *3, 4, 7, 12, 13, 14, 15, 17; D, E.*

MILWAUKEE AREA TECHNICAL COLLEGE, 1015 N. Sixth St., Milwaukee, Wisc. 53203, *1, 6, 7, 9, 13; D, F, I.*

MILWAUKEE-DOWNER COLLEGE, 2512 E. Hartford Ave., Milwaukee, Wisc. 53211, *3, 6, 7, 12, 18, 21.*

MILWAUKEE INSTITUTE OF TECHNOLOGY, 1015 N. Sixth Street, Milwaukee, Wisc. 53203, *1, 3, 6, 7, 9, 10, 13; A, D, E, F, H.*

MOUNT MARY COLLEGE, 2900 North Menomonee River Parkway, Milwaukee, Wisc. 53222, *3, 4, 6, 7, 11, 12, 14, 15, 16, 17; C, D, E, F, I, K.*

MOUNT ST. PAUL COLLEGE, 500 Prospect Ave., Waukesha, Wisc. 53186, *4, 7, 12, 15; D, G.*

RIPON COLLEGE, Ripon, Wisc. 54971, *3, 7, 12, 14; A, D, E.*

SAINT NORBERT COLLEGE DEPT. OF ART, West De Pere, Wisc. 54178, *3, 4, 6, 7, 12, 14, 15, 17; A, D, E, F, G, I, K.*

SCHOOL OF EDUCATION, 455 North Park, Madison, Wisc. 53706, *3, 4, 6, 7, 12, 13, 14, 15, 17; D.*

STOUT STATE UNIVERSITY, Menominie, Wisc. 54751, *1, 2, 3, 4, 6, 7, 9, 10, 11, 12, 13, 14, 15, 17; A, D, F, H, I, K.*

STOUT STATE UNIVERSITY AT RICE LAKE, Rice Lake, Wisc. 54868, *3, 7, 12, 17; I.*

UNIVERSITY OF WISCONSIN AT GREEN BAY, Green Bay, Wisc. 54305, *1, 3, 4, 7, 9, 10, 12, 13, 14, 15, 17; D, I.*

UNIVERSITY OF WISCONSIN AT KENOSHA, 3700 Washington Road, Kenosha, Wisc. 53140, *4, 7, 12, 14, 15, 16, 17; D, I.*

UNIVERSITY OF WISCONSIN AT MADISON ART DEPARTMENT, 970 Observatory Drive, Madison, Wisc. 53706, *1, 3, 4, 6, 7, 11, 12, 13, 14, 15, 16, 17; A, D, E, F, I, K.*

UNIVERSITY OF WISCONSIN AT MARSHFIELD, PO Box 487, Marshfield, Wisc. 54449, *7, 12, 14, 15, 17; D, E, I.*

UNIVERSITY OF WISCONSIN AT MENASHA, Fox Valley Campus, Midway Rd., Menasha, Wisc. 54952, *3, 4, 5, 7, 12, 14, 15, 17; A, E, F, H, I.*

UNIVERSITY OF WISCONSIN AT MILWAUKEE, 3203 N. Downer Avenue, Milwaukee, Wisc. 53201, *1, 3, 4, 6, 7, 9, 12, 13, 14, 15, 17; A, D, E, F, H, I.*

UNIVERSITY OF WISCONSIN—PARKSIDE, Wood Rd., Kenosha, Wisc. 53104, *3, 4, 6, 7, 12, 13, 14, 15; A, D, I.*

UNIVERSITY OF WISCONSIN AT SHEBOYGAN, Sheboygan County Center, Lower Falls Road, Box 719, Sheboygan, Wisc. 53081, *3, 7; A, G.*

UNIVERSITY OF WISCONSIN—STOUT, Menominie, Wisc. 54751, *3, 4, 6, 7, 11, 12, 14, 15; A, D, H, I, K.*

VITERBO COLLEGE, 815 S. 9th St., LaCrosse, Wisc. 54601, *3, 4, 6, 7, 12, 14, 15, 17; C, D, F, I, K.*

WISCONSIN STATE UNIVERSITY AT EAU CLAIRE, Eau Claire, Wisc. 54701, *1, 3, 4, 6, 7, 12, 14, 15, 16, 17; A, D, E, F, I, K.*

WISCONSIN STATE UNIVERSITY AT LA CROSSE, 1725 State St., La Crosse, Wisc. 54601, *4, 6, 7, 14, 15; D.*

WISCONSIN STATE UNIVERSITY AT OSHKOSH, 800 Algoma Blvd., Oshkosh, Wisc. 54901, *3, 6, 7, 10, 12; D, I.*

WISCONSIN STATE UNIVERSITY AT PLATTEVILLE, Platteville, Wisc. 53818, *1, 3, 4, 6, 7, 12, 13, 14, 15, 17; A, D, E, F, I, K.*

WISCONSIN STATE UNIVERSITY AT RICHLAND, Richland Center, Wisc. 53581, *3, 4, 6, 7; I.*

WISCONSIN STATE UNIVERSITY AT RIVER FALLS, River Falls, Wisc. 54022, *3, 4, 6, 7, 12, 14, 15; A, D, E, H, I, K.*

WISCONSIN STATE UNIVERSITY AT STEVENS POINT, Stevens Pt., Wisc. 54481, *3, 4, 6, 7, 12, 14, 15, 17; A, F, H, I, K.*

WISCONSIN STATE UNIVERSITY AT SUPERIOR, Superior, Wisc. 54881, *1, 3, 4, 6, 7, 12, 13, 14, 15, 17; A, D, E, F, H, I, K.*

WISCONSIN STATE UNIVERSITY AT WHITEWATER, Whitewater, Wisc. 53190, *1, 2, 3, 4, 6, 7, 12, 14, 15, 16; A, D, F, I, K.*

Wyoming

CASPER COLLEGE, Community Dr., Casper, Wyo. 82601, *1, 3, 4, 6, 7, 8, 9, 11, 12, 15, 16; A, D, I, K.*

CENTRAL WYOMING COLLEGE, Riverton, Wyo. 82501, *1, 3, 6, 7, 12, 13, 14, 15; A, D, H.*

EASTERN WYOMING COLLEGE, 3200 West C St., Torrington, Wyo. 82240, *3, 6, 7, 12, 13, 14, 15; A, D, H, K.*

LARAMIE COUNTY COMMUNITY COLLEGE, 1400 E. College Dr., Cheyenne, Wyo. 82001, *1, 3, 6, 7, 12, 15, 17; A, D, H, I.*

NORTHWEST COMMUNITY COLLEGE, Powell, Wyo. 82435, *1, 4, 6, 7, 8, 9, 12, 13, 14, 15; A, D, H, K.*

SHERIDAN COLLEGE, Sheridan, Wyo. 82801, *1, 6, 7, 12, 17; A, D, E, F, H, K.*

UNIVERSITY OF WYOMING, University Station, Box 3138, Laramie, Wyo. 82070, *1, 3, 4, 5, 6, 7, 12, 13, 14, 15, 17; A, D, F, H, I, K.*

WESTERN WYOMING COLLEGE, Rock Springs, Wyo. 82901, *3, 6, 7, 12, 13, 15; A, D, H.*

CANADA

Alberta

ALBERTA COLLEGE OF ART, 1301 16th Ave. N.W., Calgary, Alberta 41; *1, 3, 6, 7, 8, 9, 13, 14, 15, 16, 17; A, E, H, I.*

BANFF SCHOOL OF FINE ARTS, Banff, Alberta, *6, 7, 12, 13, 14, 17; A, D, E, J.*

MOUNT ROYAL COLLEGE, Seventh Ave. & 11th St., Calgary, Alberta, *2, 3, 6, 9, 11, 12, 17; A, D, I.*

RED DEER COLLEGE, Red Deer, Alberta, *3, 6, 7, 9, 10, 12, 13, 15; A, D, H, I, K.*

UNIVERSITY OF ALBERTA, Arts Bldg., 112 St. & 90th Ave., Edmonton, Alberta, *1, 3, 7, 10, 12, 13, 14, 15; A, D, E, I.*

UNIVERSITY OF CALGARY, 24th St. & 24th Ave. NW, Calgary, Alberta, 44, *3, 4, 7, 12, 14, 15; A, D, I.*

UNIVERSITY OF LETHBRIDGE, Lethbridge, Alberta, *3, 4, 6, 7, 12, 13, 14, 15; A, D, H, I.*

British Columbia

KOOTENAY SCHOOL OF ART, Box 480, Nelson, B.C., *1, 3, 4, 5, 6, 7, 8, 9, 12, 13, 14, 15, 16, 17; A, F, I.*

NOTRE DAME UNIVERSITY OF NELSON, 10th St., Nelson, B.C., *3, 4, 6, 7, 12, 14, 15, 16, 17; A, D, F, I.*

SELKIRK COLLEGE, Box 480, Nelson, B.C., *1, 3, 4, 6, 7, 9, 10, 11, 12, 13, 14, 15, 16; A, D, H.*

SIMON FRASER UNIVERSITY, Burnaby Mountain, Burnaby, B.C., *2, 3, 7, 12, 13, 14.*

UNIVERSITY OF BRITISH COLUMBIA, Vancouver, B.C., *8, 3; A, D.*

UNIVERSITY OF VICTORIA, Box 1700, Victoria, B.C., *7, 13, 14, 15; A, D, E.*

VANCOUVER CITY COLLEGE, LANGARA, 100 W. 49th St., Vancouver, B.C., *1, 3, 6, 7, 8, 12, 13, 14, 15; A, D, H, I.*

VANCOUVER SCHOOL OF ART, 249 Dunsmuir St., Vancouver, B.C., *3, 6, 7, 8, 9, 12, 13, 14, 15, 17; A, I.*

Manitoba

UNIVERSITY OF MANITOBA, Winnipeg, Manitoba, *1, 3, 4, 7, 9, 12, 14, 15; A, D.*

New Brunswick

COLLEGE SAINT-LOUIS-MAILLET, Edmundston, N.B., *3, 6, 7, 12, 15; A, D, E, I, K.*

LE COLLEGE DE BATHURST, Bathurst, N.B., *1, 3, 7, 9, 12, 13, 14, 15, 17; A, D, I.*

MOUNT ALLISON UNIVERSITY, Sackville, N.B., *3, 7, 12, 13, 14, 15, 17; A, D, E.*

NEW BRUNSWICK HANDCRAFT SCHOOL, Hut 3, Woodstock Rd., Fredericton, N.B., *6, 16; A, J.*

UNIVERSITÉ DE MONCTON, Moncton, N.B., *3, 4, 12, 14, 15, 17; A, D.*

UNIVERSITY OF NEW BRUNSWICK, Fredericton, N.B., *4, 6; A, I.*

Newfoundland

MEMORIAL UNIVERSITY OF NEWFOUNDLAND, Elizabeth Ave., St. Johns, Newfoundland, 7, 12, 14, 15, 17; A, I.

Nova Scotia

MOUNT ST. BERNARD COLLEGE, Antigonish, N.S., 3, 4, 7, 8, 12, 14, 15, 16, 17; A, F.

NOVA SCOTIA COLLEGE OF ART AND DESIGN, 6152 Coburg Rd., Halifax, N.S., 1, 3, 4, 6, 7, 9, 11, 12, 14, 15, 17; A, D, J.

NOVA SCOTIA TECHNICAL COLLEGE, PO Box 1000, Halifax, N.S., 2, 6, 7, 10, 13; A, D, K.

Ontario

ARTISTS' WORKSHOP, 296 Brunswick Ave., Toronto, Ont., 3, 7, 12, 13, 14, 15, 17; A, F, I.

CARLETON UNIVERSITY, Colonel by Drive, Ottawa, Ont., 1, 3; A, D, I.

CENTRAL TECHNICAL SCHOOL, 725 Bathhurst St., Toronto, Ont., 4, 1, 3, 6, 7, 9, 12, 13, 14, 15, 16, 17; A, G, I.

GEORGE BROWN COLLEGE OF APPLIED ARTS AND TECHNOLOGY, Box 1015, Station B, Toronto, Ont., 1, 3, 7, 9, 14; A, D, H.

HOCKLEY VALLEY SCHOOL, 296 Brunswick Ave., Toronto, 179, Ont., 6, 7, 12, 13, 14, 15, 17; A, J.

HUMBER COLLEGE OF APPLIED ARTS & TECHNOLOGY, Humber College Blvd., Rexdale, Ont., 1, 2, 3, 6, 7, 8, 9, 10, 11, 12, 13, 14, 15, 16; A, D, H, I.

MADOC-TWEED ART & WRITING CENTER, Madoc-Tweed, Ont., 3, 4, 6, 7, 12, 13, 17; A, E, J.

MC MASTER UNIVERSITY, Hamilton, Ont., 3, 7, 12, 14, 15; A, D, I.

NEW SCHOOL OF ART, 296 Brunswick Ave., Toronto, Ont., 179, 3, 7, 12, 13, 14, 15, 17; A, F.

ONTARIO COLLEGE OF ART, 100 McCaul St., Toronto 28, Ont., 1, 3, 6, 7, 8, 9, 10, 11, 12, 13, 14, 15, 16, 17; A, F, I.

241

QUEEN'S UNIVERSITY, Kingston, Ont., 3, 7, 12; A, J.

ST. LAWRENCE COLLEGE OF APPLIED ARTS & TECHNOLOGY, Wind Mill Point, Cornwall, Ont., 3, 5, 6, 7, 9, 12, 13, 14, 15, 17; A, D, F, I.

SOUTHAMPTON ART SCHOOL, Southampton, Ont., 4, 7, 12; A.

THREE SCHOOLS, 296 Brunswick Ave., Toronto, Ont., 179, 6, 7, 12, 13, 15; A, E.

TORONTO SCHOOL OF ART, 225 Brunswick Ave., Toronto, Ont., 3, 4, 6, 7, 12, 15; A, H.

UNIVERSITY OF GUELPH, Gordon St., Guelph, Ont., 3, 7, 12, 14, 15, 17; A, D, G, I.

UNIVERSITY OF TORONTO, Toronto, Ont., 2, 3; A.

UNIVERSITY OF WESTERN ONTARIO, London, Ont., 3, 7, 12, 13, 14, 15; A, D, I.

UNIVERSITY OF WINDSOR, Windsor, Ont., 3, 7, 12, 14, 15; A, D, H, I.

YORK UNIVERSITY, 4700 Keele St., Downsview, Ont., 3, 7, 12, 13, 14, 15, 17; A, D, F.

Prince Edward Island

HOLLAND COLLEGE, PO Box 878, Charlottetown, Prince Edward Island, 1, 3, 4, 6, 7, 9, 10, 12, 13, 15, 16; A.

UNIVERSITY OF PRINCE EDWARD ISLAND, Charlottetown, Prince Edward Island, 3, 7, 15; A.

Quebec

COLLEGE DE MONTREAL, 1931 W. Sherbrooke, Montreal, Que., 6, 12, 13, 15, 17; A, D, G.

COLLEGE D'ENSEIGNEMENT GENERAL & PROFESSIONAL, 625 Blvd. Ste. Croix, Montreal, Que., 379, 2, 3; A, D, F.

COLLEGE D'ENSEIGNEMENT GENERAL & PROFESSIONAL, 42 Rue Gagne, Rouyn (Rouyn-Noranda), Que., 3, 7, 12, 13, 17; A, D, F, I.

COLLEGE DE VICTORIAVILLE, 455 Notre-Dame E., Victoriaville, Que., 3, 13, 14, 15, 17; A, D.

COLLEGE EDOUARD MONTPETIT, 945 Chemin De Chambly, Longueuil, Que., 10; A, D, F, I.

COLLEGE LAFLECHE, 1687 Blvd. du Carmel, Trois-Rivières, Que., 7, 9, 12, 13, 14, 15, 17; A, D, F.

ECOLE DES BEAUX-ARTS DE QUEBEC, 2404 Chemin Ste—Foy 10, Que., *1, 7, 12, 13, 15, 16; A, J.*

MCGILL UNIVERSITY, 805 Sherbrooke West, Montreal, Que., *2, 3, 7, 12; A, D, E, I, J.*

MONTREAL MUSEUM OF FINE ARTS, 1379 Sherbrooke St. W. 109, Montreal, Que., *7, 12, 13; A.*

SEMINAIRE ST.-JOSEPH, Trois-Rivières, Que., *3, 7, 9, 13, 14, 15, 17; B, D, F.*

SIR GEORGE WILLIAMS UNIVERSITY, 1435 Drummond St., 108, Montreal, Que. *3, 4, 7, 12, 15; A, D, I, G.*

UNIVERSITE DE MONTREAL, Ecole Polytechnique, Montreal, Que., *1, 4, 7, 10; A, D, F, I.*

UNIVERSITE DE MONTREAL, Faculte des Lettres, CP 6128, Montreal 101, Que., *3; A, D.*

UNIVERSITE DU QUEBEC A MONTREAL, Famille-Arts, 125 Sherbrooke St. W., Montreal, Que., 129, *1, 3, 4, 7, 9, 10, 11, 12, 13, 14, 15, 17; A, D, E, F, I.*

UNIVERSITY OF QUEBEC, TROIS RIVIÈRES, PO Box 500, Trois Rivières, Que., *3, 4, 6, 7, 12, 14, 15; A, D, H, I.*

Saskatchewan

UNIVERSITY OF SASKATCHEWAN, Regina Campus, Regina, Sas., *3, 4, 7, 12, 13, 14, 15, 17; A, D.*

UNIVERSITY OF SASKATCHEWAN, Saskatoon, Sas., *3, 4, 7, 12, 13, 14, 15, 17; A, D, E, F, J.*

Appendix

ART ORGANIZATIONS

There are several organizations whose membership consists entirely of artists or people concerned with related trades. The artist interested in selling his/her art work should become familiar with those organizations and with what they have to offer. The organizations listed below were selected for two reasons: first, because some of them offer valuable services to the selling artist and are worthy of his/her membership; second, because all of them can and will give the artist valuable information concerning the art field if it is requested.

The title of the organization will indicate the group served. Many of the organizations listed have affiliated branches in most of the major sections of the country. For more information about the group and to find out if there is a branch near you, write to the central office listed on pages 244-245.

243

ALLIED ARTISTS OF AMERICA, INC., 1083 Fifth Ave., New York, N.Y. 10028

AMERICAN ABSTRACT ARTISTS, 218 West 20th St., New York, N.Y. 10011

AMERICAN ARTISTS PROFESSIONAL LEAGUE, INC., 112 East 19th St., New York, N.Y. 10003

AMERICAN ASSOCIATION OF SCHOOL PHOTOGRAPHERS OF AMERICA, 3555 Cowan Pl., Jackson, Miss. 39216

AMERICAN CERAMIC SOCIETY, INC. (Design Division), 65 Ceramic Dr., Columbus, Ohio 43214

AMERICAN COUNCIL FOR THE ARTS IN EDUCATION, 115 East 92nd St., New York, N.Y. 10028

AMERICAN CRAFT COUNCIL, 44 West 53rd St., New York, N.Y. 10019

THE AMERICAN FEDERATION OF ARTS, 41 East 65th St., New York, N.Y. 10021

AMERICAN INSTITUTE OF ARCHITECTS, 1735 New York Ave., N.W., Washington, D.C. 20006

AMERICAN INSTITUTE OF GRAPHIC ARTS, 1059 3rd Ave., New York, N.Y. 10021

AMERICAN MANAGEMENT ASSOCIATION, 135 West 50th St., New York, N.Y. 10020

AMERICAN SOCIETY OF INTERIOR DESIGNERS, 730 Fifth Ave., New York, N.Y. 10019

ARCHIVES OF AMERICAN ART, 41 East 65th St., New York, N.Y. 10022

ART DIRECTORS CLUB, c/o Jo Yanow, 488 Madison Ave., New York, N.Y. 10022

ART INFORMATION CENTER, INC., 189 Lexington Ave., New York, N.Y. 10016

ARTISTS EQUITY ASSOCIATION, 2813 Albemarle St., N.W., Washington, D.C. 20008

ARTISTS EQUITY ASSOCIATION OF NEW YORK, INC., 1780 Broadway, New York, N.Y. 10019

ARTIST GUILD OF CHICAGO, INC., 54 East Erie St., Chicago, Ill. 60611

ASSOCIATED COUNCIL OF THE ARTS, 1564 Broadway, New York, N.Y. 10036

ASSOCIATION OF FEDERAL PHOTOGRAPHERS, 7210 Tyler Ave., Falls Church, Va. 22042

ASSOCIATION OF MEDICAL ILLUSTRATORS, 6650 Northwest Hwy., Chicago, Ill. 60631

CARTOONISTS GUILD, 156 West 72nd St., New York, N.Y. 10023

CATHOLIC ART ASSOCIATION, c/o Mrs. William G. Finin, Exec. Secy., Box 113, Rensselaerville, N.Y. 12147

COLLEGE ART ASSOCIATION OF AMERICA, 16 East 52nd St., New York, N.Y. 10022

COUNCIL OF AMERICAN ARTIST SOCIETIES, 112 East 19th St., New York, N.Y. 10003

INDUSTRIAL DESIGNERS SOCIETY OF AMERICA, 1750 Old Meadow Rd., McLean, Va. 22101

INTERNATIONAL FOUNDATION FOR ART RESEARCH, INC., 654 Madison Ave., New York, N.Y. 10021

KAPPA PI INTERNATIONAL HONORARY ART FRATERNITY, Box 7843, Midfield, Birmingham, Ala. 35228

NATIONAL ART EDUCATION ASSOCIATION, 1916 Association Dr., Reston, Va. 22091

NATIONAL ASSOCIATION OF SCHOOLS OF ART, 11250 Roger Bacon Dr., Reston, Va. 22090

NATIONAL CARTOONISTS SOCIETY, 9 Ebony Court, Brooklyn, N.Y. 11229

NATIONAL ENDOWMENT FOR THE ARTS, Washington, D.C. 20506

NATIONAL FREE LANCE PHOTOGRAPHERS ASSOCIATION, 4 East State St., Doylestown, Pa. 18901

NATIONAL PRESS PHOTOGRAPHERS ASSOCIATION, Box 1146, Durham, N.C. 27702

NATIONAL SOCIETY OF INTERIOR DESIGNERS, 315 East 62nd St., New York, N.Y. 10021

PACKAGE DESIGNERS COUNCIL, PO Box 3753 Grand Central Station, New York, N.Y. 10017

PICTORIAL PHOTOGRAPHERS OF AMERICA, c/o Mr. Manuel Taber, 333 Pearl St., Apt. 6-B, New York, N.Y. 10038

PROFESSIONAL PHOTOGRAPHERS OF AMERICA, 1090 Executive Way, Des Plaines, Ill. 60018

SCREEN PRINTING ASSOCIATION, INTERNATIONAL, 150 S. Washington St., Suite 200, Falls Church, Va. 22046

SOCIETY OF ANIMAL ARTISTS, 151 Carroll St., City Island, Bronx, N.Y. 10464

SOCIETY OF ILLUSTRATORS, INC., 128 East 63rd St., New York, N.Y. 10021

SOCIETY OF PHOTO TECHNOLOGISTS, PO Box 19308, Denver, Col. 80219

SOCIETY OF PHOTOGRAPHERS AND ARTIST REPRESENTA-
TIVES, PO Box 845, FDR Station, New
York, N.Y. 10022

THE SOCIETY OF PHOTOGRAPHERS IN COMMUNICATION,
60 East 42nd St., New York, N.Y. 10017

SOCIETY OF TYPOGRAPHIC ARTS, 18 South Michigan
Ave., Chicago, Ill. 60603

SOUTHERN ASSOCIATION OF SCULPTORS, INC., Ap-
palachian State University (Art Dept.),
Boone, N.C. 28607

STAINED GLASS ASSOCIATION OF AMERICA, c/o Ken-
neth Urschel, Gen. Secy., 701 Elmhurst,
Valparaiso, Ind. 46383

ART PUBLICATIONS

The art field is not stagnant. On the contrary, it is a vibrant, changing, dynamic force that must be constantly watched and studied if
one is to participate in it and succeed. There are new styles, trends,
techniques, and materials constantly coming to the fore. Only the
artist alert to these changes can understand their impact and use
them to his/her advantage. The best way to stay abreast of the
changing conditions is to regularly look to the art magazines that
are available.

The following magazines can be found in most libraries. Foreign
magazines listed will be in the larger libraries.

Publication times: (A) annual; (M) monthly; (W) weekly; (Q) quarterly;
(Bi) occurs twice.

*These magazines can be found in most libraries.

#These magazines are particularly good for commercial artists.

#*Advertising Age* (W), Crain Communications, 740 Rush St., Chicago,
Ill. ($12/yr)

American Art Journal (Bi-A), 40 W. 57th St., New York, N.Y. 10019
($10/yr)

American Art Review (Bi-M), Box 65007, Los Angeles, Cal. 90065
($18/yr)

*American Artist (M), 1515 Broadway, New York, N.Y. 10036
($15/yr)

American Graphic Artists of the Twentieth Century, Brooklyn
Museum, Brooklyn, N.Y. 11238 ($4/yr)

Antiques (M), 551 Fifth Ave., New York, N.Y. 10017 ($18/yr)

Appollo Magazine (M), 22 Davies St., London, W.1, Eng. ($32/yr)

Architectural Record (M), 1220 Ave. of the Americas, New York,
N.Y. 10020 ($12/yr)

245 *Art Bulletin* (Q), 16 E. 52nd St., New York, N.Y. 10022 ($15/yr)

#*Art Direction* (M), 19 W. 44th St., New York, N.Y. 10036 ($11/yr)

Artforum (M), 667 Madison Ave., New York, N.Y. 10021 ($22.50/yr)

The Art Gallery Magazine (M except Aug & Sept), Ivoryton, Conn. 06442 ($13/yr)

*Art in America (Bi-M), Whitney Communication Corp., 150 E. 58th St., New York, N.Y. 10022 ($16.50/yr)

Art in Focus (M Oct-June), 131 N. 20th St., Philadelphia, Pa. 19103 ($6/yr)

Art Index (Q), The H. W. Wilson Co., 950 University Ave., New York, N.Y. 10452 (write for rate)

Art International (10/yr), Maraini 17-A, Lugano, Switzerland ($36/yr)

*Art Journal (Q), 16 E. 52nd St., New York, N.Y. ($8/yr)

Art Magazine (Q), 2498 Yonge St., Suite 18, Toronto, Ont. M4P 2H8 ($7/yr)

*Art News (M Sept-May, Q June-Aug), 750 Third Ave., New York, N.Y. 10017 ($15/yr)

Art Quarterly (Q), Detroit Institute of Arts, 5200 Woodward Ave., Detroit, Mich. 48202 ($16/yr)

Artist (M), 155 W. 115th St., New York, N.Y. 10011 ($8/yr)

Artist's Proof (A), Pratt Center for Contemporary Printmaking, 831 Broadway, New York, N.Y. 10003 (Membership $12.50)

*Arts Magazine (M Nov-June, Bi-M Sept-Jan), 23 E. 26th St., New York, N.Y. 10010 ($20/yr)

Artweek (W Sept-May, Bi-M June-Aug), 1305 Franklin St., Oakland, Cal. 94612 ($8/yr)

Avalanche (Q), Center for New Art Activities, 93 Grand St., New York, N.Y. 10013 ($10/yr)

*Ceramic Monthly (M), Professional Publications, Inc., Box 4548, Columbus, Ohio 43212 ($8/yr)

Cimaise (Bi-M), Wittenborn & Co., 1018 Madison Ave., New York, N.Y. 10021 ($36/yr)

Contemporary American Painting and Sculpture (Bi-A), University of Illinois Press, Urbana, Ill. 61801 (write for price)

*Craft Horizons (Bi-M), 44 W. 53rd St., New York, N.Y. 10022 ($10/yr)

Design Quarterly (Q), Walker Art Center, Vineland Place, Minneapolis, Minn. 55403 ($5/yr)

Feminist Art Journal (Q), 41 Montgomery Place, Brooklyn, N.Y. 11215 ($5/yr)

Graphic Design (Q), Wittenborn & Co., 1018 Madison Ave., New York, N.Y. 10021 ($24.50/yr)

#*Graphis Annual* (A), Dufourstrasse 107, CH-8008, Zurich, Switzerland (single $19.50)

Graphis Magazine (Bi-M), Dufourstrasse 107, CH-8008, Zurich, Switzerland ($39/yr)

Handweaver & Craftsman (Q), 220 Fifth Ave., New York, N.Y. 10001 ($5/yr)

Illustrator Magazine (Q), 500 S. Fourth St., Minneapolis, Minn. 55415 ($3/yr)

#*Illustrators Annual: The Annual of American Illustration* (A), Hastings House Publishers, 10 E. 40th St., New York, N.Y. 10016 ($19.50/yr)

#*Industrial Design* (10 issues), 130 E. 59th St., New York, N.Y. 10022 ($10/yr)

Interior Design (M), 150 E. 58th St., New York, N.Y. 10022 ($14/yr)

Interiors (M), One Astor Plaza, New York, N.Y. 10022 ($15/yr)

International Poster Annual (Bi-A), Hastings House Publishers, 10 E. 40th St., New York, N.Y. 10016 ($16/yr)

Journal of Aesthetics & Art Criticism (Q), Temple University, Department of Philosophy, Philadelphia, Pa. 19122 ($10/yr members, $15/yr nonmembers)

Marayas (Irreg), Institute of Fine Art, New York University, 1 East 78th St., New York, N.Y. 10021 (single $8)

Metropolitan Museum of Art Bulletin (Q), Fifth Ave. at 82nd St., New York, N.Y. 10028 ($10/yr)

Mobilia (M), Wittenborn & Co., 1018 Madison Ave., New York, N.Y. 10021 ($27.50/yr)

Museum News (M), American Association of Museums, 2233 Wisconsin Ave., N.W., Washington, D.C. 20007 ($15/yr incl. membership)

National Endowment for the Arts, Guide to Programs, National Endowment for the Arts, Superintendent of Documents, U.S. Government Printing Office, Washington, D.C. 20402 ($1)

National Sculpture Review (Q), 75 Rockefeller Plaza, New York, N.Y. 10019 ($3/yr)

New Jersey Music & Arts Magazine (M Sept-June), P.O. Box 567, Chatham, N.J. 07928 ($6/yr)

Opus International (Bi-M), 16 Rue Paul Fort, Paris (14e), France (15F./yr)

Pantheon (Q), Wittenborn & Co., 1018 Madison Ave., New York, N.Y. 10021 ($12.50/yr)

#*Penrose Annual* (A), 10 E. 40th St., New York, N.Y. 10016 (price varies)

Photographis: International Annual of Advertising Photography (A), Dufourstrasse 107, CH-8008, Zurich, Switzerland ($27.50/single)

Pictures of Exhibit (M Oct-May), 30 E. 60th St., New York, N.Y. 10022 ($5/yr)

Praxis (3/yr), 2125 Hearst Ave., Berkeley, Cal. 94709 ($8/yr)

#*Print, American Graphic Design Magazine* (Bi-M), 19 W. 44th St., New York, N.Y. 10036 ($14/yr)

Pro: The Voice of the Cartooning World (M), 1130 N. Cottage, Salem, Ore. 97301 ($10/yr)

Progressive Architecture (M), 600 Summer St., Stamford, Conn. 06904 ($7/yr)

Royal Society of Arts Journal (M), 6 John Adam St., Adelphi, London W.C.2, Eng. ($11.55/yr)

School Arts Magazine (M Sept-June), Davis Publications, Inc., Printers Bldg., Worcester, Mass. 01608 ($8/yr)

Sculpture International (Bi-A), Maxwell House, Fairview Park, Elmsford, N.Y. 10523 ($10/yr)

Southwest Art Magazine (M except July), P.O. Box 13037, Houston, Tex. 77019 ($15/yr)

Southwestern Art (Q), Box 1763, Austin, Tex. 78767 ($8.50/yr)

Stained Glass (Q), 1125 Wilmington Ave., St. Louis, Mo. 63111 ($8/yr)

Structure (Irreg), Wittenborn & Co., 1018 Madison Ave., New York, N.Y. 10021 ($2.75/yr)

Structurist (A), Wittenborn & Co., 1018 Madison Ave., New York, N.Y. 10021 ($4.50/issue)

Studio International (6/yr), Studio International Publications Ltd., 14 W. Central St., London WC1A, Eng. ($29/yr)

Washington International Arts Letter (M except July & Dec), 1321 Fourth St., S.W., Washington, D.C. 20024 ($6/yr)

SCHOLARSHIPS, FELLOWSHIPS AND AWARDS

Receiving an art scholarship, fellowship, or award can be the most important event in the life of the novice or artist. It is wrong to assume that art grants are assigned on the basis of ability alone. They include many different considerations, such as school or organization affiliation, field of specialization, language abilities, college training, test results, age, sex, residence, and nationality. It is wise to know the full particulars or you may waste your time, effort, and money working for something outside your qualifications.

In an earlier section entitled "Art School Directory," colleges and universities that offer grants to their students are listed. Following are listed additional scholarships, fellowships, and awards that have been granted in recent years by organizations other than schools. Compiling a list of scholarships, fellowships, and awards in the field of art is not an easy task. There are many grants offered by schools, foundations, and organizations that have strong financial backing and are therefore repeated year after year. Others are announced by different organizations and after a year or two fade out of existence.

The following list of grants was compiled by contact with several organizations and notation of announcements in recent editions of the leading art magazines. *The only way to know the complete, up-to-date details on any of the grants is to write directly to the sponsor indicated.*

Sponsor	Offering	Qualifications	Frequency
Academy of the Arts, Harrison & South St., Easton, Md. 21601	$100 per year (for 1 year)	H.S. student attending art school	Annual
Alabama Art League, Montgomery Museum of Fine Art, 440 S. McDonough St., Montgomery, Ala. 36104	$100 (for 1 year)	Student	Annual
Alaska Assoc. of the Arts, P.O. Box 2786, Fairbanks, Alaska 99707	$200 & up (for 1 year)	H.S. or college student	Annual
Alberta Assoc. of Architects, 217 Revillon Bldg., Edmonton, Alb., T5J 1B2, Canada	$250 (for 1 year)	Architec. student at N. or S. Alberta Inst. of Technology	Annual

Sponsor	Offering	Qualifications	Frequency
Alberta Culture, Visual Arts, Govern. of the Province of Alberta, Edmonton, Alb., Canada	$100-750 (for 1 year)	Resident of Alberta	Annual
Allied Artists of America, Inc., 1083 5th Ave., New York, N.Y. 10028	$200 (for 1 year)	Student at National Academy School of Fine Art	Annual
American Academy, 41 E. 65th St., New York, N.Y. 10021	$600 plus residency	U.S. citizen	Annual
American Antiquarian Society, 185 Salisbury St., Worcester, Mass. 01609	$1200-1600 per month	Qualified scholar	Annual
American Assoc. of University Women, 240 Virginia Ave., N.W., Washington, D.C. 20037	$1400 (for 1 year)	Woman	Annual
American Numismatic Society, Broadway at 155 St., New York, N.Y. 10032	$3500 fellowship $750 grants	Graduate student	Annual
American Oriental Society, 329 Sterling Memorial Library, Yale Station, New Haven, Conn. 06520	$5000 for student of history of Chinese painting	Student must complete 3 years Chinese language study & requirements for Ph.D. in Chinese painting	Variable
American Scandinavian Foundation, 127 E. 73rd St., New York, N.Y. 10021	$500-4000 (for 1 year)	Applicants with B.A. degree for Denmark, Finland, Iceland, Norway, & Sweden	Annual
American Watercolor Society 1083 5th Ave., New York, N.Y. 10028	Variable (for 1 year)	Outstanding student of watercolor painting	Annual
Armstrong Museum of Art & Archaeology, Olivet College, Olivet, Mich. 49076	Variable	Present & future college students	Annual
Art Assoc. of Richmond, Indiana, McGuire Memorial Hall, Whitewater Blvd., Richmond, Ind. 47374	$350 (for 1 year)	H.S. senior in art	Annual
Art Center Assoc., 100 Park Rd., Anchorage, Ky. 40223	$7500 (total)	Student	Semi-annual
Art Club of Washington, 2017 Eye St., N.W., Washington, D.C. 20006	$600 (for 1 year)	Local college or university student	Annual
Art in Architecture, Joseph Young, 1434 S. Spaulding Ave., Los Angeles, Cal. 90019	$200-500 (for 1 year)	Graduate student	Annual
Art Institute of Chicago, Michigan Ave. at Adams St., Chicago, Ill. 60603	$3000 (for 1 year)	Needy full-time student	Annual

Sponsor	Offering	Qualifications	Frequency
Art Institute of Fort Lauderdale, 3000 E. Las Olas Blvd., Fort Lauderdale, Fla. 33326	Variable	Graduating H.S. senior	Annual
Art Patrons League of Mobile, Inc., Box 8055, Mobile, Ala. 36608	$1000	Mobile area college student	Annual
Artists' Guild, c/o Art Museum of the Palm Beaches, Inc., P.O. Box 2300, West Palm Beach, Fla. 33402	$300 (for 1 year)	H.S. graduate art student of S. Florida	Annual
The Arts & Crafts Society of Portland, 616 N.W. 18th Ave., Portland, Ore. 97209	Work exchange scholarship for tuition	Student in financial need	Each term
Asheville Art Museum, Civic Center, Asheville, N.C. 28801	Variable	Needy person	Semester
Assoc. of Medical Illustrators, 6650 Northwest Hwy., Chicago, Ill. 60631	$100 (for 1 year)	2nd-year medical illustration student	Annual
Berkshire Art Assoc., P.O. Box 385, Pittsfield, Mass. 01201	$100	Art major	Annual
Birmingham-Bloomfield Art Assoc., 1516 S. Cranbrook Rd., Birmingham, Mich. 48009	Variable	Art student	Per term
Boston Architectural Center, 320 Newbury St., Boston, Mass. 02115	Variable	Art student	Annual
Archie Bray Foundation, 2915 Country Club Ave., Helena, Mont. 59601	$151 work scholarships (8)	Student	Annual
British Govt., Marshall Scholarlarships, c/o British Consulate-General in Atlanta, Boston, Chicago, Philadelphia, or San Francisco (Closing date Oct. 22)	(30) in the order of £ 1750 a year. (for 2 years with possible extension)	U.S. citizen. For college graduate under age 26 for study leading to the award of a British University degree	Annual
Brockton Art Center-Art Workshops, Oak St., Brockton, Mass. 02401	$40 (per term)	Needy children	Semi-annually
California Institute of the Arts, 24700 McBean Pkwy., Valencia, Cal. 91355	$600,000 total per year (for 4 years)	Needy and/or merit students	Annual
Canadian Society for Education through Art, University of Regina, Regina, Sas., Canada	$300 (4) (for 1 year)	H.S. graduate	Annual
Center for Creative Studies, College of Art & Design, 245 E. Kirby St., Detroit, Mich. 48202	$1950 scholarship (1) (for 1 year)	H.S. senior	Annual

Sponsor	Offering	Qualifications	Frequency
Charles River Creative Arts Program, Centre St., Dover, Mass. 02030	$2000 (for 1 year)	Needy	Annual
The Charleston Art Gallery of Sunrise, 755 Myrtle Rd., Charleston, W. Va. 25314	Tuition (for 1 year)	Underprivileged & competition winner	Annual
Cherokee National Historical Society, Inc., P.O. Box 515, Tahlequah, Ohio 74464	Variable	Graduate student of Cherokee descent studying for museum & archival professions	Variable
Cheyenne Artists Guild, Inc., 1010 E. 16th St., Cheyenne, Wyo. 82001	$200 (for 1 year)	Senior H.S. student of Cheyenne	Annual
Chicago Public School Art Society, Art Institute of Chicago, Michigan Ave. at Adams St., Chicago, Ill. 60603	$130 (each semester)	Children in society's art form program	Semi-annual
The Children's Aid Society, Lower West Side Center, 209 Sullivan St., New York, N.Y. 10012	Variable (for 1 year)	Economic need	Semi-annual
Cleveland Institute of Art, 11141 East Boulevard, Cleveland, Ohio 44106	$65,000 (total) (for 1 year)	Qualified students	Annual
Community Arts Council of Chilliwack, Box 53, Chilliwack, B.C., Canada	$300 (for 1 year)	For advanced study in fine arts	Annual
Contemporary Arts Museum, 5216 Montrose, Houston, Tex. 77006	$120-125 (for each semester)	Underprivileged	Annual
Craft Center, 25 Sagamore Rd., Worcester, Mass. 01605	$60	Needy	Annual
Delaware Art Museum, 2301 Kentmere Pkwy., Wilmington, Del. 19806	Variable (for 1 year)	Public school pupil	Semi-annual
Detroit Artists Market, 1452 Randolph St., Detroit, Mich. 48226	$1000 (for 1 year)	Qualified student attending Wayne State U. and Cranbrook Academy of Art	Annual
Dumbarton Oaks Research Library & Collection, 1703 32nd St., N.W., Washington, D.C. 20007	Variable (for 1 year)	Graduate student of Byzantine & Pre-Columbian studies	Annual
El Paso Museum of Art, 1211 Montana Ave., El Paso, Tex. 79902	$500 (per year)	Junior & senior H.S. student of El Paso	Variable

Sponsor	Offering	Qualifications	Frequency
Eleutherian Mills-Hagley Foundation, Greenville, Wilmington, Del. 19807	Variable (for 2-4 years)	College grad seeking M.A. or Ph.D. in history at U. of Delaware	Annual (deadline for applications Feb. 15)
Erie Art Center, 338 W. 6th St., Erie, Pa. 16507	Tuition for one term	Financial need	Semi-annual
Essex Institute, 132 Essex St., Salem, Mass. 01970	Fellowships (for 1 year)	Graduate student in American Studies	Annual
Fine Arts Center of Clinton, 119 W. Macon St., Clinton, Ill. 61727	Tuition	Qualified students	Annual
Flint Institute of Arts, DeWaters Art Center, 1120 E. Kearsley St., Flint, Mich. 48503	Variable (for 1 semester)	Gifted children	Variable
Florida Gulf Coast Art Center, Inc., 222 Ponce de Leon Blvd., Clearwater, Fla. 33516	Variable (for 1 summer)	Junior & senior H.S. students	Annual
Folger Shakespeare Library, 201 E. Capitol St., S.E., Washington, D.C. 20003	$600-10,000 (for 1 month-1 year)	Advanced scholars	Semi-annual
Freer Gallery of Art, 12th & Jefferson Dr., S.W., Washington, D.C. 20560	Variable	Ph.D. candidate in Oriental Art	Variable
Fresno Arts Center, 3033 E. Yale Ave., Fresno, Cal. 93703	$900	Students	Variable
Great Fall River Art Assoc., 80 Belmont St., Fall River, Mass. 02720	$100 (for 1 year)	Entering students, Southeastern Mass. University	Annual
Green Country Art Center, 1825 E. 15th St., Tulsa, Okla. 74104	$750 (for 1 year)	University art students	Annual
Elizabeth Greenshields Memorial Foundation, 1814 Sherbrooke St. W., Montreal, Que., H3H 1E4, Canada	Variable (30) (for 1 year)	Anyone interested in studying painting & sculpture	Any time
John Simon Guggenheim Memorial Foundation, 90 Park Ave., New York, N.Y. 10016	Fellowships (for 1 year)	30- to 45-year-old permanent residents of U.S., Canada, & other American states & possessions	Annual
Henry E. Huntington Library & Art Gallery, San Marino, Cal. 91108	$600 per month (up to 12 months)	Scholars (not for advanced degree)	Annual
The Henry Francis du Pont Winterthur Museum, Winterthur, Del. 19735	Base stipend $3000 (for 2 years)	College graduates for fellows in Winterthur programs in Early American Culture & Conservation of Artistic & Historic Objects	Annual

Sponsor	Offering	Qualifications	Frequency
Historical Society of Delaware, Market St., Wilmington, Del. 19801	Summer internship	College juniors interested in museum work	Annual
Historical Society of York County, 250 E. Market St., York, Pa. 17403	$100-200 (for 6 weeks)	Students	Annual
Hudson River Museum, 511 Warburton Ave., Yonkers, N.Y. 10701	Variable (4)	No restrictions	Per semester
Hutchinson Art Assoc., 321 E. First St., Hutchinson, Kans. 67501	$250 (for 1 year)	Junior college art student	Annual
Incorporated E. A. Abbey Scholarship for Mural Painting in the U.S.A., 1083 Fifth Ave., New York, N.Y. 10028	$6000 scholarship	U.S. citizen under 35 interested in studying mural painting	Biennial
Industrial Designers Society of America, 1750 Old Meadow Rd., McLean, Va. 22101	Variable (for 1 year)	Practicing designers	Annual
Institute of American Indian Arts, Cerrillos Rd., Santa Fe, N.M. 87501	Full—board, room, all materials plus 2 years H.S.	Any native American	Annual
Institute of Contemporary Art, U. of Pennsylvania, 34th & Walnut Sts., Philadelphia, Pa. 19174	Cost of lecture series (for 1 year)	All applicants	Annual
Institute of International Education (Sales & Correspondence Unit), 809 United Nations Plaza, New York, N.Y. 10017	For 1 year graduate study abroad	Students in the art fields	Apply any time
International Museum of Photography at George Eastman House, 900 East Ave., Rochester, N.Y. 14607	$7200 (3) (for 1 year)	Post-masters degree	Annual
Jackson Art Association, Jackson, Tenn. 38301	$75 (for summer)	Talented, handicapped child wanting art lessons.	Annual
Junior Arts Center, 4814 Hollywood Blvd., Los Angeles, Cal. 90027	Variable	Promising artist	As requested
Kappa Pi International Honorary Art Fraternity, Box 7843, Midfield, Birmingham, Ala. 35228	$500 (for 1 year)	Student members	Annual
Maude Kerns Art Center, 1910 E. 15th Ave., Eugene, Ore. 97403	$600 per year	Qualified applicant	Any time

Sponsor	Offering	Qualifications	Frequency
Kimbell Art Museum, Will Rogers Rd. W., Fort Worth, Tex. 76107	Variable (for 1 year)	Those in curatorial, conservation programs	Annual
Lafayette Art Center, 101 S. Ninth St., Lafayette, Ind. 47901	Up to $500 (for 1 semester)	Student of low income & merit	Semi-annual
Lahaina Art Society, 649 Wharf St., Lahaina, Hawaii 96761	$1000 per year (for 1 year)	H.S. senior	Annual
Las Vegas Art Museum, 3333 W. Washington, Las Vegas, Nev. 89107	Class tuition (for 1 year)	Graduating H.S. senior	Annual
Le Musée Regional de Rimouski, 35 ouest Saint-Germain, Rimouski, Que., Canada	$500 (for 1 year)	Artists - groups	Annual
Little Gallery of Arts, 155 E. Main, Vernal, Utah 84078	$100 (for 1 year)	H.S. senior	Annual
Loch Haven Art Center, Inc., 2416 N. Mills Ave., Orlando, Fla. 32803	Variable (Class tuition)	Qualified applicants	Quarterly
Los Angeles County Museum of Art, 5905 Wilshire Blvd., Los Angeles, Cal. 90036	$1200 (for 1 year)	Young local artists	Annual
Lyman Allyn Museum, 100 Mohegan Ave., New London, Conn. 06320	$45 for art class	Needy children	Annual
The MacDowell Colony, Inc., 145 W. 58th St., New York, N.Y. 10019. (Att: Shirley Blanchard)	Resident fellowships for maximum of 3 months	Professional painters, writers, sculptors, filmmakers, printmakers, & composers	On request
Maitland Art Center, Research Studio, 231 W. Pacwood Ave., Maitland, Fla. 32751	$500 each (for 1 year)	Open to all	Annual
Manitoba Assoc. of Architects, Winnipeg 2, Manitoba, Canada	$300 (for 1 year)	Architecture students at U. of Manitoba	Annual
Marion Art Center, Main St., Marion, Mass. 02739	$250 (for 1 year)	H.S. senior	Annual
The Memphis Academy of Arts, Overton Park, Memphis, Tenn. 38112	Variable (for 1 year)	H.S. graduates & college transfers	Annual
National Collection of Fine Arts, Smithsonian Institution, Washington, D.C. 20560	$9000 (for 1 year; limited stipend)	Ph.D. candidates in art history	Deadline: Feb. 15
		College seniors & graduate students in art	Deadline: Feb. 15
National Endowment for the Arts, Washington, D.C. 20506	$3000-10,000 (nonacademic fellowships for 1 year)	Professional artists and those in other forms of art	

Sponsor	Offering	Qualifications	Frequency
National Gallery of Art, Constitution Ave. at 6th St., Washington, D.C. 20565. Offers following fellowships:		(to qualify, applicant must be recommended by chairperson of graduate department of art history)	
David E. Finley Fellowship	(2 years plus 8 months)	Ph.D. candidates	Annual
Samuel H. Kress Fellowship	(1 year)	Ph.D. candidates	Annual
Chester Dale Fellowship	(1 year)	Ph.D. candidates	Annual
Robert H. & Clarice Smith Fellowship	(1 year)	Ph.D. candidates or holders	Annual
National Institute of Arts & Letters, American Academy of Arts & Letters, 633 W. 155th St., New York, N.Y. 10032	$3000 awards	Painters, sculptors, graphic artists	Annual
North Shore Art League, Winnetka Community House, 620 Lincoln, Winnetka, Ill. 60093	$1500 (for 1 year)	Art Institute of Chicago students	Annual
North Shore Arts Assoc., Rear 197 E. Main St., Gloucester, Mass. 01930	$100 (for 1 year)	Local students	Annual
The Oakland Museum, 1000 Oak St., Oakland, Cal. 94607	$1000 (for 1 year)	California artists	Annual
Oklahoma Art Center, 3113 Pershing Blvd., Oklahoma City, Okla. 73107	$150 (for 1 year)	Young talent in Oklahoma winners	Annual
Old Sturbridge Village, Sturbridge, Mass. 01566	Variable (for 1 year)	Persons interested in careers in historical, preservation & conservation agencies	Annual
Ontario Arts Council, Kitchener Waterloo Art Gallery, 43 Benton St., Kitchener, Ont., N2G 3H1, Canada	Up to $1500 (for 1 year)	Young Ontario artists	Annual
Palos Verdes Art Center & Museum, 5504 W. Crestridge Rd., Rancho Verdes, Cal. 90274	Class fees (for 1 semester)	H.S. students	Variable
Peoria Art Guild, 1831 N. Knoxville Ave., Peoria, Ill. 61603	$500 (for 1 year)	Needy talented art student	Annual
Place des Arts, 166 King Edward St., Coquitlam, B.C., Canada	Up to $400 (for 1 year)	Any artist living within the area	Annual
The Ponca City Art Assoc., Box 1394, Ponca City, Okla. 74601	$50 (2) (for 1 year)	Outstanding art student (1 boy & 1 girl)	Annual

Sponsor	Offering	Qualifications	Frequency
Pontiac Creative Arts Center, Williams St., Pontiac, Mich. 48053	$20-50 (tuitions)	Children & adults	Variable
Pratt Graphics Center, 831 Broadway, New York, N.Y. 10003	Tuition up to one year	Talented artists	Information upon request.
Prince Rupert Art Club, c/o Ms. Johan C. Woodland, Corresp. Secy., Court House, Prince Rupert, B.C., Canada	$100 (for 1 summer)	Deserving amateur or student	Annual
Providence Art Club, 11 Thomas St., Providence, R.I. 02903	Tuition and fees (3) (for 1 year)	Rhode Island School of Design students	Annual
The Provincetown Workshop, 492 Commercial St., Provincetown, Mass. 02657	$285 (20) (for 1 season)	Students of art schools	Annual & summers
Quincy Art Center, 1515 Jersey St., Quincy, Ill. 62301	Approx. $250 (for 1 year)	Underprivileged children	Semi-annual
Rensselaer County Historical Society, 59 Second St., Troy, N.Y. 12180	$1000 funded by NYSCA	Senior at Russell Sage College	Annual, if funded
Riverside Art Center & Museum, 3425 Seventh St., Riverside, Cal. 92501	$200 (for 1 year)	Based on need and talent	Quarterly ($50 each quarter)
Roberson Center for the Arts & Sciences, 30 Front St., Binghamton, N.Y. 13905	Covering class fees (for 1 year)	Talented student in art, music, dance	Information upon request.
Rogue Valley Art Assoc., P.O. Box 763, Medford, Ore. 97501	$200 (for summer)	Student	Annual
Roswell Museum & Art Center, 11th & Main Sts., Roswell, N.M. 88201	Grant provides stipend, home, studio, materials, and maintenance	Painters, sculptors, printmakers, weavers, and ceramicists	Information upon request.
The Royal Architectural Institute of Canada, Suite 1104, 151 Slater St., Ottawa, Ont., K1P 5H3, Canada	$2000 André Francou Scholarship	Graduate students of the School of Architecture at U. of Montreal	Annual
Royal Canadian Academy of Arts, 40 University Ave., Toronto, Ont., M5J 1T1, Canada	Variable (for 1 year)	Applicants	Annual
Saginaw Art Museum, 1126 N. Michigan Ave., Saginaw, Mich. 48602	Art classes tuition (for 1 year)	Students	Annual
Salem Art Assoc., Bush Barn Art Center, 600 Mission St., Salem, Ore. 97301	Class tuition (for 1 term)	Open to all	Quarterly

Sponsor	Offering	Qualifications	Frequency
Salmagundi Club, 47 Fifth Ave., New York, N.Y. 10003	Scholarship membership (for 4 years)	Artists under 30 years of age	3 examples of work must be submitted
San Bernardino Art Assoc., P.O. Box 2272, 1640 E. Highland, San Bernardino, Cal. 92406	$400	H.S. student	Annual
Santa Cruz Art League, 526 Broadway, Santa Cruz, Cal. 95060	$200 (for 1 year)	Between ages 15 and 19	Annual
Saskatchewan Art Board, 200 Lakeshore Dr., Regina, Sas., S4S 0A4, Canada	$1000	Saskatchewan artists	Semi-annual
School Art League of New York City, 1 Times Square, New York, N.Y. 10036	$100,000 annually (for 1 year)	H.S. students	Annual
School of the Associated Arts, 344 Summit Ave., St. Paul, Minn. 55102	Variable (for 1 year)	Students	Annual
Scottsdale Artists' League, P.O. Box 1071, Scottsdale, Ariz. 85252	Variable	Students at various schools, colleges, and universities in Arizona	Annual
Ella Sharp Museum, 3225 Fourth St., Jackson, Miss. 49203	Tuition to classes (for 1 year)	Open to all	Annual
Sheldon Memorial Art Gallery, Lincoln, Neb. 68508	$3450 (for 1 year)	U. of Nebraska graduate students	Annual
Smithsonian Institution, Office of Academic Studies, Washington, D.C. 20560	$10,000 (for 1 year)	Post-doctoral scholars in American, Oriental, and 20th-Century Art	Annual (deadline: Jan. 15)
Smithsonian Institution, Office of Academic Studies, Washington, D.C. 20560	$5000	Doctoral candidates in American, Oriental, and 20th-Century Art	Annual (deadline: Jan. 15)
South Bend Art Center, 121 N. Lafayette Blvd., South Bend, Ind. 46601	$300	Qualified applicants	Semi-annual
South Carolina Arts Commission, Brown Bldg., 1205 Pendleton St., Columbia, S.C. 29201	$130,000 annually (for 1 year)	Art organizations and artists	Quarterly
South County Art Assoc., 1319 Kingstown Rd., Kingston, R.I. 02881	$500 (for 1 year)	H.S. seniors majoring in art	Annual
Southwest Craft Center, 300 Augusta St., San Antonio, Tex. 78205	Class tuition and supplies (for 2-16 weeks)	Deserving student	Quarterly
Spiva Art Center, Inc., Newman & Duquesne Rds., Joplin, Mo. 64801	Variable (for 1 year or more)	Prospective college art student	Variable

258

Sponsor	Offering	Qualifications	Frequency
Springfield Art & Historical Society, 9 Elm Hill, Springfield, Vt. 05156	$300 (for 1 year)	Any student in art and/or music	Annual
Springfield Art Center, 107 Cliff Park Rd., Springfield, Ohio 45501	$25-100 (for 1 semester)	Children, some adults	Information upon request.
Springville Museum of Art, 126 E. 400 South, Springville, Utah 84663	Scholarships at Utah universities (for 1 year)	Participants in annual all-Utah H.S. Art Exhibit	Annual
Studio Workshop, 3 W. 18th St., New York, N.Y. 10011	Variable (for 1 year)	Qualified students	Annual, Semi-annual
Summit Art Center, 68 Elm St., Summit, N.J. 07901	$35-50 per session	Students in need	Per session
Sunbury Shores Arts & Nature Center, Inc., 139 Water St., (P.O. Box 100), St. Andrews, N.B., Canada	Approx. $1000 (per summer)	H.S. students	Annual
The Gallery/Stratford, 54 Romeo St., North Stratford, Ont. N5A 3C7, Canada	$200 (for 1 year)	Graduating H.S. senior for art study	Annual
Louis Comfort Tiffany Foundation, 1083 Fifth Ave., New York, N.Y. 10028	$2000 (for 1 year)	U.S. citizens of demonstrated ability	Annual
The Toledo Museum of Art, Monroe St. at Scottwood Ave., Toledo, Ohio 43609	Variable (for 1 year)	Graduate student	Annual
Truro Center for the Arts at Castle Hill, Inc., Castle Rd., Box 756, Truro, Mass. 02666	5 working scholarships in exchange for tuition	Qualified person age 20 and older	Annual
Tucson Museum of Art, 235 Walameda, Tucson, Ariz. 85701	Tuition (for 1 term)	Disadvantaged youth showing artistic talent	Variable
U.S. Government Grants for Graduate Study Abroad under Fulbright-Hays Act, c/o Sales & Correspondence Unit, Institute of International Education, 809 United Nations Plaza, New York, N.Y. 10017	Variable (for 1 year)	Graduate students who are U.S. citizens with B.A. degree or in the arts, 4 years of professional study and/or experience, and who have a knowledge of the country for which application is made	Annual
Villa Montalvo Center for the Arts, P.O. Box 158, Saratoga, Cal. 95070	Free or half, resident scholarship	Qualified artists	Information upon request.
Virginia Museum of Fine Arts, Richmond, Va. 23221	$100-250 per month (for 1 year)	Native Virginians or at least 5-year resident	Annual

Sponsor	Offering	Qualifications	Frequency
Wadeworth Atheneum, 600 Main St., Hartford, Conn. 06103	Art classes scholarship (for 2 months)	Deserving students	
Western College Center for the Arts, Inc., 1803 N. Seventh St., Grand Junction, Colo. 81501	As needed for children's class (for 10 weeks)	Applicants	Per term
Wichita Art Assoc., 9112 E. Central, Wichita, Kans. 67206	$2000 awarded through public schools and service organizations (for 1 year)	Art students in the Wichita area	Annual
Windward Artists Guild, Box 851, Kailua, Hawaii 96734	$100	H.S. student	Annual
Catharine Lorrillard Wolfe Art Club, 802 Broadway, New York, N.Y. 10003	$200 (for 1 year)	Art Students League & National School of Design students	Annual
Charles A. Wustum Museum of Fine Arts, 2519 Northwestern Ave., Racine, Wisc. 53404	$400-500	Residents of Racine	Annual

CODES CONCERNING ARTISTS

CODE OF FAIR PRACTICE

As formulated by the Joint Ethics Committee of the Society of Illustrators, Art Directors Club, and Artists Guild.

Relations between Artist and Art Director

1. Dealings between an artist or his agent and an agency or publication should be conducted only through an authorized art director or art buyer.
2. Orders to an artist or agent should be in writing and should include the price, delivery date, and a summarized description of the work. In the case of publications, the acceptance of a manuscript by the artist constitutes an order.
3. All changes and additions not due to the fault of the artist or agent should be billed to the purchaser as an additional and separate charge.
4. There should be no charge for revisions made necessary by errors on the part of the artist or his agent.
5. Alterations to artwork should not be made without consulting the artist. Where alterations or revisions are necessary and time permits and where the artist has maintained his usual standard of quality, he should be given the opportunity of making such changes.

6. The artist should notify the buyer of an anticipated delay in delivery. Should the artist fail to keep his contract through unreasonable delay in delivery, or nonconformance with agreed specifications, it should be considered a breach of contract by the artist and should release the buyer from responsibility.

7. Work stopped by a buyer after it has been started should be delivered immediately and billed on the basis of the time and effort expended and expenses incurred.

8. An artist should not be asked to work on speculation. However, work originating with the artist may be marketed on its merit. Such work remains the property of the artist unless paid for.

9. Art contests, except for educational or philanthropic purposes, are not approved because of their speculative character.

10. There should be no secret rebates, discounts, gifts, or bonuses to buyers by the artist or his agent.

11. If the purchase price of artwork is based specifically upon limited use and later this material is used more extensively than originally planned, the artist is to receive additional remuneration.

12. If comprehensives or other preliminary work are subsequently published as finished art, the price should be increased to the satisfaction of artist and buyer.

13. If preliminary drawings or comprehensives are bought from an artist with the intention or possibility that another artist will be assigned to do the finished work, this should be made clear at the time of placing the order.

14. The right of an artist to place his signature upon artwork is subject to agreement between artist and buyer.

15. There should be no plagiarism of any creative artwork.

16. If an artist is specifically requested to produce any artwork during unreasonable working hours, fair additional remuneration should be allowed.

Relations between Artist and Representative

17. An artist entering into an agreement with an agent or studio for exclusive representation should not accept an order from, nor permit his work to be shown by, any other agent or studio. Any agreement which is not intended to be exclusive should be set forth in writing indicating the exact restrictions agreed upon between the two parties.

18. All illustrative artwork or reproductions submitted as samples to a buyer by artists' agents or art studio representatives should bear the name of artist or artists responsible for their creation.

19. No agent or studio should continue to show the work of an artist as samples after the termination of their association.

20. After termination of an association between artist and agent, the agent should be entitled to a commission on work already under contract for a period of time not exceeding six months.

21. Original artwork furnished to an agent or submitted to a prospective purchaser shall remain the property of the artist and should be returned to him in good condition.

22. Interpretation of this code shall be in the hands of the Joint Ethics Committee and is subject to changes and additions at the discretion of the parent organizations.

Adopted by the Society of Illustrators, Art Directors Club, Artist Guild, National Society of Art Directors, and the American Society of Magazine Photographers.

STANDARDS OF PRACTICE IN HANDLING ARTWORK

American Association of Advertising Agencies

These standards are predicated upon the belief that adherence to a code of fair practice, agreed upon in advance, will contribute to the welfare of the advertiser, the creative craftsman, and the agency, and will reduce the opportunities for misunderstanding and inefficiency in handling artwork.

1. An artist or photographer should not be asked to speculate with or for an advertising agency, or be asked to do work on any basis which entails the possibility of loss to him through factors beyond his control.

2. An artist or photographer should not be expected to suffer any loss that is due to poor judgment on the part of the advertising agency.

3. Dealing with an artist or photographer should be conducted only through an art director or art buyer who is the authorized representative of the advertising agency.

4. Orders to an artist or photographer should be in writing and should include all details for which the supplier will be held responsible. The price, whenever possible, and delivery date should be set at this time and included in the written order.

5. Changes or alterations in drawings or photographs that are demonstrably made necessary by mistakes on the part of the artist or photographer should not be paid for by the advertising agency, but the supplier should be compensated for major revisions resulting from a change in agency plans or instructions.

6. If the purchase price of a drawing or photograph is based upon limited use, and later this material is used more extensively than originally planned, the artist or photographer should receive additional remuneration.

7. If comprehensive layout or other preliminary artwork or photographs are published as finished work, the price should be adjusted to include additional compensation.

8. If preliminary drawings, photographs, or comprehensives are bought from an artist or photographer with the intention or possibility that someone else will be assigned to do the finished work, this should be made clear at the time of placing the order for preliminary work.

9. Work stopped by the advertising agency for reasons beyond the control of the artist or photographer after it has been started should be paid for on the basis of the time and effort expended.

10. Should an artist or photographer fail to keep his contract with the advertising agency through unreasonable delay in delivery, or nonconformance with agreed specifications, it should be considered a breach of contract by the artist or photographer and should release the advertising agency from responsibility.

11. There should be no concealed charges in artwork as billed by the advertising agency.

12. No personal commission or rebate should be asked or accepted by the art buyer from an artist or art service.

CODE OF ETHICS

(Artists joining the Artist Equity Association subscribe to the following Code Of Ethics.)

In order to establish and build professional and public respect and confidence and to secure to the artist and the society in which he lives the benefits of economic and cultural growth, we establish this code of rights and obligations:

1. To insure high standards of conduct in the practice of the arts, and to contribute fully to the development of our American cultural heritage the creative artist must constantly strive to act so that his aims and integrity are beyond question.

2. Freedom of expression is essential for the practice of the fine arts and is the only climate in which health and growth of creative activity is possible. The artist should not, in the practice of his profession, be affected by enmities, political or religious strife, or sectarian aesthetic dissension. He should boycott professional activity involving discrimination as to race, creed, or ideology.

3. The artist shall endeavor to extend public knowledge of, and respect for, his profession through dedication to his work and discouragement of all untrue, unfair, and distorted ideas of the role of the artist and the practice of his profession.

4. The artist shall refrain from knowingly injuring or maliciously damaging the professional reputation or work of a fellow artist.

5. He shall assume full responsibility for work completed under his direction, but freely give credit to his technical advisors and assistants.

6. When acting as juror the artist shall constantly maintain the objectivity and seriousness required for this important service, taking into account local practices and instructions from those in charge, and giving each entry as careful consideration as he would expect for his own efforts.

7. When employed as teacher, the artist shall not make exaggerated claims as to his qualifications, nor permit the school or institution in question to do so in his name.

8. The artist shall vigorously oppose vandalism, censorship, or destruction of any commissioned work of art, as well as its unauthorized commercial exploitation or defacement.

9. The professional artist shall utilize the protection of existing copyright laws. He should claim all fees to which he is entitled for publication and reproduction rights.

10. The artist shall fully assume his responsibility toward his client and shall not misrepresent either the value or permanence of his work.

11. Before participating in charity fund raising sales or auctions, the artist shall assure himself that works will be properly displayed, that established prices will be maintained, and that he will receive whatever compensation is agreed upon.

12. The artist shall not enter competitions unless the terms are clearly stated, not when fees are contrary to, or below, standards currently established. Except in the case of open competition, he shall demand compensation for all sketches and models submitted.

13. When executing commercial, theatrical, or other design commissions, the artist shall familiarize himself with the codes and fair practices of allied trades to avoid misunderstandings in the execution of and remuneration for his work.

14. It is unethical for the artist to undertake a commission for which he knows another artist has been employed until he has notified such other artist and has determined that the original employment has been terminated.

15. To avoid misunderstanding in dealings with his dealer, agent, or employer, the artist should have a written contract (with the advice of an attorney).

Index